LANYER

LANYER

A Renaissance Woman Poet

Susanne Woods

New York   Oxford
Oxford University Press
1999

Oxford University Press

Oxford   New York
Athens   Auckland   Bangkok   Bogotá   Buenos Aires   Calcutta
Cape Town   Chennai   Dar es Salaam   Delhi   Florence   Hong Kong   Istanbul
Karachi   Kuala Lumpur   Madrid   Melbourne   Mexico City   Mumbai
Nairobi   Paris   São Paulo   Singapore   Taipei   Tokyo   Toronto   Warsaw

and associated companies in
Berlin   Ibadan

Published by Oxford University Press, Inc.
198 Madison Avenue, New York, New York 10016

Oxford is a registered trademark of Oxford University Press

Library of Congress Cataloging-in-Publication Data
Woods, Susanne, 1943–
Lanyer : a Renaissance woman poet / Susanne Woods.
p.   cm.
Includes index.
ISBN 0-19-512484-7
1. Lanyer, Aemilia.   2. Women poets, English—Early modern, 1500–1700—Biography.
3. Women and literature—England—History—17th century.
4. Women and literature—England—History—16th century.
5. Renaissance—England.   I. Title.
PR2296.L27Z95   1999
821'.3—dc21   98-28562
[B]

1   3   5   7   9   8   6   4   2

Printed in the United States of America
on acid-free paper

FOR MY SISTER,
VIRGINIA WOODS

PREFACE

Aemilia Lanyer was the first woman writing in English who clearly sought professional standing as a poet. This in itself gives her importance to English-speaking culture and makes her life and works, and their relation to her contemporaries, a matter of considerable interest to the history of English poetry. In her time poets were just beginning to define themselves in a print environment, but while we may debate whether Spenser or Jonson or perhaps someone else was the first true "professional" writer in English, Lanyer has no obvious challengers among Englishwomen.[1]

Women poets preceded her in England, and women writers who might be defined as professional also preceded her on the continent. Among the former: in 1560 Anne Vaughan Lock, the friend of John Knox and the wife, successively, of Puritan partisans Henry Lock, Edward Dering, and Richard Prowse, published the first religious sonnet sequence in English, a translation of Psalm 51 appended to her prose translation of one of Calvin's sermons. In 1567 and 1573 Isabella Whitney published secular poems filled with moral precepts and admonitions for minor gentry who find themselves in service. In 1589 Anne Dowrich published a Protestant version of the French civil wars and claimed serious attention as a public intellectual. In 1603 the Scots Presbyterian Elizabeth Melvill, Lady Culros, published *Ane Godlie Dreame*, a dream pilgrimage in competent and often lively ottava rima which was reprinted at least ten times between 1606 and 1737. Many women among the gentry and nobility, including the countess of Pembroke and Queen Elizabeth I, wrote poems that were widely circulated in manuscript.[2] On the continent, fifteenth- and sixteenth-century women writers were relatively more visible than they were in Britain, from (for example) Christine di Pisan and Marie de France to Gaspara Stampa and Louise Labé.[3]

One purpose of this book is to suggest what "professional writer" might mean for a Jacobean woman, but there are a few obvious indicators of Lanyer's public intent. Like Labé's *Euvres*, Lanyer's printed book, *Salve Deus Rex Judaeorum*, situated her visibly and aggressively among the professional writers of her time. The nine extant copies of her one volume suggest an effort to tailor the introductory material to specific patrons who might do her some financial good (several patronage poems are missing from three of the volumes, notably the copies given to Prince Henry and Thomas Jones, archbishop of Dublin). In addition to this apparent care with dedicatees is a recurrent formulaic *humilitas* topos much more like what we see from Ben Jonson than, for example, from the continuously self-deprecating Whitney. The publication itself, an attractive and carefully produced quarto with the certifying permission of her husband on the title page (but nowhere else), is what we would today call "mainstream." Her bookseller, Richard Bonian, was an eclectic publisher with an eye for poetry and the sensational (Shakespeare's *Troilus and Cressida* and Jonson's *Maske of Queenes* were among his offerings in 1609, as were *A mosst straunge report of two monstrous births* and *A true relacon of the birth of three monsters*), and her printer, Valentine Simmes, was someone known to take risks associated with popular genres.[4]

Because Lanyer's book is unusual, the tendency has been to theorize her either into or out of late twentieth-century feminisms. Though it is impossible for a scholar of my era to read Lanyer without being struck by her transgressions and moved by what seem her anticipations of a greater voice for women, and while she might not be read at all were it not for a new interest in recovering the voices of previously disregarded women, any just appreciation of what she has accomplished must begin with an appreciation of her context.

This book focuses on Lanyer in relation to some of the more traditionally canonical poets of her time, but recognizes that the reader lives in a different age from the writer. The facts that I deal with are both concrete and ellusive: real books printed and circulated according to specific and recoverable mechanisms of early seventeenth-century technology and society, which encode a discourse both literal and figurative that was probably fluid in its own time and sometimes seems positively misty to ours. The only way I know to do justice to the Renaissance writer and the modern reader is to take into account, as best as I can interpret them, the expectations of both 1611 and 1999. What follows is a diachronic reading.[5]

By diachronic, I mean a reading that respects differences between and among the people and ideas of two different eras. It acknowledges the epistemological problem of postromantic Western thought —our inability comfortably to separate subject from object—and adds the dimension of time to an understanding of consciousness and culture. This reading style is somewhat different from trying to interpret the Jacobean period in its own terms on the one hand, and then viewing its evidence with the values and expectations of our time on the other, which implies that eras are discrete and static. Yet how we see our heritage is to some extent what it becomes, and we are in turn changed by our backward glances. In a metaphor from modern physics, as we move into the light cone of a past event, we see the past itself and its impact on the present, but the very viewing has a fresh impact on how we see the present and what events cascade and expand their own light cones into the future. Time becomes more than a point on a continuum, more even than the unidirectional continuum itself; it becomes the track that we can travel imaginatively if not physically back and forth through a universe infinitely more multidimensional than our three-dimensional selves experience in the course of limited sensate lives.[6]

The Renaissance believed that language and symbolic systems define a culture and transcend time. Renaissance poets might point to their interaction with the classical past for exemplary culture, and their metaphysics and theology for glimpses of transcendence. As a culture we understand similar things, only in different terms and from different ontological foundations. We have moved from a largely Parmenidean to a largely Heraclitean philosophy of being, but even neoexistential postmodernism implies a definable self, if only as a tension among the many selves that flow from an individual's many stories. Chaos theory finds patterns elaborated so far beyond the binary tradition of differential equations that the whole world seems new. We live in a time of dissolving boundaries, or perhaps more accurately a time when we understand all boundaries to be always dissolving. The purpose of this book is to take a poet who is herself symbolic of boundaries and their dissolution, and both situate her in and release her from her own time.[7]

My method is modest and linear. The first chapter describes what we know about Lanyer and offers information about the literary and social context in which she lived. Subsequent chapters place her in relation to each of the three major canonical writers with whom she was roughly contemporary and whom she may have known: Spenser, Shakespeare, and Jonson. The final chapter positions Lanyer among those Renaissance English writers seeking to poeticize religious experience. Her role as a woman writing an extended narrative on the Christian passion is interesting in itself, but it is particularly so since it appears at the beginning of the great era of English religious verse. I have centered this chapter on John Donne.

I selected these male poets in part because they were well known and appreciated in their own time and have since become canonized as the principal poets of the late Elizabethan and early Jacobean periods. If Lanyer is to be contextualized, then she needs to be seen in the company of those writers who most commonly define her era for us.

There are also some important similarities between Lanyer and the others. All of these poets are from roughly the same social class: minor gentry, broadly defined, or what we would call "middle class," recognizing that this class was very much smaller in seventeenth-century England than it is in most twentieth-century English-speaking countries. All but Shakespeare were Londoners (and his working and imaginative life was spent in London). All had connections with the Elizabethan court and were old enough to be affected by the glory days of the queen. All but Spenser, who died in 1599, had some association with the court of King James. Spenser is the oldest, born around 1552 and therefore barely a generation older than Donne and Jonson, both born in 1572. Shakespeare, born in 1564, and Lanyer, in 1569, span the gap.

This book does not claim to offer a comprehensive look at Lanyer's work, much less at the work of the other poets among whom I place her. Despite the useful and interesting recent studies on Lanyer by Lorna Hutson, Barbara Lewalski, Tina Krontiris, Lynette McGrath, Janel Mueller, Louise Schleiner, and Wendy Wall, among others, we are just beginning to understand her writing and the early tradition of women writing in English. This book seeks to add information and suggest lines of further inquiry.

One brief comment on the question of value in Lanyer's poetry. While I believe early women writers would be worth our attention even if the work itself was almost entirely unskilled, since their urge to articulate their subject positions is itself of interest (even compelling interest to many women poets and scholars), Lanyer is an effective poet in traditional terms. She is mostly in charge of her craft, with large portions of her work confident, some of it dense and elegent. If her verse does not have the versatility of Spenser, Shakespeare, Jonson, Donne, or even Daniel, that says more about the educational opportunities and expectations of her time than her talent or vision. Though I could hardly rank her with Spenser and Shakespeare (few poets ascend those heights), she is a credible peer of

Jonson's and Donne's, and in some ways (her vision and original-
ity) superior to Daniel and Drayton.

Canonical placement is largely beside the point. We are still just
beginning to learn how to read early women writers, with their less
intensive educations and their often unfamiliar topics or points of
view. I want to make it clear, however, that I consider Lanyer well
worth reading not only for the light she casts on the marginal efforts
of women to speak early modern culture, but for the pleasure she
offers. She is bold, witty, sly, and joyous in her celebration of women.
As I hope the following pages will illustrate, she belongs among the
other poets of her time, her one book a substantial contribution to
the richness of our cultural history.

ACKNOWLEDGMENTS

My greatest debt is to Barbara Lewalski, who first pointed me toward Lanyer and has been a generous reader of my ongoing work on this project. She and Ken Lewalski have given me many years of warm friendship (filled with ideas and opinions), and I deeply cherish them both; they know how to dance in the street. I am also indebted to other friends and colleagues who have read portions of this work and encouraged the process: Leeds Barroll, Elaine Beilin, Jerome S. Dees, Patrick Cheney, Marshall Grossman, Suzanne W. Hull, Katherine Duncan-Jones, Elizabeth H. Hageman, Lynette McGrath, Karen Newman, John Rogers, Lauren Silberman, and especially Margaret P. Hannay. Margaret and I shared work on another project as she was finishing her Oxford edition of the countess of Pembroke's work (also collaborative) and I was struggling to complete this book. Happily this made, rather than broke, our friendship.

Anne Shaver not only read and commented on my work on Lanyer, she gave the gift of her own enthusiasm for recovering and teaching early women writers, and kept me on the right track generally. My personal and professional gratitude are permanent. I want also to express deepest thanks to the rest of the movable house party: Stuart Curran, Sarah Poyntz, Mary Ann Radzinowicz, Julia Walker, and Joseph Wittreich. Next year in Key West!

I cannot possibly include mention of all the people who have helped with this project or during its process, but I want to acknowledge at least some of those scholars who have contributed to the ongoing dialogue on Lanyer. Work by Lynette McGrath, Louise Schleiner, and Janel Mueller has been important to my own thinking. Most recently I have been invigorated by the work of Marshall Grossman and the rest of my colleagues in his recent collection, *Aemilia Lanyer: Gender, Genre, and the Canon* (Lexington: U of Kentucky P, 1998: David Bevington, Leeds Barroll, Barbara Lewalski, Kari Boyd McBride, Janel Mueller, Naomi Miller, Michael Morgan Holmes, Achsah Guibbory, and Boyd Berry. The annotated bibliography by Karen Nelson in this collection is now everyone's first resource, and I thank her particularly for obviating the need for one in this book. If I do not refer directly to these scholars in what follows, they nonetheless continue to inform my understanding of Lanyer, and this book would not have been possible without them.

My warmest thanks, too, to all those associated with the Brown University Women Writers Project, which I had the honor of founding in 1988 but has since become an international collaboration beyond the credit of any one person. I also thank my colleagues in the administration and the English departments at Brown University and Franklin & Marshall College and my students at Brown and Franklin & Marshall for keeping me focused and enthusiastic about Lanyer. I will let one excellent class, the seminar on early women writers at Franklin & Marshall in the spring of 1998, stand for them all: special thanks to Aimee Amodio, Maya Bangs, Alissa Barrett, Danielle Berkley, Alexandra Dilzer, Gillian Foster, Jamie Holloway, Beatrice Kennedy, Norell Paleologos, and Melissa Stein.

Without generous help from the staffs of the Bodleian, Folger, and Huntington Libraries this book would not have been possible. I am grateful to Mr. R. J. G. Berkeley of Berkeley Castle for permission to reproduce the portraits of Henry Carey, Lord Hunsdon and the "Unknown Woman in Black," and to Mr. David Attwood who showed me the portraits at the castle in June 1997. Those reproductions are from the Courtauld Institute, where Sarah Winbush promptly answered all of my queries and anticipated my need for the portrait of Anne Clifford at Knole. My thanks, too, to Catharine MacLeod of the National Portrait Gallery for her analysis of the portrait of the "Unknown Woman" and James Kilvington for his prompt and learned help in providing the portrait of Margaret Russell, the countess of Cumberland. I am also gratful to David Lasocki for his enormously useful book on Aemilia's paternal family, the Bassanos, and for answering several e-mail queries.

Josephine Roberts was a model of generous and careful professionalism in the effort to recover early women writers. Her work on Lady Mary Wroth established the highest standards for the rest of the enterprise, and I wish I could have shared this book with her; among the many pains of her tragic loss in August 1996, is the knowledge that she was just starting an important project on Lanyer and Milton. I honor and miss her wisdom and friendship.

This book is dedicated to my beloved sister, Virginia Woods, who started it all by reading me "The Owl and the Pussycat" long years ago, and was friend, intellectual companion, and just good fun.

CONTENTS

LANYER

I

LANYER IN HER WORLD

Aemilia Bassano was conceived in the spring of 1568, just as a much better known woman, Mary Queen of Scots, was planning her escape from Scotland into England, and Queen Elizabeth's cousin, Henry Carey, Lord Hunsdon, was made governor of Berwick and warden of the East Marches. In this role Hunsdon would put down a rebellion on Mary's behalf two years later, winning an "affectionate commendation" from Elizabeth and cementing her trust in him. This public matter would eventually have important consequences for the life of the baby born to Margaret Johnson and Baptista Bassano and baptised "Emillia Baptist" on 27 January 1569 in the church of St. Botolph's Bishopsgate, just outside the city wall of London. Some twenty years later she would experience the full glamor of the Elizabethan court, thanks to a relationship with Hunsdon.

When Mary was executed at Fotheringay on 8 February 1587, Aemilia Bassano was just eighteen, the only survivor of four children. Her father, a court musician of modest prosperity, had died when she was seven, and her mother would survive the Scottish queen by only a few months. Like Mary, whose last eighteen years marked Aemilia's first, she was attractive, strong willed, and a poet. Unlike that rare and visible public woman, she lived outside the public sphere and much of her life remains obscure. It was lived briefly near the center of the English court and thereafter on its farthest margins, and it ended twenty years into the reign of Mary's grandson, Charles I. Aemilia Lanyer was buried at St. James, Clerkenwell, on 3 April 1645.[1]

Origins

About Aemilia's mother we know very little. She may possibly be the "Margaret Johnson" who was baptised in 1544 at St. Margaret's, Westminster. She may have been a member of the musical Johnson family that later included Elizabethan lutenist John Johnson and Jacobean composer Robert Johnson, both of whom appear in lists with members of the Bassano family.[2] Her will tells us the names of a few of her friends: Stephen Vaughan and his wife, to whom she left "a ringe of twentie shillings," and Alue or Alve Dyer, who is listed as a witness to Margaret's intentions. She bore two sons who did not survive early childhood (Lewes, October 1562–November 1563, and Phillip, February 1571–November 1573), and another daughter, Angela, who by 1576 was married to "Joseph Holland, gent." and by 1587 had died, leaving one son, Phillip Holland.[3] If Margaret was born in 1544, both she and Angela would have become mothers at very young ages, unless Angela was Baptista's daughter by an earlier liaison.[4]

Aemilia's father, Baptista Bassano, was the youngest of six sons of Jeronimo Bassano, sackbut player and instrument-maker to the doge of Venice.[5] Jeronimo and his five eldest sons were from the town of Bassano del Grappa in the Veneto region, a dependency of Venice, but had settled in Venice by 1512, where Baptista reports he was born.[6] All six sons spent time in England during the reign of Henry VIII, and by 1540 all but one were established in England as royal musicians (the eldest, Jacomo, returned to Italy). The second eldest of the sons, and the first musician to receive an appointment in King Henry's court, was Alvise, also known as Lewes, after whom Margaret and Baptista's first son was presumably named. The other brothers were Jasper, John, and Anthony, the last of these the founder of a dynasty of court musicians that lasted until 1665. Anthony's daughter, Lucretia, helped form an important musical line of her own by marrying another court musician, Nicholas Lanier I. She therefore became stepmother or mother to several musicians, including John, who in turn fathered court composer Nicholas Lanier II, Ben Jonson's well-known colleague; Ellen, who married Alphonso Ferrabosco II, another friend and collaborator of Jonson's; and Alfonso, who married Aemilia Bassano. Aemilia's husband, Alfonso, was therefore her first cousin once removed, the grandson of her Uncle Anthony.

Baptista Bassano's history is interesting in itself. He may first have visited England as a sackbut player in service to Edward Seymour, earl of Hertford, in the winter of 1538. He was certainly in England by April 1540, when he and his four brothers were granted formal places as musicians in the court of Henry VIII. All five brothers became denizens of England in March 1545, a legal status roughly equivalent to permanent residency, which allowed their children born in England to inherit porperty from them under English law.

Not long after Alvise Bassano and his four brothers settled in England, Henry VIII granted them the right to live in apartments in the Charterhouse, a Carthusian monastery Henry had dissolved in 1537. These desirable accommodations with gardens and good water and sewage systems, were apparently rent-free, which may have been part of Henry's effort to entice the brothers to settle in England. Despite assurances from the king that the Bassanos could continue living there, after ten years (during the reign of Edward VI) they were forced out by Sir Edward North, who bought the Charterhouse in 1545. All the brothers except Baptista then moved into property on Mark Lane near the Tower of London, where they evidently prospered.

Baptista was not only the youngest, but apparently the most independent and anglicized of the Bassano brothers. Though he returned to Venice at least twice after 1540, he did not share in owning property in Bassano del Grappa, as his brothers did, nor was he tempted to return permanently, as did his brother John, nor marry an Italian, as did Anthony. He may never formally have married; he describes Margaret as "Margaret Bassany alias Johnson my reputed wife" in his will. However, in this context, "reputed" may simply mean "known to be," in the obsolete sense of "to repute" as "to regard, reckon, account as something."[7] She was in any case his heir; his children were treated as legitimate; and her will firmly describes her as "Margaret Bassano." After leaving the Charterhouse, Baptista became a resident of the parish of St. Botolph's Bishopsgate, roughly two thirds of a mile from his brothers on Mark Lane. Here at least three of his children were baptized, and two of them were buried, as he and his wife were.

One other intriguing bit of information has come down to us about Baptista Bassano: In 1563 "Henry Dingely, Mark Anthony, *et al.*" were sentenced to be whipped and pilloried, to have their ears cut off, and to be banished for plotting to kill him. The record is part of Sir Thomas Egerton's summary of Council and Star Chamber registers, and nothing further is known of the episode.[8] At this point it is impossible to know why the plot was hatched or how it was thwarted.

Much has been made of the possible Jewish origins of the Bassanos, although the evidence is highly speculative.[9] The argument and counter-argument run something like this: there were many Jewish Bassanos (as well as Christian Bassanos) in Northern Italy in the later Renaissance. Bassano del Grappa tried to expel its Jews in 1516, which could suggest that Jews had felt unwelcome in the town for some years before that, and perhaps explains the Bassanos' move to Venice, a more tolerant city. Though English members of the family returned to Venice from time to time, there is no evidence they ever again lived in the town of Bassano. On the other hand, Venice was a logical place for musicians to seek employment, as was the English court, so the movements of the Bassano family could reflect the fortunes of talented Renaissance musicians rather than wanderings to avoid persecution. They did continue to own a house in Bassano until 1576, which seems an unlikely privilege for a Jewish family, unless they were converts to Christianity. (In that case, however, it is less likely that their move to Venice had been provoked by anti-Jewish sentiment.)

The Bassano coat of arms may provide support for the theory that the Bassanos were originally Jewish. If it actually represents silkworms above a mulberry tree (rather than butterflies above a laurel tree, as it was originally described in Elizabethan heraldry), and if the Bassanos brought their coat of arms with them from Italy, then it would seem to reflect a heritage as silk farmers, one of the activities the *Encyclopedia Judaica* describes as a trade introduced into Italy by Jews. Yet there was apparently a "craze for raising silkworms" in England toward the end of the sixteenth century, and the earliest evidence we have of the Bassano coat of arms is a description from between 1588 and 1597.[10] While such evidence for the Bassanos' Jewish background remains suggestive rather than persuasive, there were musicians in the Tudor court with identifiable Jewish backgrounds, one of whom (Joseph Lupo) married Alvise's daughter, Laura, which may in turn suggest participation in a London Jewish community. Finally, Aemilia Lanyer's own book of poems has been offered as evidence, with its title (*Salve Deus Rex Judaeorum*) emphasizing the "King of the Jews." On the other hand, this is an unsurprising title for a poem about the passion of Christ, and depicting the poem as proof that Aemilia "had undergone a violent religious conversion" is questionable.[11] It will be clear elsewhere in this book that I read the poem differently.

Whether or not the Bassanos had Jewish origins, their religious practice was Christian at least after their move to Venice (Alvise was a member of the highly religious Scuola di San Marco), and by the time of Aemilia's birth they appear to have been observant Elizabethan Protestants. Still, there is some appeal to the idea of a Jewish background, which would give Aemilia a strong and particular heritage on the margins of Tudor England. With her English (Johnson) mother, however, she would not necessarily have been a "dark lady."[12]

More likely than a Jewish origin is the possibility that Baptista and Margaret were radical Protestant partisans. If Baptista served Edward Seymour, earl of Hertford in 1538, he would have received an early taste of English Protestantism. The earl's sympathies came to the fore ten years later when, as duke of Somerset and lord protector of his nephew, Edward VI, he was instrumental in effecting England's theological shift toward Geneva.[13] And there is evidence that Baptista and Margaret associated with the reform elements of the Protestant movement. The "Stephen Vaughan Esquier" who acts as an overseer of Margaret Bassano's will, and, with his wife, is clearly a close family friend, is also the brother of Anne Vaughan Lock, friend of John Knox and translator of Calvin.[14] Aemilia Lanyer claims to have resided as a child in the household of Susan Bertie, dowager countess of Kent and daughter of the famously Protestant dowager countess of Suffolk, Catherine Bertie, who made a spectacular escape into exile during Mary's reign. Lanyer's printer, Valentine Simmes, was implicated in the Martin Marprelate controversy, the anonymous radical Protestant pamphleteering of the 1580s.[15] These connections help to answer questions about Aemilia's own education and political and religious views.

Whatever the origins or ideologies of her parents, Aemilia Bassano grew up at the height of Elizabethan power, and her own life and work shows every evidence of having been formed by a patriotic devotion to Elizabeth and her policies. It was a life of promise, uncertainty, aspiration, and at last an achievement whose measure she very probably could not realize in her own time: a single book of poems that sets into relief major issues of gender, authority, poetry, and patronage as they shifted the English cultural landscape in the reign of James I.

Life

Aemilia Lanyer's early years are known to us only from hints in her parents' wills of 1576 and 1587, her comments as recorded by Simon Forman in 1597, and some suggestive statements within her poems. Her later years are even more obscure, although a few court documents offer glimpses. Even so, we are able to reconstruct rather more of her life than we can of most other women's from her period.

Aemilia was virtually an only child. Her older sister, Angela, was married by the time Aemilia was seven, while a baby brother lived only twenty-one months. Her upbringing had its privileges; court musicians were members of the minor gentry, with respectable incomes by the standards of the day. Her father earned over thirty pounds per year in wages and was eligible for gifts of livery and food from the court. There was also a tradition of New Year's gifts: in 1565 Baptista gave Queen Elizabeth a Venetian lute and received gilt plate or a sum of money in return.[16]

Aemilia's claim that she was educated under the aegis of the dowager countess of Kent, Susan Bertie, gives further credence to the view that her parents had close connections with England's Protestant tradition. During the reign of Queen Mary (1553–58), Catherine Brandon Bertie, dowager countess of Suffolk, joined other English Protestants, including Anne Vaughan Lock, in seeking religious freedom in continental Europe. She took her daughter Susan with her in a dramatic flight to Germany and Poland which became the stuff of Protestant legend.[17] Lanyer cites this event in the Bertie family in her poem to Susan ("To the Ladie Susan, Dowager Countess of Kent, and Daughter to the Duchesse of Suffolke," ll. 19–30), helping to establish her own place in the Reformed Protestant heritage. Even more important is her family association with Anne Vaughan Lock.

Anne Lock left her husband in England to join John Knox and his group of exiles in Geneva in May 1557. She had brought her two young children, Henry and Anne, but the daughter died almost immediately after they arrived. This tragedy may have been known to other continental exiles, including Catherine Bertie, who had a baby daughter with her as well. Whatever the nature of their connection, it was Aemilia Lanyer's earliest example of woman-to-woman dedication and patronage. In 1560 Lock published her translation of Calvin's sermons on Isaiah 38, with its appended sonnet sequence on Psalm 51, and dedicated it to Catherine Bertie: "This receipt God the heavenly Physitian hath taught, his most excellent Apothecarie Master John Calvine hath compounded, and I, your grace's most bounden and humble, have put into an Englishe box and do present to you."[18]

Lock married the famous Puritan preacher Edward Dering after her first husband's death. When he in turn died, she married an Exeter draper, Richard Prowse, who was active in Devonshire politics. In 1590, as Anne Prowse, she published a translation of Jean Taffin's *Of the markes of the children of God, and of their comfort in afflictions* (a translation from the French, as were the Calvin sermons). This work she again dedicated to a woman, Ann, countess of Warwick, the sister of Aemilia Lanyer's principal dedicatee, Margaret, countess of Cumberland. Aemilia may well have known the countess of Cumberland and her sister by 1590 when all three were at Elizabeth's court and may have encountered the translation of Taffin through either the dedicatee or Anne Lock's brother and his wife.[19] An early encounter with these (rare) dedications from one woman to another would help explain the ease with which Lanyer addresses other women in her volume of poems.

The Protestant tradition that Susan Bertie, the dowager countess of Kent, inherited from her mother, and from which Aemilia Bassano would have received her education in Susan's household, was also a richly humanistic tradition. Edward Seymour, possibly Baptista Bassano's first English patron, was the earliest leader of the Protestant party and a patron of John Cheke and Roger Ascham, the preeminent humanist educators of the mid-century. Catherine Bertie's sons by her first husband, the duke of Suffolk, were educated by John Wilson, whose *Rule of Reason* (1551) and *Art of Rhetorique* (1553) were written in her household.[20] Like Ascham, Wilson was a student of Cheke's at Cambridge, and the three represent the richest vein of English humanist education. Although young women were in general not expected to have the rigorous educations of young men, Susan Bertie's household was within a tradition that valued and admired educated women. Queen Catherine Parr, Lady Jane Grey, the daughters of Anthony Cooke, Queen Elizabeth herself (Ascham was her tutor) were models of pious Protestant humanism, with Catherine Bertie and the Vaughan family visible figures in that tradition.[21] In notable contrast to some fathers' resistance to their daughters learning Latin, these households prized their daughters' skill with classical languages.[22]

About Aemilia's education, then, we may fairly posit the following: perhaps through the influence of the Vaughan family, Aemilia Bassano entered the service of Susan Bertie, dowager countess of Kent, at some point suitable to both her intellectual and social education (possibly not long after her father's death).[23] In that service she encountered humanist learning, probably in the manner advocated by Ascham and Wilson, and a distinctly Protestant spirituality. If we believe her dedicatory poems, her spiritual education did not bear fruit until she was influenced by the countess of Cumberland some years later, though she looks back with appreciation on what the dowager countess of Kent, "the noble guide of my ungovern'd dayes," tried to accomplish.[24]

A humanist education in the tradition of Cheke, Ascham, and Wilson emphasized careful reading of specific classical texts, Latin and Greek, using the method of double translation. Ascham advocates starting the young Latin scholar off with selections from Cicero, rather than wasting the scholar's time (and patience) with grammatical drills. The master begins by presenting the context and subject of his selection, in this case a Ciceronian epistle, translates it with "the childe," then lets him work first from Latin to English, then back from the English to Latin. Praise and encouragement will help the lesson along:

> First, let [the schoolmaster] teach the childe, cherefullie and plainlie, the cause, and matter of the letter: then, let him construe it into Englishe, so oft, as the childe may easilie carie awaie the understanding of it: Lastlie, parse it over perfitlie. This done thus, let the childe, by and by, both construe and parse it over againe: so, that it may appeare, that the childe douteth in nothing, that his master taught him before. After this, the childe must take a paper booke, and sitting in some place, where no man shall prompe him, by him self, let him translate into Englishe his former lesson. Then shewing it to his master, let the master take from him his latin booke, and pausing an houre, at the least, than let the childe translate his owne Englishe into latin againe, in an other paper booke. When the childe bringeth it, turned into latin, the master must compare it with *Tullies* booke, and laie them both togither: and where the childe doth well, either in chosing, or true placing of *Tullies* wordes, let the master praise him, and saie here ye do well. For I assure you, there is no such whetstone, to sharpen a good witte and encourage a will to learninge, as is praise.

Ascham is adamant about "Jentleness in teaching" and in working with the student toward full comprehension of rhetorical as well as grammatical rules. The pedagogical technique of double translation is also an opportunity to discuss rhetoric:

> But if the childe misse, either in forgetting a worde, or in chaunging a good with a worse, or misordering the sentence, I would not have the master, either froune, or chide with him, if the childe have done his diligence, and used no trewandship therein. For I know by good experience, that a childe shall take more profit of two fautes, jentlie warned of, then of four thinges, rightly hitt.

For than, the master shall have good occasion to saie unto him:
N. Tullie would have used such a worde, not this: *Tullie* would
have placed this worde here, not there: would have used this case,
this number, this person, this degree, this gender: he would have
used this moode, this tens, this simple, rather than this compound:
this adverbe here, not there: he would have ended his sentence
with this verbe, not with that nowne or participle, &c.[25]

This technique formed the basis for a rigorous and rich education
in English as well as Latin. As the student must translate from his
(or her) own English back to a Latin that should be as much like
Cicero's as possible, the nuances of the native language become as
important as those of the classical. Lanyer's two extended prose
pieces in the *Salve Deus Rex Judaeorum* ("To the Lady *Margaret*" and
"To the Vertuous Reader") strongly suggest she received just this
sort of education. Both pieces are Ciceronian in their accumulation
of dependent clauses and parallels, and, more generally, both pieces
are at ease with rhetorical figures and constructions. In a famous
passage from "To the Vertuous Reader," for example, figures of repetition and parallelism give a long sentence impetus and rhythmic
power:

> . . . all women deserve not to be blamed though some forgetting
> they are women themselves, and in danger to be condemned by
> the words of their owne mouthes, fall into so great an errour, as
> to speake unadvisedly against the rest of their sexe; which if it be
> true, I am perswaded they can shew their owne imperfection in
> nothing more: and therefore could wish (for their owne ease,
> modesties, and credit) they would referre such points of folly, to
> be practised by evill disposed men, who forgetting they were
> borne of women, nourished of women, and that if it were not by
> the means of women they would be quite extinguished out of the
> world, and a finall ende of them all, doe like Vipers deface the
> wombes wherein they were bred, onely to give way and utter-
> ance to their want of discretion and goodnesse.[26]

This is Ciceronian hypotactic periodicity, with a series of dependent
clauses building toward a summary conclusion reinforced by a simile
("like Vipers").

Wilson's *Art of Rhetoric,* not surprisingly, is also in evidence in
Lanyer's work. This popular practical guide to the principles espoused

by Ascham went through eight editions between its first publication in 1553 and 1585, and its connection to the Bertie family makes Aemilia's acquaintance with it probable. The work is largely an Englishing of Quintilian, and it has the advantage of bringing to the vernacular the principles presumed to underlie Latin eloquence. One of its effects is to encourage the use of "figures," which Wilson defines as "a certaine kind, either of sentence, Oration, or worde used after some newe or straunge wise, much unlike to that which men commonly use to speake." Here the student will find definitions and examples for many figurative devices, beginning with their main kinds:

> There are three kindes of figures, the one is, when the nature of wordes is chaunged from one signification to an other, called a *Trope,* of the Grecians: The other serveth for words when they are not chaunged by nature, but only altered by speaking, called of the Grecians a *Scheme.* The third is, when by diversity of invention a sentence is many wayes spoken, and also matters are amplified by heaping examples, by dilating arguments, by comparing of things together, by similitudes, by contraries, and by divers other like, called by *Tully* Exornation of sentences, or colours of *Rhetorike.*[27]

What may appear to the modern eye as redundancy or excess in Lanyer's *Salve Deus* (such as the multiple examples of beautiful women threatened and betrayed) are well within the rhetorical guidelines of the age and would not be considered in the least excessive to someone trained in Wilsonian rhetoric. Rhetorical control is a distinguishing feature of Lanyer's collection, and of the title poem in particular. Its structure loosely matches the parts of oration described by Wilson: "i. The Enterance or beginning; ii. The Narration; iii. The Proposition; iv. The Devision or severall parting of things; v. The [C]onfirmation; vi. The [C]onfutation; vii. The Conclusion."[28] The entrance is the evocation of Queen Elizabeth and invocation to the countess of Cumberland. The narration is the rhapsody on the beauty of Christ (ll. 33–144), which, though the speaker describes it as a digression, grounds the importance of the poem's topic. The poem's "proposition" is that the countess of Cumberland will see in this poem a confirmation of her own virtue and consolation for her pain:

> The meditation of this Monarchs love,
> Drawes thee from caring what this world can yield. (ll. 153–54)

The "division" appears to be into simple narrative, but with the added topic of the countess's comparative virtues forming the final section of the poem:

> His death and passion I desire to write,
> And thee to reade, the blessed Soules delight. (ll. 271–72)

The confirmation is the story itself and its significance to the life of the countess, while the confutation is the concluding section that contrasts the countess with other great lovers (Cleopatra, the queen of Sheba). The conclusion situates the countess among the saints, and the poet at her service. The theme of the whole is divine versus earthly beauty, exemplified by the image and passion of Christ and the spousal soul of the countess.

These examples of rhetorical sophistication are the clearest evidence of a humanist education, with Lanyer's classical references offering further support. By the 1580s it was not difficult to learn Horace, Ovid, Virgil, and other classical writers from English translations. Surrey's translation of books 2 and 4 of Virgil's *Aeneid* appeared in 1557, Thomas Phaer's of the first seven books in 1558, and Richard Stanyhurst's odd version of the first four books in 1582. Arthur Golding's translation of books 1–15 of Ovid's *Metamorphoses* appeared in 1567, as did an anonymous translation of his *Heroical Epistles* and Thomas Drant's translation of Horace's *Art of Poetry, Epistles, and Satires*. Jacques Amyot's French version of Plutarch's *Parallel Lives* was available in 1559, while Thomas North's Englishing of Amyot appeared in 1579. Nonetheless, the ease and ubiquity of Lanyer's references to classical figures and stories strongly suggest she encountered them in their original languages, perhaps as well as in translations. There is a learned person's decorum to her use of such references; they appear prominently in her poems to Queen Anne, Arbella Stuart, and the countess of Pembroke, the latter two fine Latinists themselves, and are absent from the poem to Anne Clifford, countess of Dorset, who was not allowed to learn Latin.[29] They pervade the poem "To all vertuous Ladies in generall," suggesting that her ideal audience is an educated one, whereas the *Salve Deus* title poem leans most heavily on the Bible, then on stories recently retold by English writers such as Daniel and Drayton, and lastly on incidental references to the classics (Icarus, Phaeton, ll. 272, 285).

Ascham's schoolmaster anticipated teaching his charge for about seven years, roughly from the ages of seven to fourteen, and then passing the young man on to university.[30] University was not an option for young ladies, however privileged their upbringing, though it was possible for them to continue their tutorials less formally. Queen Elizabeth continued studying with Ascham even after she had come to the throne.[31] We have no evidence that Aemilia Bassano continued formal studies after her sojourn with the dowager countess of Kent, however, nor any specific knowledge of her studies or the years she spent on them.

We do know that Aemilia Lanyer was literate, could apparently read Latin and possibly some Greek,[32] undoubtedly knew Italian and most probably French, and cannot have escaped knowledge of music. Her work shows clear evidence of education in the rhetorical arts consistent with training in the Protestant humanist tradition of Ascham and Wilson. She appears to have been an avid reader of the poetry of her own time. Given the constraints of her situation, she was well educated.

There is some question about when Aemilia served the dowager countess of Kent.[33] The countess is presumed to have gone to Elizabeth's court not long after the death of her husband in 1573 and to have resided there perhaps until the death of her mother in September 1580, after which she apparently lived with her father, Richard Bertie, at the family home in Grimsthorpe. Aemilia may have found a place in the dowager countess's household at court, before or after her father's death in 1576, but the association probably would have ended no later than the dowager countess's remarriage in September 1581 to Sir John Wingfield of Withcoll, Lincolnshire. Aemilia's education would therefore have taken place over roughly five years, from ages seven to twelve, in the household of a woman who was herself between the ages of twenty-two and twenty-seven. A precocious daughter of musicians and a countess made dowager at age nineteen might well produce the somewhat prickly relationship Lanyer alludes to in her poem to the countess. It concludes, on the subject of reward and motivation:

> And since no former gaine hath made me write,
> Nor my desertlesse service could have wonne,
> Onely your noble Virtues do incite
> My Pen, they are the ground I write upon;
>   Nor any future profit is expected,
>   Then how can these poore lines go unrespected? (ll. 43–48)

If Aemilia left the countess's household about the time of Susan's remarriage, she probably returned to live with her mother. Her poems allude to no other youthful service, and the relationship between mother and daughter appears to have been close. Margaret Bassano signed her will with "her marke" on 27 June 1587 and died not long after. The will was probated in Aemilia's presence on 8 July 1587 and its provisions suggest a picture of the family relationships at that time. Margaret begins, in a manner not altogether formulaic, by commending her "soule unto our Lord and saviour Jesus Christ by whose death and passion I hope onelie to be saved." Next, she makes her executrix

> my welbeloved daughter Emelia Bassano unto whom I will and bequeath all my Leases goods and chattels upon condicon that she . . . shall yearlie and quarterlie paye unto Joseph Holland gent my sonne in Lawe and unto Phillipe Holland his sonne and unto the longest lyver of them tenne pound of Lawfull money of England for and dewringe as manie yeares as are yet to come and not earned of and in one Lease for yeares given unto me by Baptist Bassano my late husband deceased nowe in the tenor of Acerbo Velutellye and his assignes.[34]

When Aemilia marries, the will continues, her husband must pay two hundred pounds to Joseph and Phillip Holland to discharge this commitment. In addition, Aemilia is to pay off not only her mother's debts, but also those "that my sonne in Lawe Joseph Holland is bound with me for to paye." Aemilia therefore assumes her brother-in-law's debts insofar as they are "bounde in with [Margaret] and for [her]," which suggests she had cosigned some sort of loan with her son-in-law, though for what purpose is unstated. Margaret designates "the worshipfull Mr. Stephen Vaughan Esquier and Joseph Holland my sonne in Lawe" the overseers of her will and gives "unto Ms Vaughan a ringe of twentie shillings," her only other bequest.

Margaret's will shows confidence in her "welbeloved" eighteen-year-old daughter in naming her executrix and willing her virtually all of her property. Margaret has also taken some responsibility for her son-in-law and grandson, and hands that responsibility on to Aemilia. How much of her father's property remained is not clear, but at his death he had willed Aemilia one hundred pounds to be paid at the time of her marriage or twenty-first birthday, whichever should come first, and left Margaret the leases for three "messuages," or houses with adjoining property, one of which was presumably the source of rent from "Acerbo Vellutellye."[35] Simon Forman, the astrologer Lanyer consulted, records her report that her "father died when she was yonge and he had misfortune. and her mother did out live her father. and the welth of her father failed before he died & he began to be miserable in his estate." Yet he also reports that "she hath 40 [pounds] a yere & was welthy to him that married her / in moni and jewels."[36] Since Baptista Bassano's salary had been about thirty pounds per year, this is indeed a reasonable, though hardly princely, income. Lanyer may well have wished to plead poverty to the fashionable astrologer in the hope that she could keep his fees at a minimum.

The adult Aemilia Bassano spent some time at court, though how long is indeterminable, and whether she came there as mistress to the lord chamberlain or became his mistress after she arrived is as yet unclear. In May 1597 Forman cast a chart "for her life past," under which he describes her as "paramour" of Lord Hunsdon "that was L. chamberlaine"; she "was maintained in great pride." In June he reports that "the old Lord Chamberlain kept her longe & she was maintaind in gret pomp." In September he again records that she enjoyed a favored life in Elizabeth's court.[37]

Henry Carey, Lord Hunsdon (c. 1524–96), was Queen Elizabeth's first cousin on her mother's side and one of her most trusted courtiers. He proved his bravery and loyalty when he helped put down the border rebellion of Catholic earls sympathetic to Mary Stuart, and he continued to watch out for Elizabeth's border interests for the next fifteen years.[38] In 1577 Hunsdon was named to the Queen's Council, and in 1583 he became her lord chamberlain.[39]

The lord chamberlain was responsible for the "immediate needs of the monarch and courtiers" in the queen's household, including her chapel, music and court entertainments generally.[40] It is not surprising that he encountered Aemilia Bassano, daughter, niece, and cousin to highly prized court musicians. The relationship presumably ended with her marriage to Alfonso Lanyer in October 1592. If it were a "long" relationship, as Lanyer reports to Forman, it was surely more than a year or even two, lasting, most likely, from some time after her mother's death in 1587 until October 1592. It seems reasonble to assume that Aemilia's affair with the Lord Chamberlain had begun by the time she was twenty, in January 1589, and that the affair gave her the access to court that she claimed she had in her conversations with Forman.

Henry Carey, Lord Hunsdon, was over sixty when he began his affair with Aemilia Bassano. The portrait of him painted in 1591 when he was sixty-six and at the height of the affair (fig. 1.1) shows an attractive man in vigorous health. With his ample gold braid, staff of office, and richly jewelled knightly medallion, he presents an impressive figure. A painting of Aemilia Bassano would probably portray her like the "Woman in Black" (fig. 1.2), an unidentified woman whose portrait, done by the same painter the following year, is in the collection of Lord Hunsdon's descendants.[41] She is dressed as a gentlewoman with a fine necklace, though not the ropes of pearls affected by noblewomen (such as the countess of Pembroke) in this period. She appears to be in her early or mid-twenties (Lanyer was twenty-three in 1592). The painting's colors show the sitter to be fair,

Fig. 1.1. Henry Carey, Lord Hunsdon, in 1591, at the height of his affair with Aemilia Bassano. Portrait attributed to Marcus Gheeraerts the younger. In the collection of Mr. R. J. G. Berkeley, Berkeley Castle. Photograph courtesy of the Courtauld Institute of Art.

Fig. 1.2. "Unknown Woman in Black," 1592, showing a woman of the right age, social class, and general presentation as Aemilia Bassano, in the collection of the lord chamberlain's descendants. Attributed to Marcus Gheeraerts the younger. In the collection of Mr. R. J. G. Berkeley, Berkeley Castle. Photograph courtesy of the Courtauld Institute of Art.

with a classic "red and white" complexion, and with red hair and dark eyes.

If Aemilia Bassano looked anything like this attractive woman in the prime of her beauty, her appeal is not difficult to imagine. He had enormous power; she had youth, beauty, and intelligence. We have no reason to dispute her claim to Forman that Lord Hunsdon was the father of her son, who was born in early 1593 and whom she named Henry.[42] We know nothing directly about her relationship with Lord Hunsdon other than what she reported to Forman, but there are inferences to be made, perhaps, from works to which she refers in her own work. I'll visit some of those at the end of this chapter.

Whatever the sequence of events that brought her to court and into a relationship with this important lord, Lanyer never abandoned her longing for court and the high-born acquaintances she made there. Her access to court seems to have ended on October 18, 1592, when she married Alfonso Lanyer in the church of St. Botolph's, Aldgate, a parish with connections to her Bassano relatives.[43] Despite her complaints to Forman, the marriage was appropriate for its time.

Alfonso Lanyer was the second of six sons of Nicholas Lanier, a Huguenot flautist who came to England in 1561 after the death of Henri II, in whose musical entourage he had served in France. Aemilia's cousin Lucretia was Nicholas's second wife, whom he married in 1571. It is not clear whether Alfonso was born to Lucretia or to Nicholas's first wife, since the relevant parish registers are not available. David Lasocki argues that, judging from the order in which the Lanier sons received their appointments as court musicians, it is more likely that he was born before 1563.[44] The gap between Alfonso's appointment and that of his older brother, John (1591, 1582), might as easily mean a birth date for Alfonso of 1572 or so. His pursuit of a military career under the earl of Essex in 1597 suggests (though it does not prove) he was a man in his twenties rather than one in his thirties or older. Unfortunately his will has not been found, nor any information about his burial.

Alfonso grew up in Greenwich, where Nicholas moved with Lucretia after their marriage. Alfonso and Aemilia were certain to have been acquainted before their marriage: in addition to being the son or stepson of Aemilia's cousin, he had already become a court musician a year before their marriage, and not long afterwards formally assumed the position left vacant by the death of the recorder player William Daman, who had, in turn, assumed Baptista Bassano's place at his death in 1576.[45] Aemilia therefore married the man who had precisely her father's position at court, though the salary for the position rose to just over forty-eight pounds per year by the time Alfonso died on September 20, 1613.[46]

Aemilia reportedly told Forman that "her husband hath delte hardly with her and spent and consumed her goods and she is nowe very nedy and in debte."[47] Even if Lanyer exaggerated her financial straits, since we must take into account that it was Forman who recorded her comments, there is substantial indication that Alfonso was an adventuresome schemer. He served the earl of Essex at least twice, on the piratical trip to the Azores (the Islands Voyage) in 1597 and in

Ireland in 1599.[48] He negotiated for property and patents, and was consequently involved in petitions and litigation, yet he managed to count among his friends some very important people, including Richard Bancroft, bishop of London and then archbishop of Canterbury, and Thomas Jones, archbishop of Dublin, to whom Alfonso gave a copy of Aemilia's poems. Henry Wriothsley, earl of Southampton, was a supporter, though the earl never regained full royal favor after his implication in the Essex rebellion. (James pardoned him at his accession, and permitted his return to court.) James's preeminent minister, Robert Cecil, appears to have been helpful to Alfonso as well.[49] With all this support, it is interesting that Alfonso was never knighted. Nor did he receive the benefit of his hay and grain patent, awarded in 1604, until 1612.[50] Even granting that law courts and royal favor were notoriously slow and fickle, Alfonso seems to have attracted trouble. He appears not to have performed as a royal musician during James's reign, though he continued to be paid.[51]

Despite Aemilia's reports to Forman, and her disappointment in a life away from court, she and Alfonso were at least seemingly well suited. They were people of similar class and backgrounds who, by temperament, were ambitious for preferment and fortune. They also apparently wanted to have children together. It was for these two reasons that Aemilia Lanyer first went to see Simon Forman in May 1597.

Forman was a popular consultant on a wide variety of matters, who left extensive casebooks on his clients. He kept a folio daily professional diary which included notes on the client, a horoscope cast on the topic of the consultation, and sometimes further notes. He often added his own comments and sometimes reported the outcome of his predictions. He also kept a more personal quarto which he called *Geomantica*, consisting of a series of questions (organized by general categories, but describing specific incidents) below which he cast his own chart, followed by a record of outcomes. These are personal notes; whether they were meant for other eyes or not, they are often about Forman himself, and they are unquestionably the means by which he constructs a sense of self. A major preoccupation in these diaries—perhaps *the* major preoccupation—is sex, with Forman touting and perhaps exaggerating the ease with which he had sexual intercourse with his women clients. These diaries are not impartial records. Another reason for caution is that Forman's handwriting is extremely difficult to read, particularly in the daily folio records, and good scholars may be easily misled. With all that said, Forman's diaries are a great gift to those interested in Aemilia Lanyer, since they provide corroboration of other sources of fact and give us our one close glimpse of her effect on another person. Though disagreements remain about some readings, the overall picture is clear.

Aemilia Lanyer visited Simon Forman for his prediction and advice about her husband's (and her own) prospects for social advancement and for help with a history of miscarriages. Her first visit occurs on 18 May 1597, where she is mentioned as residing in the Longditch area of the City of Westminster.[52] There was a "long ditch" in the northwest area of Westminster, "so called," according to the contemporary surveyist John Stow, "for that the same almost insulateth the City of Westminster." This would place the Lanyers' residence near the royal deer park of St. James, and not far from the royal court (fig. 1.3).[53] There are no further notes on this first meeting, but when she returns on 25 May she is identified as "Emilia Bassana of 27 years" (she was twenty-eight), the daughter ("filia") of "Baptista Bassane" and "Margarete Jhonson," and the wife of "Alfonso Lanir." Forman casts two astrological charts side by side: one for her current situation, and one "for her life past," and records some things about her that are presumably relevant to her reasons for consulting him. These include the information that she was unchaste and "hath had a child in fornication," with the reference to being Hundsdon's mistress mentioned earlier, "and yt seemes that being with child she was for collour married to a minstrell."[54] The appellation is not necessarily derogatory. "Minstrel" most commonly referred to a musician, though its association with clowns and entertainers generally has tended to diminish its class connotations over the centuries. In Lanyer's time, however, a court musician carried the title "gentleman," and since Lanyer's heritage is richly embedded in the court music scene, even if the word is her own and not Forman's (which is doubtful), it is not to be taken as dismissive of the family profession. To be suddenly married to a musician, however, was an abrupt, rather dramatic change from life in the world of the lord chamberlain; Lanyer's desire to regain some of her lost status in income and social standing brings her to Forman. "Yt seameth she hath hard fortune in her youth," Forman writes on this same visit, noting some signs that he sees in her chart, and adding the reference to her father's death and loss of income.

Aemilia returned to Forman on 3 June, stating directly her two concerns.[55] She asks whether "her husband shall have the suit," pre-

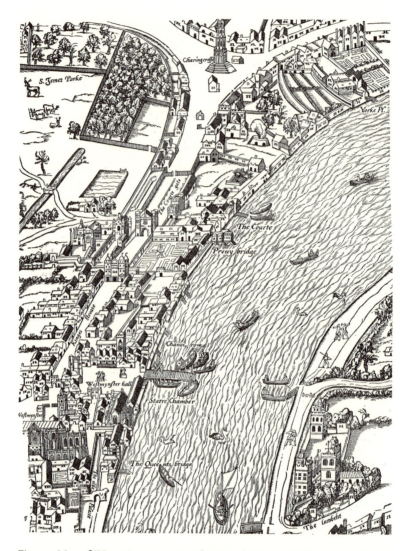

Fig. 1.3. Map of Westminster, c. 1559, showing the "long ditch" on the left near which Aemilia and Alfonso Lanyer resided when she visited Simon Forman. Note the proximity to the Queen's court of St. James, center left, and St. Margaret's parish church Westminster, the steeple just above Westminster Abbey at the bottom left. This was the Lanyers' parish church, where their daughter Odillya was baptised in 1599. Courtesy of the Guildhall Library.

sumably some form of advancement,[56] and she reports difficulty with pregnancy: "she seams to be with child of 12 daies or 12 weeks [here he would appear to be recording directly what she says, as she or he makes the correction] moch pain in the left syd." She has apparently tried some cure, "but the conception will not stai with her." After more astrological signs, Forman summarizes: "She hath mani fals conceptions. And he shall have the suet but she shalbe first in despaire of it." Following this conclusion is a summary about her education, marriage, and relationship with the lord chamberlain, including the comments that "she is hie minded. she hath som thing in the mind she wold have don for her" and "She can hardly kepe secret. She was very brave in youth / she hath manie fals conceptions. she hath a sone his name is henri." "Brave" here doubtless means "finely dressed; splendid . . . showy" (*OED*). The portrait is of an ambitious, assertive woman, probably still very attractive. The cryptic comment, "she hath som thing in the mind she would have don for her" may reflect the elusive imprecise nature of an astrological reading, or may be Forman's attempt to work toward an interpretation of this impressive woman who has come to him for help.

The notation for 16 June 1597 again presents the two reasons for Lanyer's visits, and implies that Alfonso has now left for the military adventure that became known as the Islands Voyage.[57] Ralegh's "gentlemen volunteers" would sail from Plymouth 10 July. She comes, "Mrs. Lanier for the husband," to ask whether "he shall com to any p[ref]erment before he com hom Again or no & how he shall sped." The chart for this is cast. Then Forman notes that she reports "moch pain in the bottom of the belly, womb, stomack & hed / & redy to vomit," after which he sets some more astrological figures. What follows is difficult to decipher, but the fetus appears not to be viable ("kiks not her body"), for which Forman gives her medicine ("apoth[ic] drink . . . purgat[ive] decoction").

The miscarriage seems to have taken place, probably not long after. Lanyer's gynecological problems are not mentioned again in Forman's entries, the next of which comes two and a half months later. Forman records her visit on 2 September 1597, at 2:00 PM, on the subject of whether "she shall be a Ladi. & how she shall speed" (fig. 1.4).[58] After casting her chart, he comments on her background and for the first and only time on her physical appearance. This is a passage worth presenting in full, since it shows Forman's sexual awareness of Lanyer. "She hath bin favored moch of her mati [majesty] and of mani noble men & hath had gret gifts & bin moch made

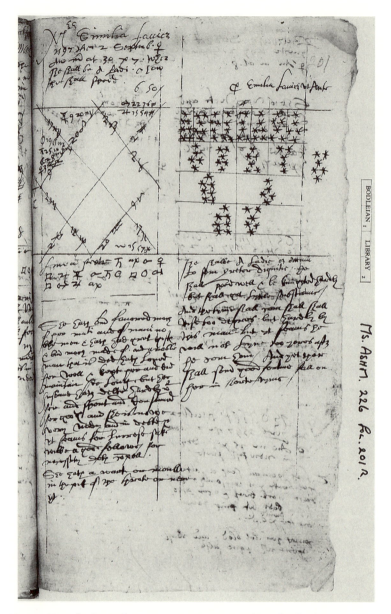

Fig. 1.4. Entry for September 2, 1597, in Simon Forman's casebook. The only known reference to Lanyer's appearance is at the bottom of the left-hand column: "She hath a wart or moulle in the pit of her throte or ner yt." Bodleian Ms. Ashmole 226, f. 201. Courtesy of the Bodleian Library.

of. and a noble man that is ded hath Loved her well & kept her and did maintain her Long. but her husband hath delte hardly wth her and spent and consumed her goods and she is nowe very nedy and in debte & it seams for Lucrese sake wilbe a good fellow for necessity doth co[m]pell. She hath a wart or moulle in the pit of the throte or ner yt." In a second column on the same page, under the heading "Emilia Lanier," he casts an arrangement of stars and predicts beneath it: "She shallbe A Ladie or attain to some greter dignitie. he shall sped well & be knighted hardly but shall get lyttle substaunce. And the tyme shall com [she] shall rise too degrees. but hardly by this man. but it seams he will not lyve too yeres after he com hom / And yet ther shall some good fortune fall on her in shorte tyme."

The 2 September and the 27 May entry, along with entries from the *Geomantica*, form the basis of A. L. Rowse's assumption that Aemilia Lanyer was sexually promiscuous.[59] If we attend to Forman's language, however, and notice the dates, a different picture emerges. Forman casts no horoscope for Lanyer after 2 September 1597, although on 29 September 1597 there is a reference to "Emilia Lanie[r] the daughter of Baptista & Margaret Bassana," and in 1600 a cryptic entry beside Forman's casting of his own horoscope "at 5 pm 7 Jan. to know whi Mrs Lanier sent for me and . . . whe[the]r she entends any mor villani / or noe."[60]

The sexual interest evident in the 2 September diary entry sparks the first entry about Aemilia Lanyer in the *Geomantica*, also dated 2 September.[61] Under the general topic "Of digniti and office," Forman poses the question from the diary, expanding somewhat on the details of the situation. "A Gentlewoman whose husband was gone to sea with therle of Essex in hope to be knighted thought there was litle cause whie he should. demaund in his absence wh[eth]er she should be a Ladie or no . . . Emilia Lanier." Below this entry two charts are cast side by side, presumably of Alfonso and Aemilia Lanyer. Beneath the first, Forman has written "he was not knighted nor [now?] worthy therof." Under the second, "she shall not nor [now?] was not now [nor?] worthi therof." The indistinguishability of "nor" and "now" makes Forman's conclusions less than crystal clear. This matters considerably less, I think, than the fact of the entry itself. September 2 represents a turning point in Forman's fascination with Lanyer and leads him to take some action.

The crux for deciphering Forman and Lanyer's relationship is the 11 September 1597 report of his visit to her, and its vexed account of an incomplete sexual encounter. He has either been led or allowed himself to believe that Aemilia, whose husband was away at sea, might entertain him sexually. If she is very "nedy and in debte," will she trade sex for money (or perhaps for free consultations with the great astrologer)? There is no evidence that she has said so. Whenever Forman prefaces a diary entry with "it seems," it is a good bet he is guessing or extrapolating from either what a client has told him or from the star chart or both. The chart he cast on 25 May led him to conclude she had had a difficult youth (I have added the emphasis): "*yt seameth* she hath had hard fortune in her youth in respect that by the" and here follows the series of astrological symbols that indicate past hardship. In the same consultation, he reports his interpretation of what she has told him of her life, and of her "child in fornication," by noting that "*yt seames* that being with child she was for collour married to a minstrell." Similarly, on 2 September, as she visits him apparently free from the pain that accompanied her May and June visits, Forman chooses to interpret her crying poor this way: "*it seams* for lucrese [i.e., money's] sake [she] wilbe a good fellow for necessity doth co[m]pell."

This, then, is the background for the 11 September *Geomantica* entry, which falls under the general topic, "Beste to doe a thinge or noe."[62] Forman's diaries make frequent reference to his sexual conquests, and he uses the word "halek" to signify sexual intercourse. On the night of 11 September, 1597, he was on the prowl. "A certain man longed to see A gentlewoman whom he loved & desired to hal[e]k with. and because he could not tell howe to com to her. & whe[the]r he should be welcom to her or noe, maied this question whe[the]r yt were beste to send to her to knowe how she did. and therbi to tri whe[the]r she wold byd the messanger byd his mr rond to her or noe. Thinking therby he might goe the bolder therby to see her." Forman then casts a chart under the name "Lanier" and beneath it reports on the result: "The [partie] sent his servante by whom she sente word that yf his mr came he should be welcom /. & he wente and supped with her and staid all nighte. and she was familiar & friendlie to him in all things. but only she wold not halek. yet he felte all p[ar]tes of her body willingly .& kyssed her often. but she wold not doe in any wise wher upon he toke some displesure & soe dep[ar]ted [i.e., stopped being] frinds. but not intending to com at her Again in haste." Then, in lighter ink and crowding the astrological analysis, an entry that appears to have been added later: "but yet they were frinds again afterward / but he never obteyned his purpos & she was a hore & delt evill with him after /."

Rowse believes that the mention of her name and parentage only in the 29 September diary entry indicates a sexual liaison. If it had, Forman would surely have said so. His freedom in announcing his sexual conquests elsewhere, and Lanyer's (at least partial) rejection on 11 September, make silence an unlikely response to success, particularly given the extent to which Forman defines himself throughout his diaries in terms of his sexual activity. More likely, Forman was frustrated and angry. He may have been hopeful after some physical contact (it is difficult to know from his description how much, since he is building a case against her as a tease). He apparently kept trying, but "she wold not halek," indeed "she would not doe in any wise," at which point he apparently left and came back; they were friends after this encounter, but "he never obteyned his purpose" and so labels her "a hore." Forman's frustration also most likely explains his violent reaction when she sends for him two and a half years later.

Far from the promiscuous courtesan of Rowse's portrait, Aemilia Lanyer was at least careful. Even with her unhappy history of miscarriages, she is not fool enough to risk intercourse at a time when her husband is quite publicly somewhere else. Given his self-construction, it makes sense that Forman would pursue the attractive former mistress of a very powerful man. Given his betrayal of her confidence in seeking his own pleasure, it is surprising that she would come by his office at all two weeks and then two and a half years later. But that is perhaps a late-twentieth-century surprise. Forman used his profession to attract distressed women and have sex with them. If they and he did not see it as the betrayal of trust that we do today, some may have been uneasy nonetheless about this exploitative behavior. The voice of Pilate's wife in Lanyer's *Salve Deus* condemns the general perfidy of men and demands that women have their "Libertie again" (l. 825). This poem and the prose dedication "To the Vertuous Reader" are peppered with references to women betrayed or exploited, or women overcoming those who would betray or exploit them: Lucrece, Octavia, Rosamond, Matilda, Hester, Judith, Susanna. Forman is not the only man in Lanyer's own life who must have inspired the poet's indignation on behalf of women—the lord chamberlain himself and those who "made moch" of young Aemilia Bassano at court are surely important to the mix. But knowing that she approached Forman for help with matters at the heart of her life and identity, and that he attempted to use that approach as a sexual opportunity, we have evidence of a specific event, or life model, that perhaps explains the transgressive language of Lanyer's poems.

Why did Lanyer come to Forman in the first place, and, having rejected his efforts to "halek," approach him again in early 1600? The answers to the first question are clear in her stated purposes for her visits. Perhaps the death of Lord Hunsdon the previous July, the last link to a time of cosseted youth among the nobility, along with Alfonso's decision to pursue advancement in service to the earl of Essex, provoked the anxiety and hope for her own future that prompted her visit to Forman. In addition, Forman appears to have been effective in soliciting trust.

The answer to the second question, why she sought to re-establish contact in early 1600, may relate to Aemilia and Alfonso's success, at last, at having a child of their own. Alfonso returned from the Islands expedition without a knighthood, but with the apparent goodwill of the Essex faction, and of his wife. "Odillya," listed as the daughter of "Alphonso Laniere," was baptised at St. Margaret's, Westminster, on 2 December 1598.[63] In March 1599 Essex went to Ireland, where Alfonso rejoined him,[64] at which point Aemilia may have moved back to one of her properties in St. Botolph's, Bishopsgate. Their daughter was buried there on 6 September 1599. Though infant mortality was high, and Aemilia had already suffered her share of losses, this must have been particularly cruel. With her husband in Ireland, it is easy to imagine her making a desperate attempt to find some help where she may have believed it came in 1597. She did, after all, carry a child to term after consulting Forman, and, if Alfonso was not yet knighted, he was still and again in pursuit of advancement. But this is mere surmise.

Alfonso Lanyer returned again without a knighthood, but survived the Essex rebellion of 1601. He may possibly have been implicated sufficiently to make his future efforts at reward more difficult, yet he seemed to have enough money and property to engage in the various deals that mark his associations with Robert Cecil, Bishop Bancroft, and other less prominent figures.[65] We do not know where he lived, or whether he and Aemilia lived together. In March 1609 Alfonso may have been living in the village of Hackney, Middlesex (about four miles northeast of the city of London), where he and another gentleman were arrested for disturbing the peace.[66] What is notable from the record of Alfonso's activities during the first decade of the seventeenth century is that he seems always to be engaged in activities with his male friends and supporters, while sometime during the decade, for how long or in what capacity we do not know, Aemilia was with Margaret Clifford, the countess of Cumberland (fig. 1.5), and her daughter Anne (fig. 1.6) at Cookham, a royal manor in the possession of William Russell of Thornhaugh, Margaret's brother. The estate was located roughly twenty-five miles west of the city of London and just a few miles from Windsor. As Barbara Lewalski notes, "the area is still a beauty spot. Located in Berkshire, a few miles from Maidenhead, it has extensive frontages on the Thames, rich woodlands, lush meadows, picturesque scattered hamlets, and high hills in the west." Margaret was apparently at Cookham during periods from about 1603 until sometime after the death of her estranged husband, George Clifford, in 1605. Lanyer may have joined them for all or part of that time.[67]

The countess of Cumberland and the sojourn at Cookham provide the impetus for Aemilia Lanyer's volume of poems. The first decade of the century, however elusive the precise details are, is therefore of crucial importance in Lanyer's definition of self and the female subject that she seeks to advance in her poetry. Her stay at

Fig. 1.5. Margaret Rusell, countess of Cumberland, c. 1585. Portrait by an unknown artist. Courtesy of the National Portrait Gallery, London.

Fig. 1.6. Anne Clifford, countess of Dorset, around the time of her first marriage (c. 1610). In the collection of the Lord Sackville, Knole. Photograph courtesy of the Courtauld Institute of Art.

Cookham may have seemed a return to the aristocratic glory Lanyer had known in her youth, though her most appropriate role in the countess's household was as a gentlewoman servant with some responsibilities for the education of Anne Clifford. Unfortunately, although Anne kept a diary and wrote a biography of her long and interesting life, the relevant diary years are missing, and there is no reference to Lanyer in any extant Clifford records.[68] These records are not abundant, though they tell us that Anne Clifford's childhood governess was one Ann Taylor, and we know that her tutor was the poet Samuel Daniel, who had earlier been tutor to the sons of the countess of Pembroke (the younger of whom, Philip, Anne Clifford would later take as her second husband). As Pamela Benson has suggested, Lanyer may have served in the Clifford household as some sort of music tutor, though she may also have helped Anne with French and Italian.[69]

The Clifford "Great Picture," which Anne commissioned when she was fifty-three (in 1643) to confirm her heritage and emblematize her life, has three panels: the center a portrait of her parents and the brothers who did not live past childhood; the right a portrait of herself at the time she commissioned the painting; and the left a portrait of herself at fifteen, the year of her father's death and what she had long asserted to be the moment of her inheritance. Each panel is rich with appropriate symbols, including the books Anne apparently read and valued at fifteen and then at fifty-three. The portrait of her at fifteen also has, set in front of her, a lute, and her hand rests on an open book.[70] Anne Clifford knew and valued music when she was fifteen, and someone must have taught her.

There are hints in "The Description of Cooke-ham" that Lanyer was at least a musical companion to the countess and her daughter. Music was among the idyllic activities at Cookham, particularly the singing of psalms.

> With lovely *David* you [Margaret] did often sing,
> His holy Hymnes to Heavens Eternall King.
> And in sweet musicke did your soule delight
> To sound his prayses, morning, noone, and night. (ll. 87–90)

More specifically, the "sport" and "recreations" Lanyer attributes to Anne sound very like the singing of madrigals, often with themes of love:

> Remember beauteous *Dorsets* former sports,
> So farre from beeing toucht by ill reports;
> Wherein my selfe did alwaies beare a part,
> While reverend Love presented my true heart:
> Those recreations let me beare in mind,
> Which her sweet youth and noble thoughts did finde. (ll. 119–24)

In this reading, the "part" Lanyer bore was a musical one, and the innocent theme of love, far from from producing "ill reports" of the young pupil, was also "true" in the heart of the loving servant. Lanyer continues to "beare in mind" Anne's delightful and inventive "recreations," perhaps of poetry as well as music. The three of them also studied books together: the majestic Cookham oak they must leave behind is a place "Where many a learned Booke was read and skand" (l. 161).

We may never know precisely what Lanyer's relationship was to Margaret and her daughter. It may be that she was, as she claims, simply a poet patronized by a countess who rewarded other poets as well, including Spenser and Daniel. This unusual and possibly unique relationship certainly emboldens Lanyer's praise of women. In any event, Lanyer's dedications to mother and daughter show she knew their principal sufferings and concerns: Margaret's grief over the unhappy relationship with her late husband, and Anne's (and Margaret's) effort to reclaim Anne's inheritance as the "sole heir" of the earl of Cumberland.[71] There is every reason to suppose the relationship, for however long and however defined, was close enough to permit both that knowledge and Lanyer's right to comment on it.

Anne Clifford sought to honor the people who had taught her and whom she and her mother had patronized by erecting a monument in the church where they were buried. She is responsible for the monument to Spenser in Westminster Abbey and the one to Samuel Daniel at the church in Beckington where he was buried. We cannot know whether she ever produced a memorial for Aemilia Lanyer, since the church of St. James Clerkenwell was thoroughly demolished in the eighteenth century to make way for the present church. Yet it is just possible that Lanyer's move to Clerkenwell may signal a continuing connection with Anne. The countess of Cumberland acquired a house on Clerkenwell Green in 1596 where Anne spent much of her childhood, and which she presumably inherited from her mother.[72]

The book of poems that, in large part, came out of Lanyer's stay at Cookham was pivotal in Lanyer's life and is, of course, her claim to our attention. Her husband died in 1613, and with him went his pension as a royal musician. She inherited the hay and grain patent but signed it over to Alfonso's brother, Innocent Lanier, with the understanding that he would get it extended and they would split the proceeds. Complications from this arrangement put her in litigation with Alfonso's relatives during the 1630s, and it is unclear what portion of the patent she received.[73]

From 1617 until the summer of 1619 Lanyer ran a school in the wealthy suburb of St. Giles in the Field, her only activity after Alfonso's death about which we have any detail. The effort was marred by a dispute over rent and repairs with her landlord, a lawyer named Edward Smith, which culminated in a suit and countersuit over who owed whom what. In her petition she describes her situation as "by the death of [her] husband beinge left in verry poore estate hee havinge spente a great parte of his estate in the servinge of the Late Queene in her warres of Ireland and other places," so that "for her maynetaynaunce and releefe [she] was compelled to teach and educate the children of divers persons of worth and under-standinge."[74] We have no record of whom or what she taught, but the disagreement with her landlord (who had a tenant he preferred) seems to have ended the enterprise.[75]

Henry Lanyer followed the family tradition and became a court musician, formally receiving an apppointment in 1629.[76] By that time he had married Joyce Mansfield, with whom he had a daughter, Mary, baptised 25 July 1627, and a son, Henry, baptised 16 January 1630, both at St. James Clerkenwell. It was there that he was buried in October 1633, leaving the care of his children to his wife, to whom they were formally granted in 1634.[77] His death may have led his mother to pur-sue the family title to Alfonso's hay and grain patent. Legal activity on this issue heats up in 1634, when Aemilia presents herself as petition-ing on behalf of her two grandchildren as well as herself.[78]

Whatever her final circumstances, when she was buried at St. James Clerkenwell on 3 April 1645, she was listed as a "pensioner," denoting someone with regular income.[79] She had lived seventy-six years, through all of the reign of James I and good portions of those of Elizabeth I and Charles I, a very long life for her time. She had been in the court, on its margins, and finally some distance from it seeking income as a teacher and a widow. It would be good to know more of her personal story, and perhaps someday we will, but she holds our interest through the book of poems she used to construct an identity as a woman poet and a woman's poet. Her publication is also an evident effort to negotiate a heightened public role for her-self in a world in which gender compounded by relatively low birth made public self-definition difficult. She was doubtless motivated by her early proximity to power, but her book shows that, beyond a desire for self-presentation, she also saw herself as an advocate for women. Her early reading may have helped her consider issues of gender. It did provide her with models for poetic narrative. The one contemporary poet she most certainly read was Samuel Daniel, and I conclude this chapter by noting some evidence of Daniel's influ-ence on Lanyer, and possibly Lanyer's influence on Daniel.

Lanyer and Daniel: Aemilia and Rosamond

Samuel Daniel's career has several important contiguities with Aemilia Lanyer's, although at first glance it is the differences that are more apparent. Born in Somerset about 1563, he spent three years at

Magdalen Hall, Oxford, beginning in 1581, where he focused much of his energy on the (noncurricular) study of modern languages. This led to his translating an Italian book of emblems in 1584 (Paolo Giovio's *Dialogo dell'Imprese*) which he dedicated to the queen's champion, Sir Edward Dymoke.[80] In 1585 he traveled to Paris, and for at least some time between 1586 and 1591 he was in Italy with Dymoke, who encouraged his interest in things Italian. In 1591, twenty-six of Daniel's "Delia" sonnets were appended to Thomas Newman's pirated edition of Sir Philip Sidney's *Astrophil and Stella,* which may have first introduced Daniel to the patronage of the countess of Pembroke. In late 1591 or shortly thereafter he joined her household at Wilton as tutor to her children, William and Philip Herbert, the future earls of Pembroke and Montgomery, and then very probably to their sister Anne Herbert and cousin Lady Mary Sidney, the future author of the *Urania*.[81]

The connections with Lanyer's life begin to appear in the 1590s but are more direct in the early 1600s. Daniel was probably at court sometime during 1589–91, as Aemilia Bassano was. His role as Dymoke's trusted servant would logically bring him with the queen's champion to the court, and he is mentioned by name in Spenser's *Colin Clouts Come Home Again*, an ostensible report of Colin/Spenser's experiences at court during those years.[82] After his service as tutor to the Herberts, Daniel became tutor to Lady Anne Clifford and resided for some time between 1599 and 1605 in the Clifford household. He may well have known the family earlier; Dymoke and George Clifford, the earl of Cumberland, doubtless encountered each other in jousts and tiltyard entertainments before the queen.[83]

Daniel's early career is closely connected to the mothers of his tutees. His first publication, and the one on which Spenser presumably based his favorable estimate of the poet's talent and best direction, was a book of poems entitled *Delia. Contayning certayne Sonnets: with the complaint of Rosamond.* Printed in early 1592 by Simon Waterson (who was to remain his friend as well as publisher), it contained a short prose preface dedicating the book to the countess of Pembroke. Among the first to develop the craze for sonnet sequences that *Astrophel* propelled, Daniel added to and corrected the sonnets published with Sidney's in 1591 and appended a "Complaint" in traditional English narrative rime royal (ababbcc). A new edition appeared in 1594, this time with the addition of a more personal verse dedication to the countess and a neoclassical drama, *Cleopatra,* presumably a companion to the countess's own translation of Robert Garnier's *Antonie*.[84]

In 1599 Daniel published his *Poeticall Essays*, including his previous poems and adding *A Letter from Octavia to Marcus Antonius*, dedicated to the countess of Cumberland and, in its focus on the abandoned wife, very probably "an oblique comment on the Countess's personal situation."[85] In 1603 he presented a *Panegyrike* to King James. It was published accompanied by *Certaine Epistles*. In order, these were to: "Sir Thomas Egerton, Knight, Lord Keeper of the Great seale of England"; "Lord Henry Howard, one of his Majesties Privy Councell"; "The Ladie Margaret, Countesse of Cumberland"; "The Ladie Lucie, Countesse of Bedford"; "The Ladie Anne Clifford"; and "Henry Wriothesly, Earle of Southampton." The connections to Aemilia Lanyer that these poems suggest go beyond the dedications to the countess of Cumberland, Anne Clifford, and the countess of Bedford, to whom she also dedicated poems. In his petition to Robert Cecil on behalf of Alfonso Lanyer, Bishop Bancroft reported to Robert Cecil that he and Alfonso "served both together the Lord Chancellor," Thomas Egerton. Bancroft also mentions that Alfonso "was put in hope of your [Cecil's] favor by the Earl of Southampton."[86] The remaining dedicatee, Henry Howard, earl of Northumberland, was second son of the poet the earl of Surrey, who was executed in 1547 in a power struggle at the end of the reign of Henry VIII, and brother of Thomas Howard, duke of Norfolk, executed in 1572 for being involved in a Catholic plot to put Mary Stuart on the throne. Henry, described by a modern historian as "a sinister figure of intrigue," was a survivor who died in his bed in 1614 at age seventy-four, despite having been (like Wriothsley) a strong partisan of the Essex faction.[87]

These poems, written and published in the first years of the new century, address a circle whose favor Alfonso sought in his hopes for advancement, at a time when he was pursuing his various schemes. Alfonso or Aemilia very probably knew all of these dedicatees. The dedications strengthen the evidence we have of Alfonso and Aemilia's circle of acquaintances from roughly 1600 to 1605.

Although Alfonso was never knighted for his service to the earl of Essex, he was made "captain" and given the opportunity to know some important members of the earl's circle, including Wriothsley and Henry Howard. Bishop Bancroft had probably served as chaplain to Sir Thomas Egerton, so Alfonso's service "together" with him may have been in some musical capacity (the chapel and musicians were part of the same administrative unit in the royal court, and presumably in the great houses as well) or it may have been in some

capacity related to the more difficult and complex events surrounding the fall of Essex, in which Egerton played an important mediating role.[88] Whatever the nature of Alfonso's service to Essex and
Egerton, he moved on the edges of the most important transition of
his generation: from the rule of an aging queen to the rule of a king,
in anticipation of which Essex and many other young men had chafed
under the old order and pushed toward the new. It is in the context
of these times that Daniel's famous dismissive comment in a letter
to Egerton may be best understood: "such hath been my misery, that
whilst I should have written the actions of *men,* I have been con-
strayned to live with *children,* and contrary to myne owne spirit, putt
out of the scene, which nature had made my parte."[89] Daniel himself never gained the preferment he wished under the king, though
he found an excellent patron in Queen Anne.[90]

The first two decades of the seventeenth century are notable for
the sharp and visible divisions that existed between men and women.
Whatever the actual relations of the sexes in the broad sweep of
English society, at court and among the would-be wits the battle was
acute. All the male longing for a court of king and men poured out
in the many panegyricks to James. The "woman controversy," documented as a literary genre by Linda Woodbridge, had faded at the
end of Elizabeth's reign but reached new heights under the king,
whose homosexual relationships parlayed handsome young favorites into key positions of influence (Robert Carr, George Villiers).
James's court was also relentlessly homosocial, allowing Queen
Anne to create a court of her own, for which Daniel wrote several
masques.[91]

While Alfonso worked to maintain his manly Essex connections,
Aemilia discovered the community of women. If she was indeed
Anne Clifford's music tutor at about the same time that Daniel was
tutoring Anne in other subjects, the two poets would have been in
frequent contact. Of all the English poets that she directly or indirectly
cites (including both Sidneys, Drayton, and possibly Shakespeare),
Daniel is the one she refers to most often. She makes specific reference to at least three of Daniel's works: *Cleopatra, A Letter from Octavia,*
and, most tellingly, *Rosamond.*

In the *Salve Deus* Lanyer's references to Cleopatra are remarkably
positive. While versions of her story were amply available, Daniel's
revised version (1609) is the one that most plays up the Egyptian
queen's virtues, particularly her constancy and stoicism. Toward the
end of her poem, Lanyer summarizes and extends her portrait of the

countess of Cumberland's loving faithfulness to Christ. "Great Cleopatra's love to Anthony," she tells the countess, "Can no way be compared unto thine [for Christ]" (ll. 1409–10). On the surface, any such comparison makes no sense in the light of the other examples, such as the queen of Sheba and martyrs for the Christian faith, unless there is a model for Cleopatra that validates her virtues as well as her failings. That model is not Daniel's 1594 *The Tragedy of Cleopatra*, which he claimed to be a sequel to the countess of Pembroke's *Antonius* but which defies the complexity of Robert Garnier and the countess's translation bring to the Egyptian queen. It is instead the 1607 version, which signals a raprochement between Daniel and the countess of Pembroke after a period of some alienation (and follows Daniel's service to the countess of Cumberland and Anne Clifford). In the later version Daniel adds the scene between Cleopatra and the dying Antony, in which "Daniel follows [the countess of Pembroke] in turning the episode, missing from his 1594 play, into an occasion for Cleopatra to negate accusations of faithlessness with an irrefutable demonstration of loyalty and love."[92]

More than her portryal of Cleopatra, however, Lanyer's references to the sufferings of Antony's wife, Octavia, place her in relation to Daniel. Early in the *Salve Deus* both Antony and Cleopatra are set in secondary relation to Octavia in a clear reference to the poem Daniel dedicated to the countess of Cumberland. The topic, and a major theme of the *Salve Deus*, is the danger of earthly beauty:

> Beautie the cause Antonius wrong'd his wife,
> Which could not be decided but by sword:
>   Great Cleopatra's Beautie and defects
>   Did worke *Octaviaes* wrongs, and his neglects. (ll. 213–16)

The later reference to Cleopatra's failure in constancy again brings in the figure of Octavia:

> That glorious part of Death, which last shee plai'd,
> T'appease the ghost of her desceased Love,
> Had never needed, if she could have stai'd
> When his extreames made triall, and did prove
> Her leaden love unconstant, and afraid:
> Their wicked warres the wrath of God might move
>   To take revenge for chast *Octavia's* wrongs,
>   Because shee enjoyes what unto her belongs. (ll. 1417–24)

Octavia is too uncommon a subject for Lanyer's emphasis to be accidental. Her debt to Daniel's *Octavia* may even extend to its verse form (eight-line stanzas riming ababababcc) and certain turns of phrase. Consider, for example, Octavia's concluding recognition that her complaint has perhaps carried her farther than her "scope" would allow:

> But whither am I carried all this while
> Beyond my scope, and know not when to cease?[93] (st. 51)

And Lanyer, reining in her efforts at a high style:

> But my deare Muse, now whither wouldst thou flie,
> Above the pitch of thy appointed straine? (ll. 273–74)

Ottava rima and the *humilitas* topos are common enough not to prove direct influence, much less imitation, but Lanyer's portrait of Cleopatra, and especially her references to *Octavia*, are sound indications that she knew Daniel's work.

While Cleopatra is the primary referent for Lanyer's theme of the dangers of earthly beauty, two other figures receive explicit attention in the *Salve Deus*, complete with sidenotes: Matilda, a woman portrayed by Michael Drayton as heroically resisting a lustful King John, and Rosamond, an early member of the Clifford family who became mistress to a much older King Henry II and was purportedly murdered by Queen Eleanor. Rosamond was well known to Lanyer's generation from Daniel's *Complaint of Rosamond*.

This was a popular poem. It derived from the complaint pattern of *The Mirror for Magistrates* and prompted Thomas Churchyard to revise and reissue his *Mirror* story of Jane Shore, *Rosamond's* most obvious model.[94] It is likely the work that led Spenser to urge Daniel to lift his sights beyond sonneteering, believing his "accent will excell / In Tragick plaints and passionate mischance" (*Colin Clouts*, ll. 426–27). *Rosamond's* popularity probably spurred Michael Drayton to write his *England's Heroicall Epistles*, modeled loosely on Ovid's *Heroides*, which included *The Legend of Matilda* and also versions of Rosamond's complaint and Henry's reply.[95] For Aemilia Lanyer, however, it may have had personal resonance.

The first edition of *Rosamond* appeared while Aemilia Bassano was still mistress of the lord chamberlain, in the time of her full glory in the court of Elizabeth. It tells the story of a beautiful young woman who has left her parents to live at court, enjoys there the effect her beauty has on others ("Soone could I teach my browe to tyrannize. / And make the world do homage to mine eyes," ll. 111–12), and falls into adultery only after much hesitation and temptation.[96] There are many elements of the story that seem far from the life of Aemilia Bassano, including the relatively high birth of Rosamond Clifford, the retirement from court as a result of her liaison with the king, and her murder by a jealous queen. Yet there are core similarities to Aemilia's situation. Rosamond has no parents to guide her. She is a young woman pursued by an old man "after all his victories . . . / Tryumphing in the honour of his deedes" (ll. 169–70). He is completely infatuated:

> No armour might bee founde that coulde defend
> Transpearcing rayes of Christall-pointed eyes:
> No stratagem, no reason could amend,
> No not his age; yet old men should be wise: (ll. 176–79)

Rosamond (like Aemilia in her report to Forman) is well aware of her effect and enjoys it ("What might I then not doe whose powre was such? / What cannot women doe that know theyr powre?," ll. 134–35), but Daniel's heroine at first holds firm to her chastity:

> The Crowne that could commaund what it requires
> I lesser priz'd than chastities attires,
>> Th'unstained vaile, which innocents adornes,
>> Th'ungathred Rose, defended with the thornes. (ll. 214–17)

She is tempted, however, not only by Henry's passion and power, but also by "One of my Sexe, of place, and nature bad" who "set upon me the smoothest speech, / That Court and age could cunningly devise" (ll. 219, 225–26). This "seeming Matrone" (l. 223) displays a fine rhetorical skill in persuading Rosamond to seize her "happy chaunce" (l. 232) and give in to the king. Her primary argument is classic carpe diem, the need to seize the day before youth fades, but she also dismisses the idea of "Fame" as mere outward show, dependent upon surfaces: "Pleasure is felt, opinion but conceav'd, / Honor, a thing without us, not our owne" (ll. 274–75). Sophisticated courtiers, the older woman tells this parentless country girl, "Esteeme them chast ynough that best seeme so" (l. 282). Rather than losing honor, a beautiful girl who gives in will find "The mightie . . . / In steed of shame doe honors great bestow," and a king, "Being sacred, sanctifies the sin" (ll. 295–96, 301). Finally, the king's very age becomes an inducement to give in:

> What, doost thou stand on thys, that he is olde,
> Thy beauty hath the more to worke uppon:
> Thy pleasures want shal be supply'd with gold,
> Cold age dotes most when the heate of youth is gone. (ll. 302–5)

Octavia, dedicated to the countess of Cumberland, was evidently meant to acknowledge her problems with the earl. *Delia,* dedicated to the countess of Pembroke, is a tribute to her brother Sidney's importance as the founder of a new English poetry. Margaret Hannay even makes a case for the countess herself as "Delia."[97] I might be tempted to make a similar case for Lanyer (Daniel's Aemilia = Delia?), if only in frivolous response to A. L. Rowse's insistence that she is Shakespeare's "Dark Lady," but it seems more reasonable to assume that the sonnets are generally fictional and an effort to exploit a popular mode. Still, the chaste beauty they honor make the countess of Pembroke an appropriate dedicatee, whether or not she would be identified with the lady of the poems. On the other hand, Daniel certainly would not want the countess to think he means to represent her by Rosamond or her situation.

I think it just possible that Daniel's observation of the affair between this other Henry of royal blood and military triumphs, the old lord chamberlain, and the beautiful young woman he had made his mistress in the late 1580s contributed to his *Complaint of Rosamond,* as the countess of Cumberland's situation later contributed to his *Octavia.* This makes neither work a roman à clef, but as the countess may have seen herself in the figure of Octavia, Aemilia Bassano, though not the poem's dedicatee, may have identified with the figure of Rosamond.

At the least, we know that she read the poem. She presents the story in some detail in the *Salve Deus*:

> Faire *Rosamond,* the wonder of her time,
> Had bin much fairer, had shee not bin faire;
> Beautie betraid her thoughts, aloft to clime,
> To build strong castles in uncertaine aire,
> Where th'infection of a wanton crime
> Did worke her fall; first poyson, then despaire,
>   With double death did kill her perjur'd soule,
>   When heavenly Justice did her sinne controule. (ll. 225–32)

In the next stanza Lanyer hastens to mention Drayton's *Matilda*, the woman who died with her virtue intact, but the lesson of both is the danger of beauty.

Influence, parallels, and intention are tricky things in literary and historical analysis, especially as we question authorial agency in a world of social constructions. All we know with reasonable certainty is that Aemilia Bassano was the mistress of the lord chamberlain at the time Daniel wrote and published *Rosamond*, which she read then or later or both, and we can easily guess that, if she read it when it first appeared, the story meant one thing to her before her forced marriage and withdrawal from court in October 1592, and came to mean something quite different afterwards.

Aemilia Lanyer had enjoyed access to the public and powerful world of court. She hoped to retrieve some of that life through her ambitious husband. As that hope faded, she sought to regain a sense of power through her affiliation with the countess of Cumberland and by seeking the patronage of other powerful women. It had worked for Daniel, who by 1611 had become a successful member of Queen Anne's entourage. Finally, the poetry itself is meant to stand as a memorial to the defining virtues of women in an aggressively masculine world. In this she achieved the sort of resurrection that the fictionalized Rosamond received from Daniel: a presence beyond sin and the grave, beyond the "double death" that loss of beauty and power had inflicted.

The book that is her memorial waited more than three hundred and fifty years to receive sustained attention. The object of the rest of this book is to place her where she herself might have done if she were reviewing the scene as we see it: among other poets of respectable birth but limited means, seeking to participate in the events of her time. Issues of influence, parallels, and even intention are less important to this project than a simple act of justice: situating the first self-proclaimed public woman poet in English among the equally ambitious men of her time.

2

LANYER AND SPENSER

Edmund Spenser left London and the Merchant Taylor's School for the fens of Cambridge in April 1569, three months after Aemilia Bassano was born. Their lives have few apparent connections, but the one they certainly have is important: both were at Elizabeth's court between 1589 and 1591, during which time Spenser very probably made himself and his *Faerie Queene* part of the court entertainments supervised by Lanyer's protector, the lord chamberlain.[1] In the thinly allegorized autobiographical poem *Colin Clouts Come Home Again*, "Colin" tells of his trip to "Cynthia's" court accompanied by "the shepheard of the Ocean" (Sir Walter Ralegh). There "that Goddesse," the queen, "to mine oaten pipe enclin'd her eare" and found the poet's performance "worth harkening to amongst the learned throng" (ll. 359–60, 68). Lanyer may well have been among those who heard Spenser read his poetry to the queen and her court "at timely houres" (l. 362).[2]

Spenser and Lanyer also both found a patron in Margaret Clifford, countess of Cumberland. Among Spenser's dedicatory sonnets to the 1590 printing of *The Faerie Queene* are verses to the Earl of Cumberland, George Clifford,[3] while the countess herself is one of the identifiable ladies praised in *Colin Clouts Come Home Again*.[4] In 1596 Spenser dedicated the *Fowre Hymnes* to the countess and her sister Anne, countess of Warwick. Margaret and Spenser had been sufficiently close that her daughter Anne erected a monument to the poet in Westminster Abbey three years after her mother's death.[5] These connections between the countess of Cumberland and Spenser had apparent consequences for Lanyer's career: the community of women Spenser portrays in *Colin Clouts* and the visions of beauty he projects in *Four Hymnes* have discernible parallels in her own foray into professional poetry.

Beyond these contiguities of acquaintance, by 1589 Lanyer would certainly have known Spenser to be among the most prominent of modern poets. By that year *The Shepheards Calendar* had been through three editions (1579, 1581, and 1586), and at least some of *The Faerie Queene* was circulating in manuscript.[6] Ralegh, one of the queen's chief favorites and most notable poets, was Spenser's sponsor at court. Spenser's poetry, and his high visibility as the new prince of poets, were very real presences in the period of Lanyer's coming of age, whether or not she was trying to write verse herself or was in attendance during his reading to the queen. He was soon being lauded as Chaucer's successor as the greatest English poet.[7] Lanyer may most reasonably be situated in her own time by considering, first, what she may have taken from Spenser, whether she consciously imitated his style or absorbed his influence from the spirit of her milieu.

There is no evidence that Lanyer ever copied Spenser directly. As far as we know she wrote no pastoral verse, sonnets, epithalamia, or romance, much less an extended allegorical epic. It would be wonderful to find verses from the 1590s that we could confidently ascribe to Lanyer, but for now all we have is her one extant book, which offers limited evidence of her exploration of genres. Yet what we do have suggests a comfortably syncretic temperament, able to compound the biblical with the classical and historical without loss of decorum. If Spenser represents the ease with which Elizabethan humanists combined Christian images with pagan, and with which they moved history toward their own rhetorical and moral ends, then Lanyer has a distinctly Spenserian approach to her materials.

There are also at least three specific areas of Lanyer's work that appear to owe something to a reading of Spenser: her approach to patrons, her analysis of earthly versus heavenly love and beauty, and her use of marginal voices to decenter and recenter narrative action. These are the areas I want to examine in some detail, both for the light they cast on Lanyer's poetry and the reciprocal light they cast on a contemporary woman's reading of Spenser.[8]

Patrons and Dedicatees

Spenser may well have provided Lanyer with her first model for eulogizing a community of virtuous women. Not only does he praise twelve court ladies, including the countess of Cumberland, in *Colin Clouts* (ll. 485–577), three of seventeen dedicatory sonnets appended to *The Faerie Queene* are to women (the countess of Pembroke and Lady Elizabeth Carey, one of the daughters of John Spencer of

Althorp and daughter-in-law to the lord chamberlain, and "To all the gratious and beautifull Ladies of the Court"). Of his twelve other published works, seven carry formal dedications to women. Lanyer may have formed something of her own approach to high-born women from what she observed in Spenser's work, though the differences between them are equally interesting.

Spenser begins his list of worthy ladies in *Colin Clouts* with the countess of Pembroke ("*Urania*, sister unto *Astrofell*"), lauding her "brave mynd,"

> More rich than pearles of *Ynde*, or gold of *Opher*,
> And in her sex more wonderfull and rare. (ll. 490–91)

Next in order are Anne Russell, the widowed countess of Warwick, also credited with a "brave mynd," and her sister Margaret, the countess of Cumberland, "the *Muses* onely darling" (ll. 496, 505). While the countess of Pembroke is a source of "bountie" as well as "intellect," she is also "the ornament of womankind" honored by the queen for her virtue, "great worth and noble governance" (ll. 498, 503). Worth, nobility, and virtue are the characteristic attributions in subsequent commendations, but beauty is always a parallel theme. The countess of Cumberland's "beautie shyneth as the morning cleare" (l. 506), while the poet's Spencer cousin, Elizabeth, Lady Carey, is so beautiful she "bereave[s] of sense each rash beholders sight" (l. 547). A brave mind, generosity, virtue, and grace may adorn a court lady, but physical beauty remains a particular and necessary glory.

Spenser's language in his dedicatory verse is generally more graceful than that of his contemporaries, but for the most part it employs commonplace stances: though the poet is humble and unworthy in relation to higher-born patrons, his public role as eternizer of the great gives him the right to link his fame to those he praises (*Faerie Queene*, Queen Elizabeth); the poet seeks the protection of the great (*Shepheardes Calender*, Sir Philip Sidney); it is the poet's role to honor the great (*Faerie Queene*, dedicatory sonnets); and the poet repays the debts he owes his patrons by dutiful dedications of his public work (*Colin Clouts Come Home Again*, Sir Walter Ralegh). Similarly Lanyer presents herself as born to praise the virtues of the countess of Cumberland (*Salve Deus*, ll. 1457–64); she appeals to Queen Anne for protection ("To the Queenes most Excellent Majestie," ll. 139–44); she honors the great (e.g., the poems to the countess of Pembroke and Lucy, countess of Bedford); and repays debts through poetic dedications (the poem to the countess of Kent and the prose dedication to the countess of Cumberland).

Spenser also makes an effort to establish a particular connection with his dedicatees. So Ladie Strange (née Alice Spencer), dedicatee for *The Teares of the Muses*, is honored for her "excellent beautie, [her] vertuous behavior, and [her] noble match with that most honourable Lord the verie Paterne of right Nobilitie," but is also thanked for "particular bounties, and also some private bands of affinitie, which it hath pleased your Ladiship to acknowledge" (presumably his kinship with her family, the wealthy Spencers of Althorp and Wormleighton). The *Faerie Queene* dedicatory sonnet to Lord Grey of Wilton acknowledges their close relationship (Spenser was his secretary). Even a poem about someone he never met, *Daphnaida*, an elegy on the death of Lady Douglas Howard, is dedicated to her aunt by marriage, whom Spenser did know. The dedication further cites the poet's closeness and admiration for Douglas Howard's husband, Sir Arthur Gorges, Ralegh's first cousin. Lanyer, too, establishes a personal connection with her dedicatees wherever possible, so that the poem to the countess of Suffolk, whom she apparently had never met, stands out as "right strange" (l. 1).

More interesting than the general similarity of their approaches and stances are contrasts between the two poets in the language and rhetorical design of their dedicatory poems to women. Two of those, the countess of Pembroke and the countess of Cumberland, are addressed by both poets, but at different enough times in the dedicatees' lives to make the poems unreliable touchstones for either comparison or contrast. Even without easy points of comparison, differences are readily visible throughout the respective body of these two poets' dedications. As in the encomia in *Colin Clouts*, in his dedicatory verse Spenser usually extols a lady's beauty and her connection to great men in her life, whatever else he may praise. Lanyer very seldom comments on a patron's external beauty, much less on the men associated with the patron. When she does, the references are brief. Praise for Sir Philip Sidney dominates Spenser's dedications to the countess of Pembroke, for example, while Lanyer's poem to that great countess mentions her famous brother only briefly.

The two poets' rhetorical emphases differ more generally as well. The encomia in the dedication to Alice (Spencer), Lady Strange is typical: Spenser praises her beauty, her virtue, and her good marriage. Similarly, in his dedication of *Mother Hubberds Tale*, to another of Sir John Spencer's daughters, "the Honourable, the Ladie Compton and

Mountegle," the poet addresses her as "Most faire and vertuous Ladie" and acknowledges his kinship with "that House, from whence yee spring." The dedication of *Muiopotmos* to the third Spencer sister, Elizabeth, Lady Carey, praised for her beauty in *Colin Clouts* and the dedicatory poem in *The Faerie Queene*, follows the established model, again lauding her beauty and family, adding specific reference to "your great bounty to my self."

In Lanyer's dedications, the lady's "virtue" is always preeminent, and the beauty she might mention is that of Christ or of the receptive soul. Even when beauty is directly attributable to ladies, it is often coupled with "virtue." There are six instances throughout the book where a form of "beauty" and "virtue" appear within ten words of each other, with "virtue" always coming first and establishing the emphasis on interior beauty. Lanyer presents her book "To all vertuous Ladies in generall," for example, addressing:

> Each blessed Lady that in Virtue spends
> Your pretious time to beautifie your soules (ll. 1–2)

and enjoins them to "Let Virtue be your guide" (l. 10).

The term "virtue" was loaded in Lanyer's time. It still bore a recognizable connotation of manly agency from its Latin definition of "manliness, valour, worth" (origins of "Virtue," *OED*), but its principal associations were with religion and courtly love.[9] In the latter tradition it carried the usual definition of "voluntary observance of the recognized moral laws or standards of right conduct" (*OED* 2a), and also, to the dismay of many a Petrarchan lover, the specific suggestion of "chastity, sexual purity" (*OED* 2c). But its (now largely obsolete) associations with religion are more to the point in Lanyer's text. The word had long referred to "the power or operative influence inherent in a supernatural or divine being" (*OED* 1a) and, by extension, "an embodiment of such power" (*OED* 1b). In this tradition, the beauty of virtue is never a function of outward appearance but of inner spiritual force.

"Virtue" as Lanyer presents it often derives from retirement and the deliberate rejection of self-display. The poet says of Susan, countess of Kent, her early model:

> In you those Noble Virtues did I note,
> First, love and feare of God, of Prince, of Lawes,
> Rare Patience with a mind so farre remote

From worldly pleasures, free from giving cause
   Of least suspect to the most envious eie,
   That in faire Virtues Storehouse sought to prie. (ll. 13–18)

The countess of Cumberland's retirement "from the Court to the Countrie" (*Salve Deus*, l. 161) is an emblem of her virtuous choice of a godly life which similarly frees her from envy and malice:

Malice must live for ever in dispaire:
There's no revenge where Virtue still doth rest. (ll. 181–82).

These differences in epideictic strategy between Spenser and Lanyer may be a function of the differences in the poems the poet is dedicating and in the relationships between dedicator and dedicatee. Even so, it is interesting that in Lanyer's poems there is none of the celebration of physical beauty that is so prominent in Spenser's poems to women patrons. This simple distinction, perhaps attributable to the genders of the poets, is less obvious than one might think. If Lanyer were merely copying the masculine patronage model, we would see more similarity than we do, an issue I will revisit in the discussion of Lanyer and Jonson. Her actual practice shows thoughtful independence from the masculine models of her time. What Lanyer's dedications do share with Spenser's are attention to relevant detail and (usually) graceful compliment, which amounts to saying that both poets do a good job.

In these examples Spenser is a model for Lanyer in only the most general sense, but his work may well have provided a more specific model for Lanyer as she sought to construct an intellectual community centered by a queen.

Colin Clouts has long been recognized as a poetic fiction based on Spenser's personal experience during his visit to court in October 1589.[10] The poem is characterized by a tension between praise of the queen and specific courtiers on the one hand, and disparagement of courtly life on the other. Poets and patrons are equally lauded as part of the same social community, women as well as men. This commingling of gender and class, brought together by a common love of poetry and centered by an enabling and beneficent monarch, is a powerful model for a woman poet constructing a similar vision of intellectual community.

The message of *Colin Clouts* seems to be that although the dangers of court life are great, within its context virtuous men and women, inspired by the queen, are able to exemplify a community of grace. Court life, Colin tells his country friends, is one

> Where each one seeks with malice and with strife,
> To thrust down other into foule disgrace,
> Himselfe to raise: (ll. 690–92)

"Deceitfull wit" and "fained forgerie" are the means of advancement at court, along with "faire dissembling courtesie" which is "not art of schoole, but Courtiers schoolery" (ll. 693, 696, 702). Fancy clothes and "vaunted vanitie" seem most glorious at first glance, but they are empty show (ll. 711–22). When Hobbinol takes him to task for being "too generall" in his blame, Colin acknowledges

> . . . there amongst them bee
> Full many persons of right worthie parts,
> Both for report of spotlesse honestie,
> And for profession of all learned arts. (ll. 751–54)

These are the poets and patrons, beginning with a queen who

> . . . to mine oaten pipe enclined her eare,
> That she thenceforth therein gan take delight,
> And it desired at timely houres to heare,
> All were my notes but rude and roughly dight. (ll. 360–63)

Not his worth, but her grace, raised this "country shepherd" to a place among "the learned throng" (ll. 364–66), including Daniel (l. 424), Drayton (l. 443), and the gracing memory of Sir Philip Sidney (ll. 450–55). Equally important to this learned community are the women, beginning with the countess of Pembroke ("Urania sister unto Astrofell," l. 497) and including, prominent among many others, Anne, countess of Warwick ("Theana," l. 492) and her sister Margaret, the countess of Cumberland ("Marian"):

> Ne lesse praise worthie is her sister deare,
> Faire Marian, the Muses onely darling:
> Whose beautie shyneth as the morning cleare,
> With silver deaw upon the roses pearling. (ll. 504–7)

The countess of Cumberland, "the Muses onely darling," would become Lanyer's principal inspiration, but if Lanyer learned from

Spenser something of how a poet represents the grace of a patron, she would find it most fully in Spenser's dedicatory verse to Queen Elizabeth.

Spenser not only dedicated *The Faerie Queene* to Elizabeth and placed her at the inspirational center of *Colin Clouts*, he alludes to her throughout his work, and the moderately generous fifty pounds per year she awarded him in 1591 effectively made him the royal poet.[11] Lanyer's primary patron was of course the countess of Cumberland, but Elizabeth is also a figure of great personal and imaginative importance to her. Although the great queen had been dead for nearly eight years, and Lanyer had been away from court for at least eighteen when *Salve Deus Rex Judaeorum* appeared, she remains a commanding if ghostly presence. Elizabeth had "favored [young Aemilia Bassano] moch" and probably been responsible for at least some of the "gret gifts" she reported receiving.[12] Spenser and Lanyer's portrayals of this royal patron make an interesting comparison.

Spenser's only formal dedication to the queen is the grandly stylized statement that immediately follows the title page to *The Faerie Queene*: "To the most high, mightie, and magnificent empresse renowmed for pietie, vertue, and all gratious government Elizabeth by the grace of God queene of England Fraunce and Ireland and of Virginia, defendour of the faith, &c. Her most humble servant Edmund Spenser doth in all humilitie dedicate, present and consecrate these his labours to live with the eternitie of her fame."[13] The forms of address, and the humility of the poet, are predictable, though the order of compliment is different from his dedications to other women. This great monarch is renowned first for her private virtues, beginning with piety, and then for her "gratious government." Religious and civil power, not beauty, take center stage in a sequence that reflects the general pattern of the *Faerie Queene*, which moves from private to public virtues across the six extant books.

Further dedicatory verses to the queen are sprinkled throughout the poem's six books, most explicitly in their introductory proems, and many of these pay tribute to Elizabeth as a Petrarchan "faire" as well as a pious ruler. The first of these follows the standard invocation to the muse, "chiefe of nine" (whether Clio or Calliope),[14] and specific invocations to Cupid, Venus, and Mars:

> And with them eke, O Goddesse heavenly bright,
> Mirrour of grace and Majestie divine,
> Great Lady of the greatest Isle, whose light
> Like *Phoebus* lampe throughout the world doth shine,

> Shed thy faire beames into my feeble eyne,
> And raise my thoughts too humble and too vile,
> To thinke of that true glorious type of thine,
> The argument of mine aflicted stile:
> The which to heare, vouchsafe, O dearest dred awhile. (1.proem.4)

Like the Petrarchan lady, this great lady's "faire beames" have the power to elevate the speaker to virtuous service, yet she is first and foremost a "Goddesse," a "Majestie divine," like the figure of "Sapience" in Spenser's *Hymne of Heavenly Beautie* (ll. 183–210).

Other moments of direct address advance the fictive or allegorical purposes of the narrative, but most of these present the queen as a model of divinity, as well as of beauty and power.[15] In this Spenser tends to reverse the emphasis of other poets who dedicate verses to the queen: for them it is her beauty and her power, mutually symbolic according to the traditions of courtly love, that receive primary emphasis.[16]

Like Spenser, Lanyer emphasizes godliness. The first reference to Queen Elizabeth occurs in the initial dedication of the *Salve Deus*, to Queen Anne. Two thirds of the way through this poem Lanyer situates herself as a sorrowful petitioner, consoled only by the story of Christ's passion:

> So I that live clos'd up in Sorrowes Cell
> Since great *Elizaes* favour blest my youth;
> And in the confines of all cares doe dwell,
> Whose grieved eyes no pleasure ever view'th:
> But in Christ's suffrings, such sweet taste they have,
> As makes me praise pale Sorrow and the Grave. (ll. 109–14)

The two stanzas that follow appear at first to refer to Queen Anne ("*this* great Ladie," the subject of the dedication), yet a closer reading suggests that Lanyer may be continuing her reference to Elizabeth, elaborating on the late queen's role as an honored inspiration to the humble petitioner who is approaching the living queen:

> And this great Ladie whom I love and honour,
> And from my very tender yeeres have knowne,
> This holy habite still to take upon her,
> Still to remaine *the same*, and still her owne:
>   And what our fortunes doe enforce us to,
>   She of Devotion and meere Zeale doth do.

Which makes me thinke our heavy burden light,
When such a one as she will help to beare it:
Treading the paths that make our way go right,
What garment is so faire but she may weare it;
    Especially for her that entertaines
    A Glorious Queene, in whom all woorth remains. (ll. 115–26)

I take this passage to mean that the suffering and piety of Queen Elizabeth provide a model for those who would bear the burden of virtue, and whoever follows that model is habited gloriously like her, which makes that follower worthy to entertain the current queen. The "great Ladie" that the poet has known from her "very tender yeeres" cannot possibly be Anne, who was in Denmark until her marriage and then in Scotland until her accession to the English crown in 1603. In 1603 Lanyer was thirty-four years old, hardly "tender yeeres." Elizabeth, however, she knew from childhood, when her father was among the queen's musicians.

These stanzas are difficult, and may include subtexts unavailable to a modern reader, but here is one reading: Elizabeth takes on the "holy habit" still (continuously, in her heavenly place as on earth), where she remains *"the same"* and "her owne"—that is, the piety that lesser people are forced to by their fortune, she is able to choose for herself "of Devotion and meere Zeale." Her example lightens the burden of those who observe her. If we follow the same path, we may wear the same holy habit, or fair "garment," which is most appropriate for one (the poet) who "entertaines / A Glorious Queene, in whom all woorth remains"—presumably Queen Anne. Yet Queen Elizabeth was a poet as well as the supreme model of piety, which makes her a complex exemplar for Lanyer, who is here a poet mediating between one queen and another. And even in my reading, questions remain. What precisely is the "holy habite"? Is it indeed the same as the "garment so faire"? And who is the "she" that may weare it? Lanyer? Elizabeth? Any pious soul? Any virtuous poet, or poet of virtuous subject matter? All of the above? Who is the "her that entertaines," and in what sense are we to take "entertaines"? The *OED* cites maintain, engage, occupy, receive, and cherish as just some of the potential synonyms current in Lanyer's time. Finally, is the reference after all to Queen Anne, who is *"the same"* as Elizabeth, because of her queenship, and yet "her owne" in her earthly body?[17]

Ambiguous references are a poetic device that Lanyer would have seen modeled all around her, including in Spenser, and she uses them throughout her own volume. It is almost impossible, for example, to tell where the voice of Pilate's wife leaves off in the *Salve Deus* and the voice of the narrator resumes (l. 841? l. 937?). This passage presenting Elizabeth (and Lanyer) to Anne is probably the most obscure passage in the entire book, however, and it is no surprise that it comes at the awkward point where the poet must maneuver between the glorious past and the glorious present, and do it in an atmosphere of piety. It may well be, too, that Lanyer intends here to conflate the sufferings of Christ and the late queen with Queen Anne's virtual exclusion from James's homosocial court, a purpose for which ambiguity is a useful strategy.

Other potential referents for "this great Ladie," such as Queen Anne herself or a personified "Sorrow," make less sense, I believe, than reading these stanzas as a claim to be authorized by Queen Anne's predecessor. In any case, the poem proceeds with the poet offering her poetic gift to Queen Anne and seeking in return inspiration and authority for her literary effort.[18]

Two other direct references to Elizabeth continue Lanyer's claim of connection. The first begins the poem to Princess Elizabeth, which predictably revolves around the conceit of her name:

> Most gratious Ladie, faire ELIZABETH,
> Whose name and virtues puts us still in mind,
> Of her, of whom we are depriv'd by death;
> The *Phoenix* of her age, whose worth did bind
> All worthy minds so long as they have breath,
>   In linkes of Admiration, love and zeale,
>   To that deare Mother of our Common-weale. (ll. 1–7)

The experience of being bound to Queen Elizabeth did not end with her death, but continues in "all worthy minds" as long as they themselves are alive. Those "linkes of Admiration, love and zeale," still active for Lanyer, make an explicit connection with female power that stands behind the easy authority of her gendered verse.

The second reference, at the beginning of the long title poem, confirms the late queen as a figure of exemplary piety. Elizabeth would have been the dedicatee and focus of the poet's praise if she were still alive, these lines say, but since she is not, the poet turns her attention to the virtues of the dowager countess of Cumberland instead:

Sith *Cynthia* is ascended to that rest
Of endlesse joy and true Eternitie,
That glorious place that cannot be exprest
By any wight clad in mortalitie,
In her almightie love so highly blest,
And crown'd with everlasting Sov'raigntie:
   Where Saints and Angells do attend her Throne,
   And she gives glorie unto God alone.

To thee great Countesse now I will applie
My Pen, to write thy never dying fame; (ll. 1–10)

The first stanza not only suggests that Lanyer may have written verse to or about Elizabeth in the past, but it actually constitutes a complete poem. Remove the "Sith," and the verses stand metrically as a memorial epigram exalting Elizabeth in her heavenly "glorious place," where "she gives glorie unto God alone."

In Spenser's great poem, the Faery Queen is "*Gloriana*," that "greatest Glorious Queene of *Faerie* lond" (1.1.3), and the "true glorious type" of Queen Elizabeth herself (1.proem.4). In contrast to Spenser, Lanyer uses the terms "glory" and "glorious" sparingly, and usually in specifically religions contexts. Christ's sacrifice is the "glorious miracle without compare" (*Salve Deus*, l. 1177); the poet leaves Christ's "perfect picture" in the heart of the countess of Cumberland, where she may see him "as a God in glory," the "Sweet of sweets, in which all glory rests" (ll. 1329, 1344). Yet the notion that women have access to God's glory, which in some way glorifies them, is an underlying premise of the whole *Salve Deus* volume. By citing Queen Elizabeth's translation to heaven as to that "glorious place," and implying a reciprocity of glory between the late monarch and God as "she gives glory unto God alone," Lanyer both draws on and shifts the Spenserian tradition of Elizabeth herself as the Glory who gives glory to those "worthy minds" who remain bound to her memory.

Lanyer uses "glory" to mean "the glory of God, the honour of God, considered as the final cause of creation, and as the highest moral aim of intelligent creatures" (*OED* 2b) and also "praise, honour, and thanksgiving offered in adoration" and "the splendour and bliss of heaven" (*OED* 4, 7). "Glory" in its more secular sense of "exalted . . . praise, honour, or admiration accorded by common consent . . . honourable fame, renown" (*OED* 2) is rare in Lanyer's verse. But the implicit and

assumed glory of the late queen, so amply affirmed by Spenser, who
consistently connects her with divinity itself, pervades Lanyer's book
of good women. Though Lanyer is more likely to use words such as
"honor," "grace," or "fame" as terms appropriate to the ladies she
praises and their effect on those around them, the very first word of
her book, and the first word in her poem to Queen Anne, suggests the
public magnificence that is synonymous with secular glory: "Renowned
Empresse, and great Britaines Queene." From this glory comes that of
all the ladies that Lanyer's volume will be praising, signified specifically
by the ladies of Anne's court, whom the poet, despite her low birth
("meannesse"), would like to join in relationship with the living queen:

> From your bright spheare of greatnes where you sit,
> Reflecting light to all those glorious stars
> That wait upon your Throane: To virtue yet
> Vouchsafe that splendor which my meannesse bars. (ll. 25–28).

Lanyer's book has the unique goal of praising women as virtuous and worthy of the honor and glory of both heavenly and earthly
fame. "Virtue" is the mediator of the two, and the voice of "Virtue" is this poet, writing in praise of these ladies to the glory of God.
In Lanyer's memorial stanza to Queen Elizabeth she becomes the
"true glorious type" of a woman's relationship with God. The countess of Cumberland, and to some extent all of the women whom
Lanyer praises in her dedications, receive and reflect divine glory
and earthly fame from and back to the poet herself. This cycle of
reciprocity is amply modeled by Spenser's *Faerie Queene*.[19] Further,
the inspiration and theoretical base for the public glorification of
women is a Neoplatonic theory of beauty whose poetic expression
Lanyer could most easily find in Spenser's *Fowre Hymnes*, verse
essays dedicated to the countess of Cumberland and her sister.

"This Taske of Beauty"

Toward the end of the *Salve Deus* Lanyer addresses the countess of
Cumberland in a way that makes explicit, though by no means simple,
the principal topic of her poem:

> Ah! give me leave (good Lady) now to leave
> This taske of Beauty which I tooke in hand. (ll. 1321–22)

Near the beginning of the poem she had defined beauty in relation to the countess herself, distinguishing between outward beauty and inward virtue, and signaling the importance of the definition by a sidenote ("An Invective against outward beuty [*sic*] unaccompanied with virtue"):

> That outward Beautie which the world commends,
> Is not the subject I will write upon,
> Whose date expir'd, that tyrant Time soone ends;
> Those gawdie colours soone are spent and done:
> But those faire Virtues which on thee attends
> Are alwaies fresh, they never are but one:
> They make thy Beautie fairer to behold,
> Than was that Queenes for whom prowd *Troy* was sold. (ll. 185–92)

When she drew attention to these lines, Lanyer could expect her patron to recall Spenser's poetic discussion of love and beauty.

In 1596 Spenser dedicated the *Fowre Hymnes* "To the right honorable and most vertuous Ladies, the Ladie Margaret Countesse of Cumberland, and the Ladie Marie [*sic*] Countesse of Warwicke," professing to amend the manuscript circulation of the first two hymns.[20] The dedication is worth quoting in full:

> Having in the greener times of my youth, composed these former two Hymnes in the praise of Love and beautie, and finding that the same too much pleased those of like age and disposition, which being too vehemently caried with that kind of affection, do rather sucke out poyson to their strong passion, then hony to their honest delight, I was moved by the one of you two most excellent Ladies, to call in the same. But being unable so to doe, by reason that many copies thereof were formerly scattered abroad, I resolved at least to amend, and by way of retractation to reforme them, making in stead of those two Hymnes of earthly or naturall love and beautie, two others of heavenly and celestiall. The which I doe dedicate joyntly unto you two honorable sisters, as to the most excellent and rare ornaments of all true love and beautie, both in the one and in the other kinde, humbly beseeching you to vouchsafe the patronage of them, and to accept this my humble service, in lieu of the great graces and honourable favours which ye dayly shew unto me, untill such time as I may by better meanes yeeld you some more notable testimonie of my thankfull mind and dutifull devotion.[21]

As commentators have noted, the first two hymns, of (earthly) love and beauty, hardly seem the sort to lead amorous gentlemen to "sucke out poyson to their strong passion," and their structural coherence with the second two hymns, of heavenly love and beauty, makes suspect the notion that the first were written much earlier.[22] It seems more likely that the published versions of the first two hymns are indeed "retractations" rather than retractions, meaning a work "undertaken anew" rather than "withdrawn," and that the four hymns together present a coherent treatise on the interrelationships of love and beauty in their several kinds.[23] It also seems likely that the project was undertaken to accommodate the objections of Margaret rather than her sister, since the earl of Cumberland was a notorious womanizer and Margaret's reputation for piety may already have been well established.[24]

Spenserian theories of love and beauty are a complex of Renaissance Platonism, Neoplatonism, Petrarchanism, and Protestantism. Except of course for the last, these ideas and influences entered England largely from Italy, through such poets as Dante, Petrarch, and Girolamo Benivieni, and such philosophers as Ficino, Pico della Mirandola (whose commentary on Benivieni's *Canzone dell'Amor Divine* describes the ladder that ascends from a lady's physical beauty to divine love), Pietro Bembo (whose views were popularized by Castiglione in book 4 of *The Courtier*), and Giordano Bruno.[25] Plato himself was a staple of the classical humanist education, much admired for his eloquence as well as his idealist philosophy.[26] It is impossible to know how familiar Lanyer was with the Italian philosophers, or whether she read Plato in any of the many available Latin translations or redactions. She certainly spoke and read Italian, though her work gives no substantial clues as to what she read in her father's native language. If she did not know Plato directly, she may well have known the work of the French Huguenot Philippe de Mornay, who was a Protestant Christian Platonist and a member of the Sidney-Pembroke circle; Lanyer very probably knew the countess of Pembroke's translation of Mornay's *Discours de la vie et du mort* (as *Discourse of Life and Death*, 1592).[27] And she was certainly acquainted with *The Fowre Hymnes*.

All four of Spenser's *Hymnes* display the idealization of love and beauty that the Platonic and Neoplatonic philosophers encouraged, though they do not represent a precise ascent from lowest to highest. Rather, the hymns of (earthly) love and beauty extol the best of the temporal, while the hymns of heavenly love and beauty translate Platonic ideals into Christian terms, extolling Christ as the source, center, and goal of all love, and God as the ineffable divine beauty. All four insist that physical beauty is but a reflection of ideal or divine beauty, and that perfect love is an appreciation for the ideal and divine that resides beyond the corporeal veil.

Put simply, Platonic theories of beauty viewed the physical world as the infusion of ideal form into base and resistant matter. The more powerful the influence of the ideal, which was often explicitly equated with the good, the more beautiful the result. One important consequence is the belief that a beautiful woman is necessarily good, although theorists (including Spenser) hasten to add that some women who have beautiful souls are confronted with a lump of clay so recalcitrant that they may not seem conventionally beautiful, and some beautiful women are so sorely tempted that they fall from the good.[28] Another consequence is a sometimes uneasy distinction between mere physical beauty and physical beauty that leads the observer inward to contemplate and understand true beauty which resides in the mind or soul. In *Hymne of Heavenly Beautie (HHB)* Spenser concludes that "Sapience" *is* the divine beauty. Both Spenser and Lanyer are very concerned with the distinction between earthly beauty and the beauty of divine wisdom, although Lanyer uses the specifically physical beauty of Christ as the agent for translating all beauty from the earthly to the heavenly, from outward shows to inward rapture.

Reflections of the *Fowre Hymnes* throughout the *Salve Deus* confirm that Lanyer had read them and expected the countess to recognize the *Salve Deus* as relating to Spenser's work, perhaps even extending or correcting it. So, for example, Lanyer's earliest references to "beauty" in the *Salve Deus* invoke a Christianized Neoplatonism that sees the beauty of the world as an emblem allowing the contemplative mind to rise to a vision of higher things, presented in language similar to Spenser's in the *Hymne of Heavenly Beautie*. Spenser explains that, while we cannot look on God directly, we may look at his works, "Which he hath made in beauty excellent" (l. 129). Contemplation of this beauty allows the "high flying mind" to

Mount up aloft through heavenly contemplation,
From this darke world, whose damps the soule do blynd,
And like the native brood of Eagles kynd,
On that bright Sunne of glorie fixe thine eyes. (*HHB* ll. 135–39)

Lanyer makes the contemplative moment specific and personal, as she recalls sharing with the countess of Cumberland a beautiful night:

> When shining *Phoebe* gave so great a grace,
> Presenting *Paradice* to your sweet sight,
> Unfolding all the beauty of her face
>   With pleasant groves, hills, walks and stately trees
>   Which pleasures with retired minds agrees.
>
> Whose Eagles eyes behold the glorious Sunne
> Of th'all creating Providence . . . (*SD* ll. 20–26)

Enid Welsford's gloss on Spenser would apply equally to this passage from Lanyer: "The aspiring mind in quest of the beatific vision needs to begin by looking intently at the created universe, and deducing from it the goodness of its Creator. This will enable him to dismiss the world from his thought and turn all his attention to God himself, just as the eagle according to traditional superstition was able to look directly at the sun."[29]

Both poets are careful to distinguish between outward show and inward beauty, with Spenser making the general case:

> How vainely then doe ydle wits invent
> That beautie is nought else, but mixture made
> Of colours faire, and goodly temp'rament
> Of pure complexions, that shall quickly fade
>
> . . . .
>
> But that faire lampe, from whose celestiall ray
> That light proceedes, which kindleth lovers fire,
> Shall never be extinguisht nor decay. (*HHB*, 64–67, 99–101)

And Lanyer applying it specifically to the countess, in the lines cited earlier:

> That outward Beautie which the world commends,
> Is not the subject I will write upon,
> Whose date expir'd, that tyrant Time soone ends;
> Those gawdie colours soone are spent and gone:
> But those faire Vertues which on thee attends
> Are alwaies fresh, they never are but one. (*SD* ll. 185–90)

The particular "gawdie colours" that Lanyer disparages are white and red, the conventional colors of female beauty and of the mix of passion and purity that Neoplatonic love sought to theorize. For Spenser these famous colors symbolize only temporal beauty:

Hath white and red in it such wondrous powre,
That it can pierce through th'eyes unto the hart
. . . .
Or can proportion of the outward part
Move such affection in the inward mynd,
That it can rob both sense and reason blynd?
. . . .
. . . that same goodly hew of white and red,
With which the cheeks are sprinckled, shal decay
And those sweete rosy leaves so fairely spred
Upon the lips, shall fade and fall away. (*HHB* ll. 71–72, 75–77, 92–95)

While Spenser sees these dangers through the eyes of the lover, Lanyer makes the same point through the eyes of the lady:

As for those matchlesse colours Red and White,
Or perfit features in a fading face,
Or due proportion pleasing to the sight,
All these doe draw but dangers and disgrace. (ll. 193–96)

Lanyer locates and makes personal the abstractions of Spenser's *Hymns*, finding clues that will glorify women and her patron. Spenser's Sapience, or wisdom, for example, the embodiment of God's perfect beauty, is the apparent model for Lanyer's portrait of the countess's internal beauty and virtue.

The fairenesse of her face no tongue can tell,
For she the daughters of all wemens race,
And Angels eke, in beautie doth excell. (*HHB* ll. 204–7)

The countess is similarly incomparable, leaving "all delights to serve a heavn'ly King" and being therefore most "wise" (ll. 170–71):

Thou faire example, live without compare,
With Honours triumphs seated in thy breast. (ll. 177–78)

Perhaps most interesting is the juxtaposition between Spenser's portrait of Christ in *Hymne of Heavenly Love* and some of the elements of Lanyer's description of the passion. Spenser offers his own abbreviated version of the passion, which is the great expression of God's love for mankind:

> And that most blessed bodie, which was borne
> Without all blemish or reprochfull blame,
> He freely gave to be both rent and torne
> Of cruell hands, who with despightfull shame
> Revyling him, that them most vile became,
> At length they nayled him on a gallow tree,
> And slew the just, by most unjust decree. (*HHL* ll. 148–53)
> And looke at last how of most wretched wights,
> He taken was, betrayd, and false accused,
> How with most scornefull taunts and fell despights
> He was revyld, disgrast, and foule abused,
> How scourgd, how crownd, how buffeted, how brusd;
> And lastly how twixt robbers crucifyde,
> With bitter wounds through hands, through feet and syde.
>   (*HHL* ll. 239–46)

Lanyer's rhythms tend to reflect Spenser's in the most dramatic parts of her version of the passion story, as if she has learned to make tumult from Spenserian lists:

> Yea for our gaine he is content with losse,
> Our ragged clothing scornes he not to weare,
> Though foule, rent, torne, disgracefull, rough and grosse,
>   Spunne by that monster Sinne, and weav'd by Shame,
>   Which grace it selfe, disgrac'd with impure blame. (ll. 1124–28)
>   . . . .
> His harmelesse hands unto the Crosse they nailde,
> And feet that never trode in sinners trace,
> Betweene two theeves, unpitied, unbewailde
>   . . . .
> His joynts dis-joynted, and his legges hang downe,
> His alabaster breast, his bloody side,
> His members torne, and on his head a Crowne
> Of sharpest Thorns, to satisfie for pride. (ll. 1153–55, 1161–64)

Lanyer's *Salve Deus* both centers and extends Spenser's treatise of beauty and love. Christ's passion makes love and beauty concrete and specific, while the poem's narrative method extends and accumulates some of Spenser's symbolic materials. The "red and white," for example, become transposed and transformed over the course of Lanyer's poem through the incarnation and sacrifice of Christ (ll. 1110–11, 1175–76, 1280, 1307–8) to what the sidenote calls the "Colours of Confessors & Martirs." At the end of the poem the poet offers her patron, now placed among the saints and figured as the perfect bride of Christ, her own vision of love and beauty:

> Loe Madame, heere you take a view of those,
> Whose worthy steps you do desire to tread,
> Deckt in those colours which our Saviour chose;
> The purest colours both of White and Red,
> Their freshest beauties would I faine disclose,
> By which our Saviour most was honoured:
>   But my weake Muse desireth now to rest,
>   Folding up all their Beauties in your breast. (ll. 1825–32)

Lanyer's "task of beautie" has been to find the true white and red in the story of Christ's passion, to present it to the countess who takes both poem and Saviour into her heart, assuring both poet and patron eternal fame. As the women of Lanyer's narrative overgo the sinful men who put their Saviour to death, so this poet has sought to overgo her countess's earlier laureate patron. Yet it is possible that Lanyer not only gathered a part of her topic, and some lessons in versification, from the great Elizabethan poet, but some key elements of her narrative technique as well.

Centering the Margins

Spenser's narrative style tends to blur traditional categories and effect solutions from the margins of a story's action. This approach to narrative, particularly as embodied by the figure of Una in book 1, may have provided a model for Lanyer's unprecedented empowerment of women in the *Salve Deus*.

The eclectic syncretism of *The Faerie Queene* is not in service to a carefully articulated worldview, but to one that questions simple doctrines and assured categories and often finds solutions from unexpected places. So the marginal (in book 5) Britomart rescues Arthegall, and Colin Clout explains the crucial doctrine of grace to Calidore on Mt. Acidale in book 6. Book 3 is neatly closed at the end of the 1590 *Faerie Queene* with the hermaphroditic union of Amoret and Scudamour, but changed in 1596 to defer all conclusion and open suddenly into a book 4 that wanders across plots, structures, and themes as if friendship itself were amorphous and solid connections always just eluding the human condition.

Yet the first three books of the 1590 edition appear more clearly defined than the last three books of the 1596 version, with book 1 the most definite of all. Relative to all the others (and I would include books 2 and 5, though that is another argument), its structure is balanced and conclusive, its themes precise, its allegory accessible. It has recognizable boundaries, and its topic is the foundational issue of Spenser's time: how does one live a godly life? But nothing Spenserian is simple, and all apparent boundaries, whether structural or thematic, blur as attention to them intensifies. Spenser's allegorical suggestions resonate like chords rather than sing like a single voice, are textured like tapestries rather than limned like etchings. This is a narrative model that a woman poet such as Lanyer might mark with interest.

Una is a particularly powerful example for a woman writing a religious narrative in celebration of good women. Her name is common in Ireland, but allegorists have long seen its many allusions in Spenser's use: to singularity, perfection, completeness, to the truth that is one, to the one true church.[30] Central as she must be to the concept of "Holinesse," the early critical tradition sentimentalized her even while acknowledging her importance as an agent in Redcrosse Knight's salvific journey (e.g., "for all her strength of endurance and of affection, she is a frail and tender being, exposed to the roughest buffetings of fortune").[31] Spenser's early commentators saw in Una the traditional heroines of medieval romance and the praying lady in the background of illustrations from the legend of St. George. As Anne Shaver has pointed out, Una's power to represent the true church is limited by the medieval Arthurian tradition from which she comes.[32] In Arthurian romance the lady is a passive inspiration at best, who does not direct her own rescue nor save her rescuer from danger. Una is neither a woman warrior, like Bradamante, nor a sorceress, like Morgan La Fay, and despite the importance of her allegorical significance, her narrative circumstances give her little ability to act on her own.[33]

Nonetheless, like the grace she sometimes receives and sometimes represents, Una blurs the traditional distinctions between active masculinity and passive femininity, and leans in from the margins to direct Redcrosse Knight at crucial moments. In the familiar approach to the battle with Error in book 1, she cautions him against foolhardy action:

> Be well aware, quoth then that Ladie milde,
> Least suddaine mischiefe ye too rash provoke:
> The danger hid, the place unknowne and wilde,
> Breedes dreadfull doubts: Oft fire is without smoke,
> And perill without show: therefore your stroke
> Sir knight with-hold, till further triall made. (1.i.12)

When he argues against the shame of retreat, she continues her warning, while acknowledging that he must now act to avoid disgrace:

> Yea but (quoth she) the perill of this place
> I better wot than you, though now too late
> To wish you backe returne with foul disgrace
> Yet wisedome warns, whilest foot is in the gate,
> To stay the steppe, ere forced to retrate.
> This is the wandering wood, this *Errours den*,
> A monster vile, whom god and man does hate:
> Therefore I read beware. (1.i.13)

Una knows how to "read," how to interpret the environment she sees. A Sophia figure here, she is able to advise and urge caution, but she does not intervene in the forward movement of her knight's adventure. Her intervention becomes more nearly direct in the battle, however, when she shouts encouragement and instruction:

> His Lady sad to see his sore constraint,
> Cride out, Now now Sir knight, shew what ye bee
> Add faith unto your force, and be not faint
> Strangle her, else she will surely strangle thee. (1.i.19)

Much like a modern coach, from the sidelines Una directs the action in the center. Perhaps, on the narrative level of Spenser's story, her aggressiveness in this encounter makes Redcrosse Knight more willing to believe in her sexual aggressiveness when the false Una importunes him in canto ii.

The true Una, however, reverts to the more traditional passive lady in distress in the middle of the book: she subdues the Lion by her beauty, accepts his protection (1.iii.5), and is subject to deception by Archimago (1.iii.30) and abduction by Sans Loy (1.iii.43–44). She seems to have lost all agency in canto vi. Her helplessness in the face of Sans Loy, her rescue by the fauns and satyrs, and the appearance of Satyrane contrast sharply with Redcrosse Knight's active adventures—the fights with Sans Foy and Orgoglio, even the dalliance with Duessa. Yet Una has a more-than-passive role even in canto vi. As she had guided Redcrosse, so she seeks to guide "the woodborne people" who "fall before her flat" (1.vi.16):

> Glad of such lucke, the luckelesse lucky maid,
> Did her content to please their feeble eyes,
> And long time with that salvage people staid,
> To gather breath in many miseries.
> During which time her gentle wit she plyes,
> To teach them truth, which worshipt her in vaine,
> And made her th'Image of Idolatryes;
> But when their bootlesse zeale she did restraine,
> From her own worship, they her Asse would worship fayn. (1.vi.19)

As she could not keep Redcrosse from hasty battle with Error, so she cannot keep the satyrs from idol worship. Nor could Sir Satyrane's human mother fully tame him by instruction (1.vi.27–28), though her influence and Una's beauty and "wisedome heavenly rare, / Whose like in womens wit he never knew" provide the wild knight with enough good instincts to inspire him to rescue the endangered damsel (1.vi.31, 33).

Yet Una is to some degree an agent of her own rescue even in canto vi, in part because of her traditional inspiring beauty, but in part because of her less traditional, but allegorically necessary, "wisedome heavenly rare." In canto vii, though she manages to swoon a theologically correct three times when the dwarf tells her the news of Redcrosse's capture, she takes heart and takes charge, "resolving him to find / Alive or dead" (1.vii.28). Her purposive wandering allows her to encounter Arthur, who rescues Redcrosse from Orgoglio's dungeon (1.vii.29, 1.viii). At first Una is the fawning lady, bemoaning the sad state (and lost innocence) of her beloved. Next she decides the fate of Duessa, choosing to let her live, but spoiled "of her scarlot robe" and therefore revealed as the disgusting creature she truly is.

Una's most spectacular intervention is in canto ix, when the tantalizing rhetoric of Despair tempts the fallen Redcrosse "to worke his finall smart." The focus of the canto has been completely on Despair and Redcrosse, two figures locked in a duel of mental anguish. Then stanza 52 shifts to Una who, after a ladylike short swoon, takes charge of the action and her knight:

> Out of his hand she snatcht the cursed knife,
> And threw it to the ground, enraged rife,
> And to him said, Fie, fie, faint harted knight.
> What meanest thou by this reproachful strife?
> Is this the battell, which thou vauntst to fight
> With that fire-mouthed Dragon, horrible and bright?
>
> Come, come away, fraile, feeble, fleshly wight,
> . . . .
> Arise, Sir knight, arise, and leave this cursed place.(i.ix.52–53)

This is a woman of authority whose brief centrality shifts the whole direction of the narrative. From the point of view of the allegory, she has of course been a central player all along, whether she is seen as truth, the true church, or God's motivating force within the Christian soul.

From this point in book i personified pieties and a holy hermit take over, preparing Redcrosse for his final duel with "that fire-mouthed Dragon, horrible and bright" that has Una's parents in thrall. Narrative moves into denser allegory in canto xi and then merges comedy and heroic poem in the concluding betrothal. Una may wait for her man to complete his quests at the end of book i's frame, but she has been anything but passive within the book's narrative adventures. Yet her active power is always balanced by traditional-romance passivity (first a quick swoon, then she takes charge), and her interventions reach into the main scene from the sidelines.

The most remarkable characteristic of Lanyer's passion story is that it is presented entirely from women's points of view, and in it women have important roles both in the central narrative and in the dedicatory frame. Spenser provides a powerful model for how the apparently marginal can center the issues and even direct the action. Lanyer interjects the active authority of female figures, who come into the picture at key times to warn or affect the actions of men. Despite the very real differences between allegorical and biblical characters, the example of Una is an important predecessor of Lanyer's effort to situate women in the Christian story.

The narrative action of the *Salve Deus* begins at line 333, as Christ goes to the Garden of Gethsemane, and ends at line 1320, after a short song of his resurrected beauty, based on the Canticles. Surrounding the story proper is a dedicatory frame to the countess of Cumberland in which her virtues and sufferings are extolled and consoled. The narrative loosely follows Matthew 26:30–28:10 and consists primarily of men who are at worst wicked, and at best misguided (Simon of Cyrene and Joseph of Arimethea are the only exceptions), contrasted with women who are the prophets and revealers of truth. Peter, James, and John fall asleep in the garden, and Peter denies Christ three times. These are the best. Judas and Caiaphas are wicked, Herod is a fool, and Pilate is the ultimate self-serving politician. In themselves, these are familiar characters who (along with the ever-present figure of the suffering Christ) center the action. Less familiar are the women who appear from the margins, take center stage long enough to make important points about the perfidy of men, and then blend their voices into that of the narrator.

The narrative voice, which has so forcefully characterized itself as female (ll. 273–96), intrudes and comments at will, even to the point of little homilies. Here, for example, is her explosive commentary on those who came to arrest Christ:

> How blinde were they could not discerne the Light!
> How dull! if not to understand the truth,
> How weake! if meekenesse overcame their might;
> How stony hearted, if not mov'd to ruth:
> How void of Pitie, and how full of Spight,
> Gainst him that was the Lord of Light and Truth:
>   Here insolent Boldnesse checkt by Love and Grace,
>   Retires, and falls before our Makers face. (ll. 505–12)

A narrator has the right to comment as well as describe, and though she does more of the former than Spenser, she does enough of the latter to keep the familiar story moving in interesting new ways. While the narrator's homiletic moments may be considered one way of centering a female voice, they are less apparently transgressive than the insertion of women into the story itself.

The first and most radical intrusion of a woman's voice is that of Pilate's wife, whose single biblical verse (Matt. 27:19) Lanyer expands into a lengthy speech in defense of Eve and all women against the terrible masculine sin of the crucifixion. Una provides a model here

as well, turning argument into action as she corrects the sophistries
of Despair:

> Come, come away, fraile, feeble, fleshly wight,
>   Ne let vaine words bewitch thy manly hart,
>   Ne divelish thoughts dismay thy constant spright.
>   In heavenly mercies hast thou not a part?
>   Why shouldst thou then despeire, that chosen art?
>   Where justice growes, there grows eke greater grace,
>   The which doth quench the brond of hellish smart,
>   And that accurst hand-writing doth deface.
> Arise, Sir knight, arise, and leave this cursed place. (I.ix.53)

Pilate's wife similarly reaches in, unasked, from the margins of the
action and, while acknowledging the power of men, makes herself
the prophetic voice that should be heeded:

> Let barb'rous crueltie farre depart from thee,
> And in true Justice take afflictions part;
> Open thine eies, that thou the truth mai'st see,
> Doe not the thing that goes against thy heart,
> Condemne not him that must thy Saviour be;
> But view his holy life, his good desert.
>   Let not us women glory in Mens fall,
>   Who had power given to over-rule us all. (ll. 753–60)

Like Una, Pilate's wife is able to "read" the situation, and she goes
on to rewrite the story of the fall. In recasting the biblical narrative
(as Una had recast Despair's version of sin and damnation), Pilate's
wife portrays an Eve who meant no harm,

> But surely *Adam* cannot be excusde,
> Her fault though great, yet hee was most too blame
> What Weaknesse offerd, Strength might have refusde. (ll. 777–79)

And just to blur the categories of ignorance and knowledge a bit more:

> If *Eve* did erre, it was for knowledge sake,
> The fruit beeing faire perswaded him to fall:
>   No subtill Serpents falshood did betray him.
>   If he would eate it, who had powre to stay him?

Not *Eve*, whose fault was onely too much love,
   Which made her give this present to her Deare

  . . . .

   Yet Men will boast of Knowledge, which he tooke
   From *Eves* faire hand, as from a learned Booke. (ll. 797–802, 807–8)

This being the case, why should not women be the best interpreters
of Scripture? Lanyer invites Queen Anne to test this reading against
the exegetical tradition, "To judge if it agree not with the Text"
("Queene Anne," l. 76). Pilate's wife, like Una, like women generally, reads aright.[34]

So it is with the daughters of Jerusalem, who read correctly the
procession of the cross:

First went the Crier with open mouth proclayming
The heavy sentence of Iniquitie,
The Hangman next, by his base office clayming
His right in Hell, where sinners never die,
Carrying the nayles, the people still blaspheming
Their maker, using all impiety;
   The thieves attending him on either side,
   The Serjeants watching, while the women cri'd. (ll. 961–68)

In their weeping, these women from the sidelines become centered
in the procession, as Christ turns to them, comforting and speaking
to them as he would not speak to his accusers (ll. 969–84). The women
are blessed (ll. 985–87) and seek by their example to turn the hearts
of the men:

They labor still these tyrants hearts to move:
   In pitie and compassion to forbeare
   Their whipping, spurning, tearing of his haire.

But all in vain, their malice hath no end,
Their hearts more hard than flint, or marble stone. (ll. 998–1002)

Like saints and martyrs, like medieval heroines, they try to inspire
by their examples, to refocus the attention of the men.

The poem turns immediately to "The sorrow of the virgin Marie,"
whose grief and tears are most directly reminscent of Una ("To see
his bleeding body oft she swouned," l. 1012). But if she swoons like
Una, like Una she can also read a scene correctly and act accordingly:

Her teares did wash away his pretious blood,
That sinners might not tread it under feet
To worship him, and that it did her good
Upon her knees, although in open street,
Knowing he was the Jessie floure and bud,
That must be gath'red when it smell'd most sweet:
    Her Sonne, her Husband, Father, Saviour, King,
      Whose death killd Death, and tooke away his sting. (ll. 1017–24)

Lanyer turns full attention to Mary, with a hymn of praise that extends the story of the annunciation and Mary's own Magnificat (Luke 1:48–49), concluding with a return to Christ's sacrifice, and then back to Mary on the sidelines of the procession (ll. 1025–1136). And so Mary fades from view, as the scene moves inexorably to the crucifixion itself. The story has two more women, "The *Maries*" who come to anoint the body of Christ and find the tomb empty, but Lanyer gives them only two lines (ll. 1287–88). The mighty act of sacrifice has been done, the resurrection and the risen Christ are next in order, and then a return to the frame of praise for the countess of Cumberland.

The narrator has in fact broken the story's forward movement before the report of Christ's resurrection, addressing the countess directly at the moment of crucifixion. "To my Ladie of Cumberland," says the marginal note:

This with the eie of Faith thou maist behold,
Deere Spouse of Christ, and more than I can write;
And here both Griefe and Joy thou maist unfold,
To view thy Love in this most heavy plight.
Bowing his head, his bloodlesse body cold;
Those eies waxe dimme that gave us all our light.
    His count'nance pale, yet still continues sweet,
      His blessed blood watring his pierced feet. (ll. 1169–76)

Like Mary and the daughters of Jerusalem, the countess enters the narrative to read the story aright ("and more than I can write"). More importantly, she enters as the "Deere Spouse of Christ," the Church born at the moment of the crucifixion, and fulfills a symbolic importance suggested in the opening frame: "Thy constant faith like to the Turtle Dove / Continues combat . . ." (ll. 157–58): ". . . thou, the wonder of our wanton age, / Leav'st all delights to serve a heav'nly king" (ll. 169–70); "Thou faire example, live without compare" (l. 177).

In the concluding frame, which is immensely rich and complex in its allusions to powerful women, Lanyer completes the circle by filling out the portrait of the countess as the perfect type of the church. The poem's structural margin—its frame—becomes its center.

Lanyer's principal device in the concluding frame is to compare the piety and devotion of the countess of Cumberland to the love and piety of a series of famous women, beginning, interestingly, with Cleopatra (ll. 1409–46), and concluding with an extended comparison with the queen of Sheba who (like the countess) sought wisdom (ll. 1569–1608). The comparisons themselves are subtle and sometimes unexpected; their net effect is to underscore the countess as the true spouse of Christ. The section that precedes these comparisons (ll. 1321–1408) is the point at which Lanyer moves from the passion narrative back to the frame, where the poet presents her gift of the passion story to the countess, who in turn becomes both the reader of the book of Christ and herself the model for all perfect piety.

First Lanyer brings the countess in from the margin of her narrative and recenters the entire passion story in her patron's heart:

> . . . (good Madame) in your heart I leave
> His perfect picture, where it still shall stand,
>   Deepely engraved in that holy shrine,
>   Environed with Love and Thoughts divine. (ll. 1325–28)

Her heart engraved with Christ, the countess is able to recognize his presence in all its guises:

> Thou call'st, he comes, thou find'st tis he indeed,
> Thy Soule conceaves that he is truly wise:
>   Nay more, desires that he may be the Booke,
>   Whereon thy eyes continually may looke. (ll. 1349–52)

Seeing Christ in the sick and poor, she performs acts of mercy that confirm her own salvation and imprint her with the power "to heale the soules of those that doe transgresse" (l. 1371). Rejecting wealth and honor if "it prooves a foe / To virtue, learning, and the powres divine" (ll. 1390–91), she brings others to him:

> . . . in thy modest vaile do'st sweetly cover
> The staines of other['s] sinnes . . .
>   That by this means thou mai'st in time recover

Those weake lost sheepe that did so long transgresse,
Presenting them unto thy deerest Lover. (ll. 1394–98)

Like Una, the countess reads the book of holiness correctly and performs right actions, then becomes herself a text by her example. Her sufferings are never merely passive, as they move her to acts of charity and mercy. The veil that hides Una's face becomes the veil the countess throws over the sins of others. The marginal figure embodies the triumph of the story's action, and both Una and the countess end up properly betrothed.

Blurring traditional categories of active and passive, story and reader, both Spenser and Lanyer privilege the marginal. In Spenser's story Una becomes the agent for Redcrosse Knight's redemption. In Lanyer's passion the scorned Christ and the apparently helpless women share the triumph. An important question in Lanyer criticism is how a nonaristocratic woman can write with such authority. Spenser provided an excellent model for Lanyer's unapologetic stance, boldly approaching great patrons and creating figures like Una and Britomart. The imposing presence of Gloriana, real and feigned, could easily have a major impact on a young woman who saw for herself the power of a queen. Spenser's narrator, himself both observer and actor, provides additionally an ungendered model for the marginal figure—the author—who centers and directs the action. Colin Clout teaches Calidore the reciprocity of grace, and Edmund Spenser may have taught Aemilia Lanyer about the authority of the poet.

Lanyer almost certainly read Spenser and his work helps to illuminate specific areas of hers. He is in many ways the great original, the new English laureate, whose presence is inevitable for any Jacobean poet. While a male poet may have a vexed relationship with Spenser (Ben Jonson comes to mind),[35] Lanyer seems at ease taking on the Spenserian "taske of Beauty." She is less concerned than Jonson (or Daniel or Drayton) about the theory and direction of poetry, and perhaps better able to pick and choose elements from the Spenserian model that suit her own purposes. How she articulates her stance as a Jacobean poet, however, is best seen in relation to her contemporaries, Shakespeare and Jonson.

3

LANYER AND SHAKESPEARE

William Shakespeare (1564–1616) and Aemilia Lanyer have been linked in many minds since 1973, when A. L. Rowse declared that he had discovered the "dark lady" of Shakespeare's sonnets.[1] There is no direct evidence for any connection between Shakespeare and Lanyer, but Rowse's identification of her with Shakespeare's Petrarchan fiction has received so much notice that I address it briefly here and return to it in more detail at the end of this chapter. More interesting than the speculation about a romantic or sexual relationship, in my judgment, is what Lanyer as a poet may have found in Shakespeare's published work. This chapter seeks to situate Lanyer fairly in relation to Shakespeare.

Shakespeare was born and raised in the Warwickshire town of Stratford-upon-Avon, made a successful career in London as an actor and playwright, and retired to Stratford around 1611, where he had acquired property and maintained contact with his countrymen throughout his career.[2] None of his known London residences was located near Lanyer's, although sometime around 1596 he resided in the parish of St. Helen's, Bishopsgate, roughly two hundred yards from her parents' parish church of St. Botolph's, Bishopsgate. Her parents were long dead, however and we know that by May 1597 she was living about three miles away from the Bishopsgate area near the long ditch in Westminster.[3]

While Lanyer and Shakespeare may be taken to have a common patron in Henry, Lord Hunsdon, since Shakespeare's acting company was "The Lord Chamberlain's Men," the dates do not suggest that the mistress and the playwright would have had any direct contact. The group of players that flourished under Lord Hunsdon and his son was "virtually a creation of the reorganization [of theatrical companies] that followed the easing of the plague in 1594"; the first documented reference to Shakespeare at Elizabeth's court refers to performances around the Christmas revels of 1594.[4] Lanyer had left court and (probably) the lord chamberlain's protection through her marriage to Alfonso Lanyer in October 1592. Records indicate that Shakespeare's first plays were performed from 1590 to 1592 under the auspices of Lord Strange's Men (the group that was later to form the core of the reconstituted Lord Chamberlain's Men), the Earl of Pembroke's Men, and possibly an earlier version of the Lord Chamberlain's Men, but there is no evidence that any of these were performed at court.[5] In 1603 this same group became the King's Men, enjoying the sponsorship of James. These theatrical and court associations were not open to Aemilia Lanyer after 1592, and there is no evidence that she attended public performances.

Lanyer refers to the stories of Lucrece and Cleopatra in the *Salve Deus*, but again there is no obvious reason to think she derived them from Shakespeare, as she apparently derived her figures of Rosamond and Octavia from Daniel. Versions of the Lucrece legend and of Antony and Cleopatra's stories were ubiquitous, while the Rosamond legend, and the focus on Octavia, were not.[6] Thomas Heywood's theatrical version of *The Rape of Lucrece*, one popular version of the Lucrece story, was published in 1608 and went through two more editions in 1609.[7] Nevertheless, as I discuss later in this chapter, Lanyer may well have read Shakespeare's *Venus and Adonis* (1593) and *The Rape of Lucrece* (1594). They are both poetic narratives about the dangers of beauty, a genre and topic that certainly interested her, and Alfonso's later relationship with their dedicatee, Henry Wriothesley, earl of Southampton, may have brought Shakespeare to the attention of both Lanyers.

Alfonso expected Southampton's help as he attempted to procure income from the hay and grain weighing patent originally awarded to him in 1604.[8] He probably had encountered the earl during his military adventures, since he was also petitioning other military associates (notably Thomas Bancroft, with whom he had served in Ireland) about the same matter. Alfonso probably met Southampton, a close associate of the earl of Essex, through military adventures begun, as Forman's diaries tell us, in the summer of 1597 with the Islands expedition.[9] Southampton, to whom Shakespeare dedicated both *Venus and Adonis* and *The Rape of Lucrece*, might have been the person behind the figure of the beautiful young man in the sonnets.[10] There is no evidence that Aemilia Lanyer was acquainted with Southampton, however, and, if she was, a more likely time for it would be after 1598, when Alfonso returned from the adventures he shared with the earl.

Although Southampton might be a potential connection between Lanyer and Shakespeare, there is nothing to show that the earl continued as Shakespeare's patron after 1594, nor any suggestion that he was close enough to Alfonso Lanyer to have encountered his wife. It is just possible that she met Southampton herself when he was a very young man at Elizabeth's court.[11] The only acquaintance we can be sure Shakespeare and Lanyer shared is the old lord chamberlain.

In sum, both Shakespeare and Lanyer were acquainted with the old lord chamberlain, though probably at different times, and both Shakespeare and Alfonso Lanyer knew Henry Wriothesley, Earl of Southampton. That is the extent of verifiable evidence for a link between the two poets.

Rowse and, more recently, Roger Prior have nonetheless argued that Lanyer and Shakespeare had a sexual relationship basing their case substantially on an interpretive reading of Shakespeare's sonnets and plays.[12] Several of our most distinguished Shakespeareans have countered Rowse's arguments (sometimes repeatedly), while Lanyer scholars have tended to dismiss the "dark lady" issue as distracting to the study of Lanyer in her own right. Rowse reads her work as showing a personal consciousness of sin and illustrating a sudden religious conversion, for example, which I find skewed and naive about the religious and poetic conventions of the time.[13] Rowse, trained as a historian, tries to make the author of the *Salve Deus Rex Judaeorum* fit the character he constructs from the sonnets, confuses his construction with the speaker of another text, and generally makes no distinctions between literary and documentary evidence.

Rowse responded to all criticism by insisting that he is right and his critics are wrong, and Roger Prior has reiterated Rowse's views and sought to add his own support through his work on a possible Jewish origin for the Bassanos.[14] I take up the arguments and counterarguments at the end of this chapter.

Red and White Once More: Courtly, Classical, and Christian

Shakespeare's *Venus and Adonis* (1593), an extraordinary version of the erotic Ovidian narrative that was also famously represented by Marlowe's *Hero and Leander* (1593, published 1598), went through twelve editions by 1636. It has two characteristics that stand out as relevant to Lanyer's own narrative poem: its systematic transformation of the iconography of "red and white" and its elegant focus on the beauty of the male body. The lustful gaze of Venus on Adonis has its ostensibly chaste counterpart in the portrait of Christ that Lanyer holds up for the embrace of her women patrons. If Shakespeare's poem takes the deferrals of desire to erotic heights, Lanyer's *Salve Deus* transubstantiates the elements of desire into the consummation of the soul.

In chapter 2 I noted that Lanyer appears to reject those "matchlesse colours Red and White" (*SD* l. 193), picking up on the rejection of the merely physical that Spenser insists upon even in his "Hymn to Love."[15] Although red and white as the colors of love have a pedigree that goes back at least as far as the early-thirteenth-century courtly love lyrics of Italy and France, *Venus and Adonis* is the most impressive example of their deployment as the iconography of mortal beauty in Elizabethan narrative verse.[16] It is quite likely that Lanyer knew the poem, although in her own long Christian narrative she scarcely mentions classical mythology. Unlike the complaint narratives that Lanyer does mention in *Salve Deus*, the Ovidian *Venus and Adonis* makes no claim to moralize or transcend the dangers of beauty. It is a story of pure passion: Venus lusts after Adonis, who is interested only in the sport of hunting. She is afraid of his plan to hunt the wild boar, and her fears are realized when he dies from the hunt. His metamorphosis into a purple flower becomes a way for his beauty to survive in the world, transcending simple mortality but neither granting nor judging Venus's passion or his refusal.

It did not take a post-Freudian age to see the parallels between Adonis's love of hunting and Venus's sexual pursuit. The hunt was one of the most popular of Petrarchan conceits, introduced into England by Wyatt's "Who so list to hounte, I know where is an hynde," but frequently deployed by sixteenth-century sonneteers (e.g., Spenser's *Amoretti 67*: "Lyke as a Huntsman after weary chace").[17] Nor was there lack of precedent for seeing the relation between lust and death.

Spenser (along with Arthur Golding, whose translation of Ovid's *Metamorphosis* appeared in 1567) may have provided Shakespeare with important models for his version of the story of Venus and Adonis. I want to pause over Spenser's Adonis stories in book 3 of *The Faerie Queene*, which provide relevant background for Shakespeare's story. A comparison with *Venus and Adonis* will clarify the traditional symbolism of "red and white" that Lanyer claims to reject, while their contrasting emphases help illustrate the difference between setting female or male characters in the line of the reader's gaze, a difference that interested Lanyer.

If red and white are the traditional colors of beauty and passion, in the *Faerie Queene* they sometimes take on a sinister character. In 3.i the story is explicitly, and in 3.ix implicitly, part of the iconography of destructive love. That iconography is balanced and centered by a more creative passion in the Garden of Adonis of canto vi, where Venus has secreted her beloved and made him "the Father of all formes" (3.vi.47) in a world not red and white but fecund green. Although he is the focus of book 3's thematic set piece, he is never seen in 3.vi, so our gaze never shifts from beautiful woman to beautiful man.[18]

In 3.i.34–38 the chaste heroine Britomart sees the story of Venus and Adonis portrayed in a tapestry that adorns the great hall of Castle Joyeous, home to unchaste Malecasta. In this version Venus succesfully seduces Adonis, with the erotic content of the tale made explicit. Red and white do not appear as the colors of love, but implicitly of death:

> Lo, where beyond he lyeth languishing,
>   Deadly engored of a great wild Bore,
>   And by his side the Goddesse groveling
>   Makes for him endlesse mone, and evermore
>   With her soft garment wipes away the gore,
>   Which staines his snowy skin with hatefull hew:
>   But when she saw no help might him restore,
>   Him to a dainty flowre she did transmew,
> Which in that cloth was wrought, as if it lively grew. (3.i.38)

In canto xi there is only a brief allusion to the story, which appears in another tapestry filled with chilling portraits of lust gone wild and Cupid gone mad in his assaults on all the gods:

> Ne did he spare (so cruell was the Elfe)
>   His owne deare mother, (ah why shoulde he so?) (3.xi.45)

Britomart's view of the second tapestry is shortly followed by the Mask of Cupid, whose red and white center is the captive Amoret, tortured by the sorcerer Busirane:

> Her brest all naked, as net ivory,
>   Without adorne of gold or silver bright,
>   Wherewith the Craftesman wonts it beautify

> Of her dew honour was despoyled quight,
> And a wide wound therein (O ruefull sight)
> Entrenched deepe with knife accursed keene,
> Yet freshly bleeding forth her fainting spright,
> (The worke of cruell hand) was to be seene,
> That dyde in sanguine red her skin all snowy cleene. (3.xii.20)

As with the fallen Adonis, the red and white of beauty lead tragically to the red of blood on ivory skin. Britomart rescues Amoret, though not before receiving her own wound, that with "little drops empurpled her faire brest" (3.xii.33).

Spenser's tale is a moral one, with lust the cause and pain the effect. Shakespeare's story is morally ambiguous, as were other Elizabethan versions of Ovidian erotic poetry.[19] While Venus's pursuit of Adonis is excessive and she seeks to entrap him against his will, it is the hunt that kills him, not the lust. Shakespeare's use of red and white in this context may borrow some of its blood imagery from Spenser's verse but not, apparently, its moral. Shakespeare appears, instead, to be exploring the range of simple iconographic terms. What can red and white mean? While Spenser's "Hymn of Love" is a philosophical poem that simply rejects them as the colors of earthly beauty personified by the traditional courtly fair, Shakespeare's *Venus and Adonis* is a story that shifts and transforms them, centering their meaning in the control, humiliation, death, and metamorphosis of a beautiful young man. As narrative technique (as opposed to moral intent) Shakespeare's model of "red and white" is much closer to what Lanyer sets out to do in the *Salve Deus*.

The sequence of iconographic transformation in *Venus and Adonis* is complex, moving eventually from passionate life to passionate death, but along the way interweaving traditional significances (fair skin, red cheeks, hot passion, cool death) to enrich and blur the symbolic values of the colors. The initial twist is to apply the traditional emblems of the lady's beauty to "rose-cheeked Adonis" (l. 3), whom Venus woos and addresses as "more white and red than doves or roses are" (l. 10). Shades of ambiguity and contradiction that will eventually infuse the traditional colors appear early on. Venus promises kisses, for example, that will make his lips "red, and pale, with fresh variety" (l. 21); she is "red and hot as coals of glowing fire, / He red for shame, but frosty in desire" (35–36). Her direct approach puts him "'twixt crimson shame and anger ashy pale" (l. 76), which is followed by the colors reverberating between the pursuer and the pursued:

> Being red, she loves him best, and being white
> Her best is bettered with a more delight. (ll. 77–78)

If red goes with lips and passion, Adonis's lips are "fair," which Venus will cure with her own lips "not so fair, yet are they red" (l. 116).

White begins to take on subtle overtones of death as Venus imprisons Adonis in her "lily fingers [locked] one in one" (l. 228) and hunts him within that white enclosure:

> "Fondling," she saith, "since I have hemmed thee here
> Within the circuit of this ivory pale,
> I'll be a park, and thou shalt be my deer." (ll. 229–31)

As she pursues him, she displays a "fighting conflict" in her coloring, as her passion and intensity destroy their traditional courtly complementarity:

> How white and red each other did destroy:
> But now her cheek was pale, and by and by
> It flashed forth fire, as lightening from the sky. (ll. 346–48)

Although we expect the flash of fire to renew the red of her cheeks, Shakespeare slips in some visual dissonance with the image of fire "as lightening," a white heat, not pallor or even the creamy beauty of the ideal courtly complexion.

Increasingly, white takes on the burden of passion usually associated with red. His hand in hers is "a lily prisoned in a gaol of snow / Or ivory in an alabaster band" (ll. 362–63). Beauty in a "naked bed" is figured as "teaching the sheets a whiter hue than white" (l. 398). In contrast, red symbolizes both Adonis's erotically enticing beauty and his cold rejection, as he speaks words she does not want to hear:

> Once more the ruby coloured portal opened
> Which to his speech did honey passage yield,
> Like a red morn that ever yet betokened
> Wreck to the seaman, tempest to the field. (ll. 451–54)

Venus turns so passionate white she faints, and "the silly boy, believing she is dead / Claps her pale cheek, till clapping makes it red" (ll. 464–65). The result is both to gain Venus some of the physical attention she has been lusting for, and to restore the traditional iconographic meaning of white and red. "Set thy seal manual on my wax-red lips" (l. 515), she says in one of the most richly sensuous metaphors of this richly sensuous poem. Her cheeks, too, are again red in their passion, as "her face doth reek and smoke, her blood doth boil" (l. 555), while mention of his plan to hunt the dangerous boar produces "a sudden pale," which, "Like lawn being spread upon the blushing rose / Usurps her cheek" (ll. 589–91).

Far past the discordant lightening of white passion, Venus points to the white fear ("Didst thou not mark my face? Was it not white," l. 643) that sees the red image of death,

> An image of thyself, all stained with gore
> Whose blood upon the fresh flowers being shed
> Doth make them droop with grief and hang the head. (ll. 664–65)

From discordant passion and the white imprisonment of lust, to red lust in action then white fear and red blood, the story itself moves with the colors it paints and the colors keep shifting their places in the emotional scene. In Venus and Adonis, red and white are more than leitmotif: they provide a structural device that links and shifts the erotic imagery of the narrative.

There is no mention of red or white for nearly one hundred lines as Venus tries to persuade Adonis not to hunt the boar, telling stories against the hunt. "Unlike myself thou hear'st me moralise," she says, explicitly doing what the author himself refuses to do, "Applying this to that, and so to so" (ll. 712–13). Shakespeare wittily makes Venus herself a bit of a bore, increasing her beloved's desire to break free. As part of her moralizing, she notes that nature mingles "beauty with infirmities" (l. 735), so that "pure perfection" is subject to such things as "burning fevers, agues pale and faint" (l. 739), an argument she turns toward a carpe diem moral: "Be prodigal" (l. 755).

This story of fear followed by attempted seduction again compounds the hunt of love with the dangerous hunt of the boar. When the reader next encounters red and white, on the frothy mouth of the successful boar, the image is both shocking and just right. Just at the point when Venus has talked herself into avoiding senseless fears, "she spied the hunted boar,"

> Whose frothy mouth bepainted all with red,
> Like milk and blood being mingled both together. (ll. 900–2)

Red and white, beauty and passion, death and life, are all intermingled in the final transformative images of Adonis himself:

> . . . the wide wound that the boar had trenched
> In his soft flank, whose wonted lily white
> With purple tears, that his wound wept, was drenched.
> No flower was nigh, no grass, herb leaf or weed,
> But stole his blood, and seemed with him to bleed. (ll. 1053–56)

The fire of passion becomes the fire of grief ("Mine eyes are turned to fire, my heart to lead," l. 1072), and, in an act that combines passion, grief, and the classical version of redemption, metamorphosis,

> . . . she falleth in the place she stood
> And stains her face with his congealed blood. (ll. 1121–22)
> .   .   .   .
> And in his blood that on the ground lay spilled
> A purple flower sprung up, check'red with white,
> Resembling well his pale cheeks and the blood,
> Which in round drops upon the whiteness stood. (ll. 1167–70)

Surveying the shifts in meaning that the ubiquitous red and white receive in this poem provides only a hint of the poem's metaphorical density, erotic wit, and thematic conflation of courtly love, passion, and death. Yet Shakespeare's various evocations of red and white provide a remarkably sturdy structure for the richness of the rest of the poem. Although this is a poem to titillate a young man and Lanyer's is a poem to validate the piety of an older woman, we see something similar in the *Salve Deus*.

As Shakespeare takes the colors of courtly love and makes them the colors of classical fame, so Lanyer takes the same colors and transforms them into the red and white of Christian redemption. Her use of them is less direct (except at two key points in the poem) and less pervasive than in *Venus and Adonis*, but nonetheless they act as a structural element that supports some of the same transformative ideas: movement from a passion for beauty to the passion of blood sacrifice to redemption and renewal. A core difference resides in the stories themselves, one pagan and one centrally Christian, and I do not want to suggest that *Venus and Adonis* was in any substantive sense a model for the *Salve Deus*. It does, however, model a technique that Lanyer would certainly have seen if she read

Shakespeare's poem, and both poems have a crucial similarity: the beauty on which our gaze is focused is the beauty of men who represent, respectively, the perfection of pagan eroticism and the erotics of perfect transcendence.

Venus and Adonis begins with the beauty of a fair and rosy beloved, whose enjoyment is frustrated by death. *Salve Deus* begins by explicitly rejecting the "gawdie colours" (l. 188) of mutable outward beauty in favor of "faire Virtues" which "are alwaies fresh" (ll. 189–90), and moving through the tragedy of pain to a sacrifice that unites the human with the divine in the glory of perfect and immutable love. The famous colors appear explicitly together at only three places in the poem. The first is toward the beginning, when the poet rejects earthly beauty. The colors and what they represent are presented in the abstract, to dismiss their concrete mutability:

> As for those matchlesse colours Red and White,
> Or perfit features in a fading face,
> Or due proportion pleasing to the sight,
> All these doe draw but dangers and disgrace. (ll. 193–96)

The second is after the crucifixion, when it seems the death of the beautiful Christ will be simply another sad and lovely natural event like the death of Adonis, and the colors are appropriately represented together in their usual substantiated pairing of lilies and roses. Joseph finds a tomb in which he lays the crucified Christ and embalms him in the natural images of courtly beauty, but the narrative shifts abruptly toward the miracle of the resurrection:

> There this most precious body [Joseph] incloses,
> Imbalmd and deckt with Lillies and with Roses.
>
> Loe here the Beautie of Heav'n and Earth is laid,
> The purest coulers underneath the Sunne,
> But in this place he cannot long be staid,
> Glory must end what horror hath begun. (ll. 1279–84)

Red and white have moved from "gawdie" to "purest" colors, a process achieved by the imagery of Christ's red blood. At first it comes metaphorically from his agonized prayer, when "pretious sweat [comes] trickling from the ground / Like drops of blood" (ll. 407–8). Next it is "innocent blood" that Judas has betrayed and Pilate threatens to spill (ll. 741, 750). Finally there is the actual blood of Christ, "pretious" (l. 896) and redemptive:

His sacred blood must grace that loathsome field,
To purge more filth, that that foule place could yield. (ll. 1143–44)

And also starkly vivid:

His blessed blood watring his pierced feet. (l. 1176)

The lilies and roses of his tomb hold Christ no more than the cross, however, and blood becomes the sign of Christian triumph and grace, uniting God to humankind once again. Instead of an ardent Venus pursuing the youthful red and white body of a reluctant Adonis, at Christ's resurrection he is greeted

       . . . by his faithfull Wife
The holy church; who in those rich attires,
Of Patience, Love, Long suffring, Voide of strife,
Humbly presents those oyntments he requires:
    The oyles of Mercie, Charitie, and Faith,
    She only gives that which no other hath. (ll. 1291–96)

Drawn from Mary Magdalene and "the other Mary" approaching Christ's tomb (Matt. 28:1), this is a dutiful female figure who "washeth cleane / The soares of sinnes, which in our Soules abounds," becoming a virtual co-redeemer (ll. 1297–1300). Lanyer hastens to put the focus back where tradition must have it:

Yet all the glory unto Christ redounds,
His pretious blood is that which must redeeme. (ll. 1301–2)

She then shifts the reader's gaze to that exquisite "briefe description of his beautie upon the Canticles":

This is the Bridegroome that appeares so faire,
So sweet, so lovely in his Spouses sight,
That unto Snowe we may his face compare,
His cheekes like skarlet, and his eyes so bright
As purest Doves that in the rivers are,
Washed with milke to give the more delight. (ll. 1305–10)

Red and white appear explicitly once more at the very end of the poem, as the "Colours of Confessors & Martirs," the new transformed beauty whose dross has been sublimated and whose meaning has been forever transformed by the blood sacrifice of the pale man on the cross:

> Loe Madame, heere you take a view,
> Whose worthy steps you doe desire to tread,
> Deckt in those colours which our Saviour chose;
> The purest colours both of White and Red,
> Their freshest beauties I would fain disclose,
> By which our Saviour most was honoured:
>   But my weake Muse desireth now to rest,
>   Folding up all their Beauties in your breast. (ll. 1825–32)

Like Adonis, the Christ of *Salve Deus* is beautiful, passive, and surrounded by the traditional colors of courtly love. Instead of a lustful Venus to enclose, demand, terrorize, and tempt him, Christ faces a sequence of sinful men and loving women, with the final agency of the poem residing in the hearts of the virtuous women to whom Lanyer dedicates her poem. The countess of Cumberland becomes the bride of the perfect lover, and red and white become the outward and visible signs of an inward and spiritual grace.

Inward and outward beauty, passive and active virtue, honor, shame, guilt, and despair are all features of the world described in the *Salve Deus*. They are also issues that surface in Shakespeare's only other published narrative poem.

Lucrece and Matilda: Desire, Power, and Agency

The false red and white, Lanyer assures her reader, deceives and distracts from gazing on the purity and life-giving blood of Christ, whose sacrificial grace transforms the mutable world and destroys death. Along the way, as I have noted in this chapter and the preceding one, her narrative poem stresses the dangers of external beauty, particularly to beautiful women. While warnings against the dangerous lure of beauty can be found throughout the history of Western poetry from well before the proud fair of the courtly love tradition to well after Keats's "Belle Dame Sans Merci," the desires it elicits are almost always described from the male point of view. The motivating force of those desires may be sexual, a drive of nature that culture must control, but they are described in terms of a longing for the beautiful, and often, as well, the urge to conquer or master the beautiful object. An inchoate and insatiable desire, as Catherine Belsey has argued, pervades Western culture.[20]

Lanyer, by contrast and in concert with other Jacobean writers, shows the allure of beauty from the woman's point of view. Elizabeth Carey and Lady Mary Wroth have much to say on the subject (in *Mariam,* 1613, and *Urania,* 1621, respectively), but male Jacobean playwrights also have women characters speak their view of the equations of desire. Implicit in these works is a critique of male desire and the power that stands behind it, along with a search for female agency. Shakespeare's *Lucrece,* with its unresolved moral dilemmas and its internal disputations, stands behind a part of that critique.

The story of the rape of Lucretia, purportedly occurring around 510 BCE, is the founding myth of the Roman republic. The tale had descended from Livy's *Early History of Rome* (I.57–58) through the Italian Renaissance to several English versions by the time Lanyer's *Salve Deus* appeared.[21]

Though the details and emphasis vary, the basic legend goes like this: During the Roman siege of Ardea, men of the Roman camp carouse and begin bragging about their wives. One, Collatine, insists that his wife, Lucretia, is the best, and a group sets out to test his claim. After visiting the wives of several of the company, each of them "sporting themselves" and not tending to household chores, they find Lucretia "not as the other before named spending time in idleness, but late in the night occupied and busy amonges her maids in the middes of her house, spinning of wool."[22] One of the ruling king's sons, Sextus Tarquinus, develops such a passion for this image of wifely perfection that he determines to have her. Later he returns to Collatine's house and is hospitably and chastely received. When all have gone to bed he creeps into her bedchamber where he threatens to kill both Lucretia and a servant and leave them in bed together if she does not allow him his way. Sextus rapes her and departs. Lucretia immediately calls for both her husband and father, who come accompanied by Junius Brutus, thought to be something of a fool. Lucretia tells them what happened, and although her husband absolves her of any guilt, she chooses to kill herself so that her death will bear witness to her innocence. As husband and father grieve, Brutus, now revealed to have feigned foolishness to avoid the attention of the Tarquin rulers, pulls the knife from her breast and vows revenge. The house of the Tarquins is shortly thereafter overthrown, and the Roman republic established, with Brutus one of the first consuls.

This is very much a Roman story, whose message of shame and honor is blurred in Renaissance versions, which raise the issue of Christian guilt. It is also a political story, with a chaste wife sacrificed for the birth of the republic. Lucretia is a valued possession whose destruction sparks rebellion. Yet her destruction also has something in it of agency; her husband absolves her, but she decides on the appropriate testimony to her own virtue. Among recent critics, Ian Donaldson has ably analyzed issues of shame and guilt and the political uses of the story over its long life in Western culture, while Stephanie Jed has observed the myth's role in the construction of Italian humanism and its abstraction of textuality.[23]

Lanyer's reference to it is brief and occurs as part of a larger context:

> 'Twas Beautie bred in *Troy* the ten years strife,
> And carried *Hellen* from her lawfull Lord;
> 'Twas Beautie made chase *Lucrece* loose her life,
> For which prowd *Tarquins* fact was so abhorr'd:
> Beautie the cause *Antonius* wrong'd his wife,
> Which could not be decided but by sword:
> > Great *Cleopatraes* Beautie and defects
> > Did work *Octaviaes* wrongs, and his neglects. (ll. 209–16)

Shakespeare's *Lucrece* may bear some relation to this glancing reference in Lanyer's catalog of exemplary beauties who put themselves or others in danger. She would have encountered the story in any number of sources. Its conjunction with the legend of Antony and Cleopatra might suggest Shakespeare as a principal source, but, as I showed in chapter 1, the Cleopatra story was also ubiquitous in Lanyer's time, and Samuel Daniel's narrative poems *Cleopatra* and *Octavia* are more likely to have been backdrops for her interest in and angle on the tale than is Shakespeare's play.

Yet it is quite possible that Lanyer's interest in the story was aroused by Shakespeare's *Lucrece*. It is a verse narrative of the sort she certainly read. Like Michael Drayton's *Matilda*, a story in some ways similar (and to which I shall turn shortly), Shakespeare's *Lucrece* was published in 1594 and may be seen as part of the rage for titillating stories about tragic women set off by Daniel's *Rosamond*. The focuse of the Lucretia story nearest in time to Lanyer's reference, Thomas Heywood's popular play, *The Rape of Lucrece* (1608), is entirely on the tyranny and fall of the Tarquins. Heywood's Sextus Tarquinus never explicitly mentions Lucrece's beauty (though he calls her the "bright enchantress that hath dazed my eyes," 4.iii), but instead claims to be motivated principally by a desire to possess "her modesty" and her "virtue, grace, and fame" (4.i).[24] Collatine's bragging and the viciousness of the Tarquin clan are the real motivators in this play.

Shakespeare, on the other hand, has a great deal to say about Lucrece's beauty and, like Lanyer, makes it the explicit motivation for Tarquin's act.[25] As he waffles back and forth between his moral sense and his passionate desire, her beauty argues for his lust:

> Why hunt I then for colour or excuses?
> All orators are dumb when beauty pleadeth; (ll. 267–68)
>
> .   .   .   .
>
> Desire my pilot is, beauty my prize. (l. 279)

He even assigns her the blame for the rape:

> . . . The fault is thine,
> For those thine eyes betray thee unto mine.
> Thus I forestall thee, if thou mean to chide:
> Thy beauty hath ensnared thee to this night. (ll. 482–85)

Unlike Painter or even Heywood, Shakespeare gives his Lucrece intelligence, moral complexity, and rhetorical space. Only after a great deal of internal debate does she decide that her only possible moral action is suicide (ll. 1023–29). Her decision, though registered in the grossest patriarchal terms, allows her to be active rather than passive. Her rape means that she risks "bastard graff," that she is no longer the spotless property she had been before, and she resolves that Tarquin

> . . . shall not boast, who did thy stock pollute,
> That thou art doting father of his fruit. (ll. 1061–63)

Caught in this grim social construct, she asserts the paradox of her choice; it is both an affirmation of her personal agency and a recognition that the rape has forced her into the worst possible offence, that of threatening the due familial order of inheritance:

For me, I am the mistress of my fate,
  And with my trespass never will dispense,
    Till life to death acquit my forced offence. (ll. 1069–71)

If the founding of the Roman republic is inscribed through the rape of a chaste woman, at least, in this version, that woman is a conscious participant in the process.[26]

If Lanyer did not read Shakspeare's version of the story, she nonetheless derived some of the same issues from it. Whatever else Lanyer is doing in her discussion of the dangers of beauty, she is struggling with the complexities of female agency in the face of masculine power. Her first step is to warn her female readers to beware of putting trust in the power of beauty, since it unleashes destructive male desire:

For greatest perills do attend the faire,
What men do seeke, attempt, plot and devise,
  How they may overthrow the chastest Dame,
    Whose Beautie is the White whereat they aime. (*SD*, ll. 205–08)

Beware, too, of the effects your beauty may have on others. Lanyer blames Cleopatra for not keeping Antony in check, for "giving consent" to Antony's passion:

What fruit did yield that faire forbidden tree,
But blood, dishonour, infamie and shame?
Poore blinded Queene, could'st thou no better see,
But entertaine disgrace, in stead of fame?
Doe these designes with Majestie agree?
To staine thy blood, and blot thy royall name.
  That heart that gave consent unto this ill,
    Did give consent that thou thy selfe should kill. (ll. 217–24)

There are some ironies here: the "disgrace" is also part of the "fame" of Cleopatra's beauty; if Lucrece's sacrifice founded the Roman republic, Cleopatra's adultery lost it (Octavius's victory spells the end of republican Rome), yet the reward for both is suicide.

The litany of beauties continues with

Faire *Rosamund*, the wonder of her time,
[Who] had bin much fairer, had shee not bin faire;

> Beautie betraid her thoughts, aloft to clime,
> To build strong castles in uncertaine air,
> Where th'infection of a wanton crime
> Did worke her fall; first poyson, then despaire,
>   With double death did kill her perjur'd soule,
>   When heavenly Justice did her sinne controuble. (ll. 225–30)

Lanyer blames neither Lucrece nor Cleopatra for the sin of suicide, which Augustine had raised as a serious objection to the standard Roman praise of Lucrece.[27] Rosamond, however, whose situation was closest to Lanyer's own, comes in for the accusation of "double death," ostensibly because she despaired, unquestionably a mortal sin, but then so was suicide. One could say that the Christian imperative did not extend back before Christ, but (as with Shakespeare's *Lucrece*) moral anachronisms were more common than not in Renaissance writers. Furthermore, the next and last in Lanyer's procession of tragic ladies is Matilda, the thirteenth-century beauty who committed suicide rather than give in to the lust of King John.

Lanyer's source for this story is certainly Michael Drayton's *Legend of Matilda* (1594), a tale he liked so well that he took it up again when he came to write his *Englands Heroicall Epistles* (1597). The *Legend* is an avowed imitation of *Rosamond* and Churchyard's *Jane Shore* (ll. 19, 36), carrying forward the theme of female beauty as impetus for desire and the cause of male lust. King John sees the beautiful Matilda, "And of my Sovereigne, him my subject made" (l. 114). Her father, worried about the king's intentions, warns Matilda not to give in to him ("Kings use their Loves as Garments they have worne," l. 190). When King John woos her ("Hoord not thy Beautie, when thou hast such store," l. 232), she finds herself tempted by the riches and honour he can bestow and so leaves court secretly, returning to her father's house. In a rage the king seeks to disgrace her father and, when that does not work, exiles him. Still pursued, she makes her way to a cloister.

> The King, who heard Me safely thus to bee,
> Set in my Cloyster, strongly discontent,
> That me from thence he had not power to free, (ll. 442–43)
>   . . . .
>   . . . past hope then, ever to enjoy me,
> Resolv'd, by some meanes, lastly to destroy me. (ll. 447–48)

He sends an emissary who enters the cloister by deceit, conveying Matilda's options: give in to the king, or die. She refuses, and he poisons her with "a Poyson murd'ring by the scent" (l. 539),

> Which for the same, when fittest time He spy'd,
> Into my nostrils forcibly did strayne. (ll. 541–42)

And so she dies, but not before affirming her chastity: "O, let the Grave mine Innocencie hold" (l. 587). Drayton may have thought to contrast his virtuous Matilda with Daniel's fallen Rosamond, but the result is the same for the beautiful young women: each is poisoned by an enemy.

Lanyer at first seems to be emphasizing a contrast, but not the contrast that Drayton is making. To be sure, Matilda is the only one in Lanyer's list of famous beauties who dies with her chastity intact. Like Lucrece, who has managed to avoid the guilt if not the shame of the act, Lanyer's Matilda martyrs herself on the altar of chastity, the one place a woman's honor could be completely understood:

> Holy *Matilda* in a haplesse houre
> Was born to sorow and to discontent,
> Beauty the cause that turn'd her Sweet to Sowre,
> While Chastity sought Folly to prevent.
> Lustfull King *John* refus'd, did use his pwre,
> By Fire and Sword, to compasse his content:
> But Friends disgrace, nor father's banishment,
> Nor Death it selfe, could purchase her consent. (ll. 233–40)

Lanyer goes on to describe Matilda as "the height of all perfection," and to present her sacrifice as if it were an act of religious communion:

> Here beauty in the height of all perfection,
> Crown'd this faire Creatures everlasting fame,
> Whose noble mind did scorne the base subjection
> Of Feares, or Favours, to impaire her Name:
> By heavenly grace, she had such true direction,
> To die with Honour, not to live in Shame;
> And drinke that poyson with a cheerefull heart,
> That could all Heavenly grace to her impart. (ll. 241–48)

This is not Drayton's version, though Lanyer's readers likely would have his popular poem in mind. His Matilda leaves court for fear she might give in to King John's promise of "favours"; Lanyer's Matilda is steadfast. Drayton's heroine is passively surprised by the inhalation of poison. Lanyer's Matilda, like Lucrece, drinks poison "with a cheerefull heart." She, like Shakespeare's Lucrece, is in the only sense her vulnerability and subjection can permit, "master of [her] fate."

The picture Lanyer paints of male desire and power is a familiar one, but her take on it is different enough to make this poem by and for a woman an interesting contrast to the many contemporary male-authored tragedies about female beauties. Instead of indulging in the description of female beauty, or in the pathos of female passivity, she rejects beauty as a topic for praise precisely because it makes women so vulnerable. In rehearsing the popular stories of her time, she also seems to commend female agency. Lucrece and Matilda have it, Rosamond does not, and Cleopatra should, but gives it over.

Of all the contemporary popular works implicit in Lanyer's rehearsal of the dangers of beauty, Shakespeare's Lucrece comes closest to suggesting female agency in the face of male power and desire. Its exercise may be limited and its options not very attractive, but at least it exists. In the *Salve Deus* a woman may have fewer apparent options, but it is the beautiful man who dies. Like a transcendent Adonis, who was transformed to beautify nature, Lanyer's Christ creates true and enduring beauty in his bride, the Church, who Lanyer's readers may choose to be. She presents her passionate Christ as the true object of female desire, and the choice of steadfast virtue as a new female freedom.

Lanyer and Shakespeare's "Dark Lady"

Many years of debate about Shakespeare and his sonnets stand behind efforts to identify the dark lady, leading Stephen Booth to conclude that "speculation on her identity has ranged from wanton to ludicrous and need not be illustrated."[28] I do not wish to rehearse that range, but only to consider the case for offering Aemilia Lanyer this dubious prize. My hope is to make very clear why most Lanyer scholars find the case weak and irrelevant, and so lay the topic to rest as much as possible. (Readers already persuaded may choose to go directly to the next chapter.)

First some basics. Competing assumptions about the sonnets that have affected approaches to identifying the dark lady include that: the sonnets are primarily autobiographical, or are primarily Shakespeare's reaction to the sonneteering fad set in motion by Sidney's *Astrophil and Stella* (1591); the sonnets imply a coherent narrative, or have related sequences but are essentially experimental and episodic; the sonnets are personal poems that reveal the heart and soul of their author, or are exercises in poetics. They represent fact, or they are constructed fictions.[29]

There is no reason why the sonnets cannot be all of these at once, but the degree to which one favors one emphasis over another is likely to affect one's opinion of the merit in Rowse's arguments. Prior accuses Rowse's critics of dismissing him because he is a historian rather than a literary professional, and because the literary profession has been busily trying to eliminate the author from literary studies. "Modern literary criticism is dedicated to removing the author from the text," Prior asserts. "The author's thoughts and intentions can never be known, it is claimed, and are in any case quite irrelevant to our understanding of his work. . . . It is this doctrine that is threatened by Rowse's discovery and fuels much of the hostility to it."[30]

This seems to me a very serious misreading of the objections to Rowse's theory, as well as a misreading of recent critical theory. There are a good many literary historians who are interested in literary biography, and who believe it can help illuminate literary texts, but who find the idea of one-to-one correspondence between the author's life and what he or she may write in a creative work simplistic and are not persuaded by Rowse's arguments. As David Bevington has recently commented, Rowse's assertion of biographical necessity behind all Shakespeare's work produces judgments such as, "an artist like Shakespeare writes beautifully when he is in love and less so when he is merely carrying out apprenticeship exercises." Bevington adds the useful comparison that "romantic biographies like Sullivan's about Beethoven used to pursue similar sorts of antitheses: happiness produces the symphonies in a warm key, especially 2, 4, 6, and 8, while suffering produces the Eroica, 5, 7, and 9."[31] In practice, this approach leads to circular arguments. Beethoven must have been happy when he wrote the eighth symphony. If Lanyer is the dark lady of the sonnets, then we can attribute to her the characteristics described in them and attribute to Shakespeare's plays biographical references consistent with both Aemilia Lanyer's known biography and what is assumed about her from reading the sonnets.[32]

This is exactly what Rowse and Prior do: they see a certain kind of person described (more or less) in Shakespeare's sonnets, they use a few facts about Lanyer to assert that she must be that sort of person, they then attribute all the characteristics described in the sonnets to Lanyer, and they take that composite portrait and read it into the plays. Despite Prior's attack on the literary profession in defense of Rowse, the issue is not the obtuseness or hostility of Rowse's critics; it is whether his case meets reasonable standards of logic and evidence.

Shakespeare does describe a particular sort of mistress in sonnets 127–52, making her most deliberately a parody of the traditional virtuous fair that (for example) Spenser celebrates in the *Amoretti* and the "Hymn to Love." The eyes of Shakespeare's mistress, we famously recall, "are nothing like the sun" (130). And in response to the usual "red and white," she is dark of hair ("black wires," 130), eye ("raven black," 127), and complexion ("thy breasts are dun," 130). He is enchanted by her beauty ("Thy black is fairest," 131; "beauty herself is black," 132) but nonetheless uses her darkness metaphorically to insinuate a deceiving character ("as black as hell, as dark as night," 147; "I have sworn thee faire: more perjured eye," 152). He portrays her as enticing, but recklessly promiscuous ("the bay where all men ride," 137; "I do believe her though I know she lies," 138; "thou lov'st elsewhere," 139; "She that makes me sin awards me pain," 141; "Robd others beds revenues of their rents," 142; "In act thy bed-vow broke," 152). To those of us steeped in the sonnet tradition, much of this language seems a witty response to the conventional virtuous beauty of courtly love, an extension of Sidney's assertion of Stella's black eyes, tantalizing kisses, and frustrating preference for someone else.[33] The whole point of sonnet writing was to weave variations on common themes and to overgo predecessors; whether or not a real dark lady inspired Shakespeare's sonnets, they are an immediately recognizable (often delightful, sometimes provocative) response to a popular and well-understood set of conventions.[34]

Pace Prior, most critics have been willing to grant that there may well have been a real person behind the portrait Shakespeare chose to draw in his post-Petrarchan exercise. Assuming the reward is worth the effort, we would need to make the following assumptions about Aemilia Lanyer to begin arguing any association between her and the picture Shakespeare gives of the dark lady in the sonnets: she had dark hair and eyes and was dark complected by English standards; she was promiscuous; and she knew Shakespeare. I want to take these in reverse order, which takes us from what I believe to be the weakest to the strongest evidence about Lanyer herself.

Originally Rowse believed he had found his dark lady in Simon Forman's diaries, because Forman, who was visited at one point by Shakespeare's landlady, Mary Mountjoy, and who himself attended plays, described a client who had been the lord chamberlain's mistress; who, Rowse initially believed, was married to someone named William; and who had been "very brown in youth." When other scholars looked at the Forman entries, they found that "very brown" was actually "very brave," and what he had read as a visit from a "William Lanier" on 13 May 1597 was actually the first visit from "Millia Lanier." This forced Rowse silently to expunge two key pieces of his "evidence" from subsequent discussions of Lanyer as the dark lady.[35] Although the connection between Lanyer and Shakespeare initially rested in large part on two false readings, the discovery that she was a poet and from a musical family allowed him to make much of sonnet 128, which has the lady playing a musical instrument.

There remain some important mitigating features of Rowse's combined evidence. Hundreds of people visited the popular Forman. There was no particular correspondence in the timing of Lanyer's affair with the lord chamberlain (c. 1588–92) and Shakespeare's membership in his company (1594 ff.), nor of Mary Mountjoy's visits to Forman (November 1597 to 1598) and Shakespeare's residence in her household (c. 1600–1602), nor of Forman's reports of his own attendance at Shakespeare's plays (1611) and his references to Lanyer (May to September 1597). Further, the ability to sing and play an instrument was an almost universal requirement for educated ladies in the 1590s. What Rowse had actually discovered was one intriguing contiguity between the life of a gentlewoman near Shakespeare's age (she was five years younger) and William Shakespeare: an association with Henry Carey, Lord Hunsdon.

Lanyer's affair with the lord chamberlain underlies all other interpretations of her promiscuity. There is no reason to question Forman's report of the relationship: it is detailed, repeated, and born out by records of her marriage and the birth of her son, Henry, apparently named after the real father. The question is whether this fact, and Forman's further descriptions of her sexual behavior, merit the charge of promiscuity. Interestingly, while most critics of Rowse's case have pointed out its logical weaknesses, no one has challenged his assertion that Lanyer was, as he phrased it, "no better than she should be."[36]

The case for Lanyer's promiscuity has rested, first, on the fact of her relationship with the lord chamberlain, and, second, on reports by Forman that some have taken to indicate Lanyer's continuing sexual availability. The first is hardly an argument for promiscuity; if anything, it is the reverse. Gheerhaerts's portrait of Henry Carey, Lord Hunsdon, painted in 1591 when he was sixty-six and his relationship with Aemilia Bassano was at its height, shows a handsome older man of commanding presence, whose authority it would be unwise to challenge (see fig. 1.1). One can assume this is an image he wished to convey, and the parentless young woman to whom he gave many gifts would do well to respect it. It was neither unusual nor demeaning for a member of the minor gentry to be the mistress of a great lord.[37]

But what of Aemilia Lanyer in 1597? Some of the evidence for her promiscuity that Rowse finds in Forman is simply her frankness about her affair with Hunsdon. To say that she had a child in fornication, for example, is Forman's own (precise) description of her liaison with the lord chamberlain (for Hunsdon the affair was technically "adultery," since he was married); it does not suggest that she had more than the one affair, as Rowse seems to assume. Other evidence Rowse simply misreads. He originally declares, for example, that Forman himself records having had sexual intercourse with Lanyer, but not only is this not true, Forman is adamantly frustrated by her refusal to "halek." Prior continues to insist on Lanyer's promiscuity, though he concedes that, with Forman, her sexual relationship was "perhaps not sexual intercourse."[38]

What, then, remains of the evidence of Aemilia Lanyer's promiscuity? It is possible to find some in Forman's record, though only, I believe, by a willful misreading of some of his comments, and an equal willingness to take Forman at face value on others. To illustrate this point, let me juxtapose Prior's reading with my own on some key passages, on whose transcription we both agree (except for some very minor points, in which I have allowed his readings; it is well to remember how difficult Forman's handwriting can be to decipher).

Here are what I believe to be Prior's crucial misreadings: he claims that "there is no doubt" that "the Dark Lady" Shakespeare describes and Aemilia Lanyer "both were promiscuous."[39] As evidence, he cites the lord chamberlain (no quarrel there) and suggests that Lanyer traded sex for money: "Hunsdon paid her, since she 'was wealthy to him that married her, in money and Jewels' [from Forman]." He certainly gave her gifts, but she also had some inheritance of her own, and Forman's record hardly suggests an Elizabethan call girl. Prior believes that the report of an arranged marriage "for colour" means that the relationship with Hunsdon continued after her marriage, but the phrase more likely refers to a marriage that would give legitimacy to their mutual son. (Although Rowse and Prior refer to both Lanyer and her son, Henry, as "bastards," they were in fact both considered legitimate.)[40] It is possible that Lanyer's relationship with the lord chamberlain continued, but I think it unlikely. She reports her husband's dissipation of the gifts she had received, which suggests that they were not replenished after her marriage.

Prior also seems to believe that Lanyer's report to Forman that she "hath been favored much . . . of many noblemen" means that she granted them sexual favors in return. But he omits the context (which I give here in full in modern spelling, as Prior does his selections): "She hath been favored much of her Majesty and of many noblemen and hath great gifts and been made much of. And a nobleman that is dead hath loved her well and kept her and did maintain her long. But her husband hath dealt hardly [i.e., harshly] with her and spent and consumed her goods and she is now very needy and in debt, and it seems for Lucres sake will be a good fellow for necessity doth compel. She hath a wart or mole in the pit of the throat or near it."

It was usual for the queen and nobility to give gifts to attractive young people at court, but it was not usual for the queen or others to expect sexual favors in return, unless, as is explicit here, one is keeping and maintaining a particular mistress. The particularity of the lord chamberlain's position among the rest seems quite clear, and it is unlikely that others would invade the territory of so powerful a peer. As I noted in chapter 1, Forman appears to use "it seems" when he is interpreting rather than recording. I read this as an example of his wishful thinking, completely consistent with the satyriasis evident throughout the diaries, and suggestively placed before his one physical observation about Lanyer.[41]

We have only Forman's word for how physical Lanyer allowed their relationship to become, and he explicitly acknowledges his inability to get her to have intercourse, a cause of considerable frustration. "She was familiar and friendly to him in all things but only would not halek. Yet he felt all parts of her body willingly and kissed her often, but she would not do in any wise. Whereupon he took some displeasure and so departed friends. But not intending [interdicting?] to come at her again in haste. But yet they were friends again afterward. But he never obtained his purpose and she [was] a whore and dealt evil with him after."

Forman has just three further references to Lanyer, none of them suggesting a sexual relationship. On 23 September 1597 he casts his own horoscope to try to decide whether "to go to Laniere today or no," but as he is about to go he is detained by other business. Forman adds that "the next day at afternoon she sent her maid to me and I did go with her to her," but it is not clear that this refers to Lanier. Next to this comment is a horoscope cast with the notation: "Jone Harrington," with whom he visited "and did halek" on 29 October 1597. A last reference in 1597 is simply the record of her name and ancestry, "Emilia Lanie[r] the daughter of Baptista and Margaret Bassana," following other casebook notes dated 29 September 1597. Finally, on 7 January 1600 he casts his own horoscope to try to discover "why Mrs. Laniere sent for me . . . and whether she intends any more villany or no."

We don't know what Forman considered Lanyer's evil dealing to have been, but it was not sexual intercourse; he is careful to record every successful "halek." His calling her a whore and, later, referring to her as intending "villainy" is consistent with Forman's outbursts about others elsewhere in the diary. People he does not like or who do not do his will are always villains, and a woman who frustrates him would naturally be called a whore. Forman does not present himself as a temperate man.[42]

To refer to Forman as Lanyer's "known lover," as Prior does, is therefore stretching matters considerably, even if she allowed him some liberties while her husband was away. Nor is Prior correct in seeing Lanyer as the instigator in his frustrating night with her. In this same entry, in which Prior and Rowse see so much and I see considerably less about Lanyer's morals, it is clear that Forman himself set up the encounter. "A certain man longed to see a gentle-woman whom he loved [and] desired to halek with. And because he could not tell how to come to her and whether he should be welcome to her or no, made this question: whether it were best to send to her to know how she did. And thereby to try whether she would bid the messenger bid his master round to her or no, thinking thereby that he might go the bolder thereby to see her."[43] After casting a "Lanier" horoscope for 11 September 1597, he reports the result: "The party sent his servant by whom she sent word that if his master came he should be welcome. And he went and supped with her and stayed all night." From here we pick up the rest of the story ("And she was familiar and friendly . . ."). Lanyer may have sent for him on September 24 or visited him on September 29 (though neither is certain), but we have no record of what happened between them. If intercourse had taken place, he would have recorded it.

In sum, there is no evidence that Lanyer ever had intercourse with Simon Forman, or with any men except her husband and the lord chamberlain. Prior's conclusion that she was a woman well known for loose morals results from the circular reading of Lanyer's character from Shakespeare's sonnets, not from the record.

Prior's further evidence that Lanyer must have been the woman of the sonnets rests on reading "pride" in those poems to refer to the high-mindedness and social aspiration that are apparent from Forman and in Lanyer's own verse. Although I read her approach to patrons differently from Prior, I concede the point that Lanyer (like Samuel Daniel, Ben Jonson, and countless others) sought to connect with patrons of higher social class. Prior makes too much of the lady's pride in Shakespeare's sonnets, however; the "proud fair" was a commonplace of the tradition, upon which Shakespeare plays in several interesting ways. There is nothing particular, nothing outside of well-understood literary conventions, that characterizes Shakespeare's poetic variations on the lady's pride or Lanyer's poetic pursuit of reflected glory from her high-born patrons.[44]

The case for Lanyer's promiscuity is the most complex of the dark lady arguments. To believe it requires both believing and disbelieving Forman. We must believe all his angry denunciations and disbelieve his report that Lanyer refused to "halek." We must credit his lust as her lack of virtue. Counter to the claim of promiscuity is the unchallenged report that Queen Elizabeth "made much" of the attractive young woman. Elizabeth did not tolerate public sexual transgression; she tended to throw unmarried pregnant ladies and their miscreant lovers into prison, a fate which Lanyer's relatively low birth and marriage to Alfonso spared her.[45] It is difficult, too, to believe that the dowager countess of Cumberland, long renowned for her piety and forbearance in the face of her own husband's promiscuity, would be quick to sponsor a woman with an equally distasteful reputation.

I am not claiming a case for Aemilia Lanyer's sacred purity. She was open about her relationship with Lord Hunsdon, and there is no way to prove that she did not have other lovers. But it takes a leap far beyond common rules of evidence and logic to assert with uncompromising assurance that Lanyer was promiscuous.[46] Yet even if Aemilia Lanyer had slept with half of London, it would not prove her to be the dark lady of the sonnets. I find Daniel's portrait of *Rosamond* a much more likely picture of the relationship between

Aemilia Bassano and Lord Hunsdon than the one Rowse imagines by way of Shakespeare's sonnets.

It should be clear that I believe the case has not been made either for Lanyer's association with Shakespeare nor her promiscuity. What about the evidence that Lanyer was "dark"? It is certainly possible. David Lasocki has found a report from 1584 that describes two of her cousins as "a little black man who was booted" (probably Arthur Bassano) and "a tall black man." As Lasocki notes, "'Black' here must refer to their dark complection and black hair, typical of Italians but rare in England at that time."[47] This may appear to make Aemilia Lanyer almost certainly "dark," but two parents contribute to the mix. Arthur and his brothers' parents were both Italian (Baptista's brother Anthony Bassano and Elina de Nazzi), while Aemilia's mother, Margaret Johnson, was English. If Aemilia Lanyer's coloring was unusually dark, Forman does not mention it. It is possible she was not dark at all, and it is quite possible that she had dark hair and eyes but a typically fair English complexion. In the expression "black Irish," we still find the term used to describe dark-haired people who are otherwise fair-skinned.[48]

Was Aemilia Lanyer Shakespeare's dark lady? Assuming such a person existed, we have no evidence that Lanyer knew Shakespeare, no convincing evidence that she was promiscuous, and only reasonable conjecture about her coloring. I discount all arguments from the sonnets back to Lanyer as logically absurd. What is left is a matter of faith. Some readers, such as Prior, would like her to be the dark lady because they believe that identification actually gives them useful insights into Shakespeare's work. This would be unobjectionable if it were not accompanied by a continuing insistence on the certainty of the biographical identifications (they are not proven, no matter how loud the shouting) and if they truly led to new perceptions about the literary works. I find Prior's readings of both the sonnets and plays naive about the literary conventions of the period and unpersuasive in their claim for the value of simple biographical correspondences, but that is another debate, and better engaged in by dedicated Shakespeareans.[49]

It would be interesting to know whether Lanyer and Shakespeare ever met. It is possible. Whether they did or not, Lanyer was likely to have read his two narrative poems, since the *Salve Deus* shows her to have been interested in the genre (sometimes called *epillyon*, a nineteenth-century coinage meaning "little epic") and to have been reading others of the same general type. She may also have attended or read the published plays, but I leave that question for others.

4

LANYER AND JONSON

Aemilia Lanyer and Ben Jonson (1572–1638) have a number of things in common, including the genres and apparent purposes of many of their poems. The two were almost exact contemporaries (she was roughly three years older than Jonson and lived seven years longer) and in some ways seem very much alike. Jonson's well-documented aspirations—to rise to higher rank, to be part of and have influence on the court circle, to claim friendship with those of high birth and chronicle their virtues, and, above all, to gain from his patrons the authority to speak for his culture—have parallels in what we know of Aemilia Lanyer.

It is remotely possible they were related. Jonson's origins remain obscure, but until about 1604 he spelled his name "Johnson," and Lanyer's mother was one Margaret Johnson. However "Johnson" was then, as now, a common surname, and since Margaret Johnson was very possibly associated with a family of court musicians, a kinship between Jonson and Lanyer seems unlikely.[1] If Ben Jonson's family had musical connections, there is no record of it. The two poets did have common acquaintances, and very probably some personal contact.

Contiguities between the Jonson and Lanyer circles are particularly notable during the crucial period in which Aemilia Lanyer was putting together her one extant book. Appropriately enough, the common thread is music and musicians, especially through the Lanier family, as her husband Alfonso's relatives commonly spelled it. Jonson worked closely with several musicians, including the most eminent composers of the Jacobean court, in the production of masques. Of those, three stand out: Alfonso Ferrabosco, Nicholas Lanier, and Robert Johnson. The first two had close family connections with Alfonso Lanyer and the last may have been related to Aemilia.

Ben Jonson referred to Alfonso Ferrabosco the younger (1575–1628) as his "excellent friend."[2] Alfonso Ferrabosco the elder, a court musician like his namesake, came to England in the early 1560s, around the same time as Alfonso Lanyer's father, Nicholas Lanier the elder. Alfonso Lanyer may have been named for the elder Ferrabosco. By about 1610 Alfonso Lanyer's sister, Ellen, was married to the younger Alfonso Ferrabosco. The Lanyer, Ferrabosco, and Bassano families were all closely aligned by that time.[3] Ellen's mother, and probably Alfonso's as well, was Lucretia Bassano, Aemilia's first cousin, who lived until 1634. Alfonso Ferrabosco and Ellen Lanyer Ferrabosco also named their second son Henry, probably for Prince Henry, the popular heir to the throne whom Alfonso Ferrabosco tutored in music, but perhaps also with a glance at Henry Lanyer, Aemilia's son, who was about twenty when Henry Ferrabosco was born.[4]

Jonson worked with Ferrabosco on several masques, including *Hymenaiei* (1606), *Masque of Queens* (1609), *Oberon* (1611), and *Love Freed from Ignorance and Folly* (1611). Jonson also wrote him two appreciative epigrams, prefaced to two of Ferrabosco's publications, his *Ayres* and *Lessons*, both published in 1609.[5] The first poem lists the virtues of music, assuring "my lov'd *Alphonso*" that:

> . . . when I have said, The proofes of all these bee
> Shed in thy Songs; 'tis true: but short of thee. (ll. 17–18)

The second poem gives Ferrabosco advice on what to expect once his book is published, advice Aemilia Lanyer may well have read:

> When we doe give, Alphonso, to the light,
> A work of ours, we part with our own right;
> For, then all mouths will judge, and their owne way:
> The learn'd have no more priviledge, then the lay. (ll. 1–4)

Nicholas Lanier the younger was Alfonso Lanyer's nephew, son of his older brother, John. Traditionally believed to have been Prince Henry's court musician, Nicholas certainly served Queen Anne and was to have a long and prominent place in court culture. Jonson credited him with introducing recitative into the music of the masque, and art historians credit him with introducing Van Dyck to England.[6] He worked with Ben Jonson on *Lovers Made Men* (1617), *Vision of Delight* (1617), *The Gypsies Metamorphosed* (1621), and *Masque of Augurs* (1621, with Ferrabosco).

Robert Johnson was a close associate of Ferrabosco and Lanier, working with Ferrabosco on Ben Jonson's *Oberon* and *Love Freed from Ignorance and Folly*, and with Lanier on *The Gypsies Metamorphosed*.

Robert was the son of John Johnson, a court lutenist from 1579 to 1594 and apparently a favorite of Queen Elizabeth. Her affection for John extended after his death, when she gave his widow, Alice, a considerable amount of country land "in consideration of her husband's services." His son, Robert, was indentured from 1596 to 1603 to the household of the new lord chamberlain, Sir George Carey (son of Aemilia's lover), where he learned his musical trade.[7]

Robert Johnson may have been related to Aemilia Lanyer, since a musical Johnson family most easily explains Margaret's marriage into the musical Bassano family, and John Johnson's is the most prominent. Whether or not he was a blood relative, Robert Johnson was part of the close circle of court musicians that was the core of Aemilia Lanyer's family and society, and part of the coterie of court artists that included Ben Jonson.

Particularly given her Ferrabosco in-laws, it stretches credence to believe that Aemilia Lanyer did *not* encounter Ben Jonson.[8] Her acquaintance with him, whether tangential and negligible or substantial and influential, probably began earlier than 1609–10, which is about when Ellen Lanyer married Ferrabosco and when Jonson and Ferrabosco produced the *Masque of Queens*. Three of those masquers were among the dedicatees of Lanyer's book: Queen Anne, Lucy, countess of Bedford, and Lady Anne Clifford.[9]

Whatever the connection between Jonson and Lanyer, their poems are particularly interesting to compare because of their similar aspirations and circle of acquaintances yet different genders and access to the court. In this chapter I want to focus primarily on Lanyer's dedicatory verse and "The Description of Cooke-ham," since they have close affinities to Jonson's "To Penshurst" and the poems he dedicated to patrons, published in the *Epigrammes* and *Forrest* sections of his *Workes* (1616).

Patronage and Authority

Both poets sought the support and approval of higher-born patrons. While Ben Jonson thrived as a poet within the Jacobean patronage system, we have no evidence that Aemilia Lanyer had any measure of success. Gender is certainly relevant here. Even his modern editors, C. H. Herford and Percy Simpson, cite Jonson's "virility" to help explain his attractiveness to court patrons, particularly women. However skeptical one might be about this view of Jonson's success, there is no doubt that men were allowed and expected to speak, even to their betters, while the tradition (if not the reality) of women's behavior assumed chaste silence.[10] Although women patrons, as in the courtly love tradition, could act as "mi dons," as lords with masculine authority, the patronage system was part of the general fabric of a hierarchical society and was essentially patriarchal. With all authority derived from the idea of the father, Jonson's gender implicitly allowed him to receive and enact the authority of his dedicatees, whether men or women.[11]

David Riggs argues that "the dominant motifs of Jonson's professional life are social and literary ambition," which come together in Jonson's manipulation of the patronage system.[12] These motifs are certainly present, but he manipulates the patronage system as much to establish his authority as the definer of English culture as to seek social or financial advancement. When Jonson acknowledges his superiors, his social distance becomes a ritual to enable that reciprocity of grace by which the worthiness and virtues of the patron empower the poetic voice.[13] In the process, Jonson creates an identity between his patrons' virtues and his own, an Aristotelian friendship of mutually admiring virtue.

Since the empowering conceit Jonson uses with his patrons is based on social distance overcome by reciprocal virtue, the patron may as easily be a man or a woman. Gender matters nonetheless. In epigram 76, on Lucy, countess of Bedford, for example, Jonson gives her "a learned, and a manly soule" so that she might have the freedom of her own destiny and the authority of her own virtue. In epistle 13 of *The Forrest* ("To Katherine, Lady Aubigny") the writer's conventional conceit of holding a mirror of virtue up to the patron plays off the supposition of female vanity:

> I, *Madame*, am become your praiser. Where,
>   If it may stand with your soft blush to heare,
> Your selfe but told unto your selfe, and see
>   In my character, what your features bee,
> You will not from the paper slightly passe:
> No lady, but at some time, loves her glasse. (ll. 21–26)

The pun on "character" (as handwriting and as strongly developed moral qualities) is an example of Jonson's frequent claim that, as a writer, he inscribes but also shares his patrons' virtues.[14]

In Jonson's poems to women, virtue tends to be contingent on connection with famous men (as in epigrams 79 and 103, to Sir Philip Sidney's daughter, the countess of Rutland, and his niece, Lady Mary Wroth) or to be defined, at least in part, by overcoming the limits of gender (as in the poem to Lucy, countess of Bedford). In the ode "To the immortall memorie, and friendship of that noble paire, Sir Lucius Cary, and Sir H. Morison," on the other hand, Jonson situates himself in the middle of the Cary-Morison friendship and participates in a virtue that is uncontingent and absolute: "Nothing perfect done, / But as a CARY, or a MORISON" (ll. 115–16).[15] He even makes his connections with his greatest dedicatees seem somehow commensurate with their greatness. Epigram 4, to King James, praises him as a fellow poet, for example, while epigram 43, to "Robert Earle of Salisburie," praises him for not needing flattery and, by implication, the poet for not flattering.[16]

For all the praise and deference he gives his social superiors, whether men or women, Jonson speaks to his patrons as an equal. As Riggs notes, "Jonson projected his own code of values on his prospective patrons," creating a coterie of virtuous like-minded intellectuals which he both defined and celebrated.[17] He derives his authority through the community he creates.[18]

Lanyer also seeks to create authority through community—a distinctively and assertively female community. While many of the strategies she uses are familiar from Jonson and the patronage poetry of her time, there are some interesting differences. The first is her apparent inability to bridge the social gap between herself and her dedicatees, and her use of that inability to obscure the audacity of "A Womans writing of divinest things."[19] The second is her set of strategies for rendering female gender a source of authority.

Despite the important differences I noted in chapter 2, Lanyer's approach to her patrons is in many ways more Spenserian than Jonsonian.[20] As Spenser appeals to Queen Elizabeth to "raise my thoughts too humble and too vile" (*Faerie Queene*, 1.proem.iv), Lanyer relies on the virtues of her patrons to inspire her abilities and diffuse her inadequacies. So she "humbly" wishes that the "Estate and Virtue" of Queen Anne

> . . . may light on me:
> That so these rude unpollisht lines of mine,
> Graced by you, may seeme the more divine. (ll. 34–36)

In disclaiming any monetary motive to her dedication, she tells Susan, countess dowager of Kent,

> Onely your noble Virtues do incite
> My Pen, they are the ground I write upon. (ll. 45–46)

Since Lanyer received her education in the countess's household, this is no hyperbole.

The acknowledged distance between herself and her patrons allows Lanyer to obscure the question of gender. In the first stanza of the book's first poem, to Queen Anne, gender is contained within the bestowal of grace which is the conventional empowering gift of social distance:

> Renowned Empresse, and great Britaines Queene,
> Most gratious Mother of successding Kings;
> Vouchsafe to view that which is seldom seene,
> A Womans writing of divinest things:
>   Reade it faire Queene, though it defective be,
>   Your Excellence can grace both It and Mee. (ll. 1–6).

By collapsing her unworthiness as a woman into the general unworthiness of the lower-born in relation to the higher, and by seeking elevation from another woman, Lanyer effectively transcends the gender issue altogether.

The authority Lanyer attains throughout the book therefore comes in part from her ability to diffuse gender as an impediment to speaking publicly. Unlike Jonson, who situates himself within the coterie of his patrons and gains his authority from being part of their club, Lanyer keeps her social distance. The question of authority remains primarily an issue of social class and becomes a familiar Spenserian convention rather than the intrusion of an alien female voice. Objections to her speaking out become as dismissable for Lanyer as they were for Spenser.

This negative strategy is not the only means by which Lanyer asserts her authority. Her most fundamental authorization comes from her religious theme, the passion of Christ. Protestantism declared that God channels his will through the unmediated conscience, so that piety becomes its own authority, and women's souls were generally conceded to be as directly accessible to God as were men's.[21] Lanyer claims not merely her right, but her destiny to "speak of divinest things." God has not simply removed an impediment, he has issued a positive command that she speak for all virtuous women.

Lanyer tells Katherine, countess of Suffolk, that the poet's "starre" of destiny has "guided me to frame this worke of grace." Everything is in God's power, and "his powre hath given me powre to write" (ll. 13–14). She dedicates to Lady Anne Clifford "this worke of grace," which is "blest by our Saviours merits, not my skill." In her concluding envoy, "To the doubtfull Reader," she tells of hearing the phrase "Salve Deus Rex Judaeorum" in a dream and taking it as "a significant token, that I was appointed to performe this Worke."

Most interesting, however, is Lanyer's ability to dilate her avowed calling as a religious poet into a more comprehensive poetic vocation. So, for example, she uses several authorizing strategies in her poem to that most famous of all women patrons, Mary Sidney, the countess dowager of Pembroke. The poem purports to describe a dream, it appeals to the grace of the high-born dedicatee, and it asserts the authority of divine subject matter. Waking from her dream vision of the virtue and artistic power of the countess, Lanyer offers both the dream vision and the "feast" of her poem on Christ's passion:

And Madame, if you will vouchsafe that grace,
To grace those flowres that springs from virtues ground;
Though your fair mind on worthier workes is plac'd,
On workes that are more deepe, and more profound;

Yet it is no disparagement to you,
To see your Saviour in a Shepheards weed,
Unworthily presented in your viewe,
Whose worthinesse will grace each line your reade. (ll. 213–220)

Whose worthiness will grace each line? Christ, the figure and topic of the *Salve Deus* poem, or the countess herself? In this ambiguity, whether deliberate or not, Lanyer derives authority from both her potential patron and her God, and praises the excellence of both.

Lanyer also conflates the grace of the patron with divine grace throughout the *Salve Deus* poem. "Sith *Cynthia* is ascended to that rest / Of endlesse joy and true Eternitie," the poem begins, the poet will dedicate her great work to the praise of the countess of Cumberland. Queen Elizabeth I, representing grace both secular and divine, is a powerful symbol with which to begin her poem, and again invokes the ghost of Spenser. Like Spenser before his queen, so Lanyer before her countess must acknowledge the inadequacy of the poet to the task:

> Pardon (deere Ladie) want of womans wit
> To pen thy praise, when few can equall it. (ll. 15–16)

Few can equal thy praiseworthiness? Few can portray thy praise adequately? Few can equal thy ability to praise? This nicely ambiguous ritual assertion ironically crushes the gender reference under the force of Queen Elizabeth's magnificence and the countess of Cumberland's virtues. Lanyer's stance in relation to her patron has a parallel in the Pauline argument, which Lanyer also uses, that weakness better shows divine strength:

> But my deare Muse, now whither wouldst thou flie,
> Above the pitch of thy appointed strain? (ll. 273–74)
> . . . .
> But yet the Weaker thou doest seeme to be
> In Sexe, or Sence, the more his Glory shines. (ll. 289–90)

Queen Elizabeth, Queen Anne, the countess of Pembroke, the countess of Cumberland, and "all vertuous Ladies in generall" combine to authorize Lanyer's voice. Their authorizing power, in turn, derives in part from social position, and even more from their devotion to Christ, which Lanyer assumes and shares. Like Jonson's fictive participation in a coterie of virtuous friendship, Lanyer identifies with the Christian devotion that she ascribes to her community of virtuous women. The Christ whom Lanyer portrays in the *Salve Deus* valorizes the specifically female voices and perspectives, from Pilate's wife to the daughters of Jerusalem to Mary. The grace of God and the grace of Lanyer's patrons are conflated in the process, and she becomes the voice for both.

Margaret, countess of Cumberland, appears throughout the poem as the representative bride of Christ and the key figure for a united, authorizing grace. She is both the bride and "co-heir" of Christ:

> This Grace, great Lady, doth possesse thy Soule,
> And makes thee pleasing in thy Makers sight;
> This Grace doth all imperfect Thoughts controule,
> Directing thee to serve thy God aright;
> Still reckoning him the Husband of thy Soule,

Which is most pretious in his glorious sight:
    Because the Worlds delights shee doth denie
    For him, who for her sake vouchsaf'd to die.

And dying made her Dowager of all;
Nay more, Co-heire of that eternall blisse
That Angels lost, and We by *Adams* fall. (ll. 249–59)

As Christ's bride and "Dowager of all" she shares with him the full glory of redemption, "eternall bliss." Such a "Co-heire" both inspires and transcends even Lanyer's assured poetic vision:

This with the eie of Faith thou maist behold,
Deere Spouse of Christ, and more than I can write. (ll. 1169–70)

Though the glories of salvation may be ineffable, the poet still asserts her role as giver of the gift of vision, portrayer of the passion, "Which I present (deare Lady) to your view" (l. 1265). That gift returns the grace that has inspired it:

Therefore (good Madame) in your heart I leave
His perfect picture, where it still shall stand,
    Deepely engraved in that holy shrine,
    Environed with Love and Thoughts Divine. (ll. 1325–28)

In this context Lanyer again affirms her vocation and the divine grace from God and patron that infuses it:

And knowe, when first into this world I came,
This charge was giv'n me by th'Eternall powres,
Th'everlasting Trophie of thy fame,
To build and decke it with the sweetest flowres
That virtue yeelds; Then Madame, doe not blame
Me, when I shew the World but what is yours,
    And decke you with that crowne which is your due,
    That of Heav'ns beauty Earth may take a view. (ll. 1457–64)

Until publication of the *Salve Deus Rex Judaeorum*, women writing in English tended to use self-effacement or indirection as authorizing strategies.[22] Lanyer gives ritual nods to both ("want of womans wit," the dream device), but more persuasive and impressive are her assertions of a poetic vocation, supported by claims of grace from high-born patrons and from God. While her language never quite bridges the social gap between her and her dedicatees the way Jonson's language frequently does, her assurance in her art is comparable to his.

Richard Helgerson has shrewdly noted that Jonson's "labor of self-presentation" centers his works and gives them "much of their troubling power."[23] His effort to present himself as the poet of his culture, defining a laureateship unlike the Virgilian model that Spenser had achieved, pervades his poems to patrons as it does his masques and plays. He has the authority of gender, if not of social class, and he uses it assertively to define culture in terms of praiseworthy virtues that he claims to share with his social superiors.

Lanyer similarly defines a culture of good women and establishes herself as its portrayer. She has authority of gender to speak of her own gender, and in doing so comments directly and indirectly on the world of men (the Eve's apology section of the *Salve Deus* and the prose dedication "To the Vertuous Reader" are the most direct). Lanyer's effort to present a woman's voice gives her volume much of *its* troubling power. While her self-presentation does not have Jonsonian "agon, an unresolved struggle of the self against its very conditions of its expression,"[24] it does have heightened self-consciousness in relation to the cultural condition of her time and place.

Gendered Portraits

Lanyer and Jonson's epideictic poetry has a common purpose: to portray the ideals of the culture by portraying the virtues of specific persons. All of Lanyer's, and many of Jonson's, verbal portraits are of women. I have noted Jonson's tendency to praise women by their relation to famous men, a standard Spenserian device, while Lanyer's reference to Sir Philip Sidney in "The Authors Dreame" is the only such occasion in her extant work, and even that is direct praise of Sidney himself rather than praise of the countess of Pembroke by means of her brother. Jonson praises women differently. This in itself is no surprise, but some of the differences are counterintuitive, with Jonson admiring virtues not usually considered feminine, and Lanyer seeming to laud female retirement. This, at least, is the picture from their one directly comparable figure, Lucy, countess of Bedford, and from Jonson's generalized portrait of retiring virtue,

"To the World" (*The Forrest*, 4) which has some counterpart in Lanyer's praise of the countess of Cumberland.

Three of Jonson's epigrams (76, 84, and 94) are dedicated to the countess of Bedford, Queen Anne's favorite courtier and a well-known patron and intellectual of the Jacobean court.[25] She often took the chief role (next to the queen) in court masques, and Samuel Daniel, John Donne, and the musician John Dowland, along with Jonson, were among her clients.[26] Lanyer may have hoped to be better noticed by so important a sponsor of English poetry and music. Nonetheless, Jonson's poems show more knowledge of and appreciation for the countess's intellectual stature than does Lanyer's one poem. This may be simply a function of his easier access, through his masques, but it may also reflect the greater freedom the male poet has in defining, even against gender expectations, the value of the people he praises.

In epigram 84 Jonson treats the countess of Bedford with familiarity. She is the perfect patron for whom he is and will continue to be the witty friend:

> Madame, I told you late how I repented,
>> I ask'd a lord a buck, and he denyed me;
> And, ere I could aske you, I was prevented:
>> For your most noble offer had supply'ed me.
> Straight went I home; and there most like a *Poet*,
>> I fancied to my selfe, what wine, what wit
> I would have spent: how every *Muse* should know it,
>> And *Phoebus*-selfe should be at eating it.
> O *Madame*, if your grant did thus transferre me,
>> Make it your gift. See whither that will beare mee.

The countess's gift of venison has made the poet think he must respond, making it a "grant" which requires a return, presumably this poem. But if she were to make it truly a "gift," which would require no return, his muse will be even more inspired. The wit depends on irony, but presumes the free gift of grace, the standard fare of the patronage relationship. While the poem acknowledges social difference in the petitionary position of the poet, the tone is appreciative and familiar, suggesting an intellectual peer. A deeper level of irony, therefore, is that the social inferior might think himself the superior in gender, but the very familiarity of the tone again certifies the countess's own "manly soul."

Jonson portrays something similar in epigram 94, "To Lucy, Countess of Bedford, with Mr. Donnes Satyres." This poem establishes a coterie of intellectuals that includes Bedford, Donne, and Jonson, even as it acknowledges and praises the countess as the perfect center of poetic activity in a (rare, for Jonson) beginning and ending refrain:

> *Lucy*, you brightness of our spheare, who are
>   Life of the *Muses* day, their morning-starre! (ll. 1–2)

(The last line completes the circle by varying the refrain slightly: "The *Muses* evening, as their morning-starre.") The poem argues that since satire's subject is "the most of mankind" (l. 7), only the best few dare to request such poems:

> They, then, that living where the matter [of satire] is bred,
>   Dare for these poemes, yet, both aske, and read,
> And like them, too; must needfully, though few,
>   Be of the best: and 'mongst those, best are you. (ll. 11–14)

Epigram 76 remains Jonson's fullest portrait of Lucy and one of his finest epigrams. It presents the poet as passionate servant of the most virtuous:

> This morning timely rapt with holy fire
>   I thought to forme unto my zealous *Muse*,
> What kind of creature I could most desire,
>   To honor, serve, and love; as *Poets* use. (ll. 1–4)

The creature he would "forme" should be "faire, free, and wise / Of greatest bloud, and yet more good than great" (ll. 5–6). She should be "curteous, facile, sweet" and resist pride (ll. 99–100). She should of course be feminine, but with the famous "manly soule" as well:

> I meant each softest vertue, there should meet,
>   Fit in that softer bosome to reside.
> Onely a learned, and a manly soule
>   I purpos'd her; that should, with even powers,
> The rock, the spindle, and the sheeres controule
>   Of destinie, and spin her owne free houres. (ll. 11–16)

But there is no need to invent such a person:

> Such when I meant to faine, and wish'd to see,
>> My *Muse* bad, *Bedford* write, and that was shee. (ll. 17–18)

In none of these three epigrams to Lucy is there any specific mention of religion. The countess of Bedford has the courtly and classical virtues of beauty, wit, learning, and control of her own destiny. Since the learned poet both represents and shares these virtues, he has the right and even duty to blazon them in others. In Jonson's portrait, the great Countess ("more good than great") is not genderless, but transgresses the limits of her gender, which becomes part of the compliment.

Lanyer's poem to the countess of Bedford suggests no personal famliarity and, somewhat surprisingly, makes no reference to Bedford's famous wit or learning (as does the poem to Arbella Stuart). Lanyer's opening strategy is similar to the one she uses in her dedication to the countess of Pembroke, which immediately precedes it. Like that poem, and to a lesser extent like Jonson's epigram 76, Lanyer dreams or feigns an image ("Methought I saw," "Me thinkes I see"). In the poem to Lucy what she imagines is personified Virtue, serving as a mediator between the poet, who is offering the gift of her passion poem, and the virtuous and grand countess of Bedford. The language is indirectly petitionary, allowing Virtue to knock on the door of the place (the heart) where the countess's "selfe doth rest":

> Me thinkes I see faire Virtue readie stand,
> T'unlocke the closet of your lovely breast,
> Holding the key of Knowledge in her hand,
> Key of the Cabbine where you selfe doth rest,
> To let him in, by whom her youth was blest
>> The true-love of your soule, your hearts delight,
>> Fairer than all the world in your cleare sight. (ll. 1–7)

The poem's second stanza invites the reader to view the picture of Christ crucified. Not until the third stanza is the compliment to the countess of Bedford made more specific than her presumed piety:

> You whose cleare Judgement farre exceeds my skill,
> Vouchsafe to entertaine this dying lover. (ll. 15–16)

The speaker asks no particular grace or favor from the countess, however, and there is no reference either to the poet's unworthiness (as in the poems to Queen Anne and the countess of Pembroke) or the dedicatee's reputation for learning. Lanyer seems to be using the countess of Bedford to represent a presumed female receptivity to Christ, "The Ocean of true grace," offering her a place of rest in the "blessed Arke" of her poem:

> There may your thoughts as servants to your heart,
> Give true attendance on this lovely guest,
> While he doth to that blessed bowre impart
> Flowres of fresh comforts, decke that bed of rest,
> With such rich beauties as may make it blest:
>   And you in whom all raritie is found,
>   May be with his eternall glory crownd. (ll. 22–28)

Compared with Jonson's personalized praise, this portrait is not of the countess of Bedford at all. Yet the mediating figure of Virtue is, like Jonson's Muse or his gift of Donne's Satires, an emblem of shared knowledge. The "cleare Judgement" and "raritie" of the countess allows the poet simply to assume that the countess will be a receptive audience for the poet's devotional work. Jonson describes Lucy's classical virtues; Lanyer assumes her Christian piety. Jonson is therefore the poet, in this case, who challenges gender expectations, while Lanyer uses the presumption of female virtue as inward and spiritual to claim a shared point of view. For Lanyer, Bedford is part of the coterie of virtuous women whom Lanyer serves with her vision of Christ and memorializes in her dedication.

Much of the difference between Jonson and Lanyer's approach to the countess of Bedford can be attributed simply to Jonson's greater access to the countess. The result are poems that feel much more personal, even as they idealize their subject. The tables are turned, it would seem, if we compare Jonson and Lanyer's two extended portraits of the virtuous lady retired from the vices of court life. In Jonson's poem "To the World," subtitled "A Farewell for a Gentlewoman, Vertuous and Noble" (*The Forrest*, 4), an anonymous lady retires from court life to a Stoic contemplation of life's vanities. Lanyer's several addresses to the countess of Cumberland in the *Salve Deus* portray a Christian stoicism, but also emphasize the Countess's active rejoicing in the contemplation of Christ.

Jonson's poem is in the voice of a woman renouncing the tempta-
tions of the world in favor of retreat into a contemplative life.[27] "False
world, good-night," begins sixty-eight lines of tetrameter quatrains,

> since thou hast brought
> That houre upon my morne of age,
> Hence-forth I quit thee from my thought,
> My part is ended on thy stage. (ll. 1–4)

The bulk of the work is a criticism of the world. The lady is credited
with no particular virtues that might have led to her wise observa-
tions and conclusions about the world's vanity. Perhaps it is simply
that she sees clearly:

> I know thou [the world] whole are but a shop
> Of toyes, and trifles, traps, and snares,
> To take the weake, or make them stop:
> Yet art thou falser than thy wares.
> Yet knowing this, should I yet stay[?] (ll. 17–21)

Like her virtues, the lady's sufferings are also indistinct, but a sign of
her stoicism:

> But, what we'are borne for, we must beare:
> Our fraile condition it is such,
> That, what to all may happen here,
> If't chance to me, I must not grutch. (ll. 53–56)

She shares the human condition, seeing no particular escape, expect-
ing no "miracle [to] be wrought" for her sake:

> No, I doe know, that I was borne
> To age, misfortune, sickness, griefe:
> But I will beare these, with that scorne,
> As shall not need thy [the world's] false relief. (ll. 60–64)

Lanyer similarly praises the countess of Cumberland for her retreat from the world:

> Thou from the Court to the Countrie art retir'd,
> Leaving the world, before the world leaves thee: (ll. 161–62)

As in Jonson's poem, Lanyer's world is dangerous, "That great Enchantresse" who appeals to weak minds who "yeeld themselves as prey to Lust and Sinne" (ll. 163, 167). Lanyer's countess, however, has a specific "miracle," the salvation of Christ, which is the story Lanyer intends to tell:

> To set his glorie forth whom thou lov'st best,
> Whose wondrous works no mortall eie can see;
> His speciall care on those whom he hath blest
> From wicked worldlings, how he sets them free. (ll. 147–50)

This central miracle prompts the countess's virtuous retreat from the world, and rewards it:

> The meditation of this Monarchs love,
> Drawes thee from caring what this world can yield. (ll. 153–54)
> .   .   .   .
> Thou faire example, live without compare,
> With honours triumphs seated in thy breast. (ll. 176–77)

Like Lanyer's countess, Jonson's lady finds solace in staying at home and contemplating her own virtue:

> Nor for my peace will I goe farre,
>   As wandrers doe, that still doe rome,
> But make my strengths, such as they are,
>   Here in my bosome, and at home. (ll. 65–68)

The countess of Cumberland, too, stays away from court and keeps her strength in her heart. The *Salve Deus* poem, however, leaves in the countess's heart the "perfect picture" of Christ's sacrifice (ll. 1325–26), which continually renews both her virtue and her joy:

> Oft times hath he made triall of your love,
> And in your Faith hath tooke no small delight,
> By Crosses and Afflictions he doth prove,
> Yet still your heart remaineth firme and right;
> Your love so strong, as nothing can remove,
> Your thoughts beeing placed on him both day and night,
>   Your constant soule doth lodge betwene her brests,
>   This Sweet of sweets, in which all glory rests. (ll. 1337–44)

Jonson's lady retreats from vanity to a stoic mastery of affliction. Lanyer's countess retreats from vanity through affliction to Christ.

These are heavily gendered portraits. The virtue of the lady in both cases comes from her retirement from the world and her choice to lead a contemplative life at home. Yet Jonson's lady bears no resemblance to the real ladies he praises, notably the countess of Bedford, whose virtue may be singular but is certainly not retiring. Lanyer's real countess of Cumberland, on the other hand, has endured genuine unhappiness and achieved admirable strength. Jonson's imaginary lady is an idealized, one might even say masculinized, stoic figure. Lanyer's countess is a realized ideal Christian. Her Christian virtue is not particularly distinct from the modest and retiring womanhood that Lanyer might be thought to praise in her. It is true that Lanyer praises women generally as closer to Christ, but it is more for what they see and understand (Jonson's value, too) than for a conventional retiring modesty.

When both poets are describing, in however an idealized fashion, real people they know reasonably well (Jonson's Bedford, Lanyer's Cumberland), the portraits are complex ones that confound or at least extend cliches of gender. Even in their more generalized portraits (Lanyer's Bedford, Jonson's lady) the poets cannot resist imposing the complexity of their own gendered view of virtue (Jonson gives his lady a brave stoicism, Lanyer assumes that the countess of Bedford, like all virtuous women, has a special affinity for the image of Christ). Comparing these poets, if it does nothing else, should complicate our expectations about how gender was viewed in the early seventeenth century. Differing views of gender nonetheless play a real part in the worldviews these poets bring to their poems, as a look at their most comparable poems, "The Description of Cooke-ham" and "To Penshurst," will indicate.

Founding a Genre

Ben Jonson is usually credited as the originator of a major seventeenth-century poetic genre, the country-house poem.[28] This is an important claim, since the genre embodied and characterized an ideal of English patriarchal society that caught the imaginations of several generations of gifted poets. In a book on the origin and development of genre, Alastair Fowler sees in Jonson's poem a rare example of attributable generic invention:

It remains true that a single writer's creativity can play a decisive part in originating a new kind. . . . *To Penshurst* began, in some sense, the country house poem. Because of its high value . . . it had an almost paradigmatic function. This status is not a matter of formal value only, but of content and personal worth. Such a work becomes institutionalized and leads to change: it generates not only faithful imitations but original works that nevertheless relate to it rather than to its predecessors. Before *To Penshurst* there were less successfully experimental antecedents, such as the river encomia of Leland, Camden, Vallans, and no doubt others much dimmer. Had they been brilliant, a very different genre might have developed. As it is, estate poems by Carew, Waller, and Herrick, and more distantly Denham and Marvell, allude to Jonson and each other, but not to Jonson's largely occluded predecessors. He is the founder of a new line.[29]

Many students of seventeenth-century English poetry would concur with this judgment. I agree with it myself, up to a point.

There is one poem, however, that precedes Jonson's in publication (and most likely in composition), that uses the iconography of the country estate fully and with considerable skill, and that Jonson may well have read before taking his own approach: Lanyer's "Description of Cooke-ham."[30] The two poems are close enough together in time and type that they are rapidly becoming a standard teaching pair, and, as "Cookham" has moved away from being "largely occluded," it has become easier to see them both (rather than Jonson's poem only) as the earliest English constructions of a classical and continental mode. Barbara Lewalski has ably situated "Cookham" in the context of the seventeenth-century country-house poem and offered a paradigmatic comparison of "Cookham" and "Penshurst" as "male and female conception[s] of an idealized social order."[31]

These poems are rapidly becoming classroom paradigms of some important gender differences in early seventeenth-century poetry, and their comparison will likely have long currency in Jacobean studies. Here I want to do something slightly different in rehearsing the comparison. Until now the main work of the poets I have set in relation to Lanyer preceded her volume. Jonson's "Penshurst," on the other hand, was probably written after Lanyer's "Cookham," and both poems were produced during the time when the two poets might well have had some contact (at the Ferrabosco-Lanyer wedding if nowhere else). Instead of suggesting what Lanyer may have found in Jonson, or comparing the two as different examples of the same basic model, I want to ask what Jonson might have learned from Lanyer.

Throughout this book I have tried not to presume that any given work influenced a specific work of another poet. The realities of intention and causality are simply unknowable, even assuming they were of any interest or value to a reader of the poems. However, as T. S. Eliot so famously insisted, we see a literary tradition in the relationships among individual talents, and since my purpose is to situate Lanyer in that tradition, I have been trying to place her and her work in relation to her contemporaries, in particular those poets most visibly "canonical."[32] This has meant suggesting, along the way, that she may have read or probably read works by her contemporaries, that in any case she produced her poems in conscious recognition of the poetry of her time. Whether her awareness was in fact of these very poets or poems is in most instances unverifiable (although her list of narratives in *Salve Deus*, ll. 209–48, provides strong evidence for a few), and it is not finally the point. What is important is that Lanyer be seen as part of the vigorous cultural production of Renaissance England.[33]

In practice so far this has meant placing Lanyer in relation to the male authors of her time. Now I want to turn the tables, and place a poem by Jonson in relation to a poem by Lanyer. The reasons are partly chronological and partly strategic. I want to review "Cooke-ham" and "Penshurst" in their probable chronological sequence, and posit an unanswerable but instructive question: what if Jonson read Lanyer's poem, as well as his recorded classical models? What might he have taken from "Cookham" to create his country house poem which would go on to serve the "paradigmatic function" Fowler claims for it?

As I noted in chapter 1, Cookham was a crown manor near Windsor, leased to the countess of Cumberland's brother, William Russell of Thornaugh. The countess resided there periodically during her estrangement from her husband before his death in 1605 and probably for a short time after.[34] If the evidence of the poem can be trusted, it was a place special to the heart of Margaret, countess of Cumberland, and an environment in which the social differences between the poet on the one hand and the countess and her daughter, Anne Clifford, on the other were subdued by an idealized order of exercise, contemplation, and conversation. Lanyer's poem is a nostalgic valedictory to the place and the ideal, but also the first in a line of seventeenth-century poems that sought to paint a verbal por-

trait of a place and time that was both an affirmation of social values and, for the patron, a memento and celebration of a beloved
place. A country-house poem was like a verbal video that, unlike a
static painting, could travel the landscape and give it movement
and interaction.

One might claim that "Cookham" sets standards for this genre that
Jonson borrows, transforms, and transmits to his literary descen-
dents. Lanyer's poem is a stately survey of a stately place, a celebration of hospitality and noblesse oblige by a poet who has experienced
that hospitality and whose vocation has been reinforced as a result.
In 210 lines of iambic pentameter couplets, the poem is structured
with an invocation (ll. 1–16), entry and description (17–80), meditation and memorial (81–126), valediction and departure (127–204), and
envoy (205–10).

"Cookham's" invocation begins with a valedictory, anticipating
the outcome of the poem and personalizing the place as one where
the poet first enjoyed a relationship with the Countess and found her
vocation as a religious poet:

> Farewell (sweet *Cooke-ham*) where I first obtain'd
> Grace from that Grace where perfit Grace remain'd;
> And where the Muses gave their full consent,
> I should have powre the virtuous to content. (ll. 1–4)

Cookham itself is a muse, a place whose royal magic encourages piety
and poetry, presumably leading the poet to produce her story of
Christ's passion:

> Where princely Palace will'd me to indite,
> The sacred Storie of the Soules delight. (ll. 5–6)

The most important muse of all is the "great Lady" (l. 11) who
centers the place and inspires the poem. While the setting recalls
Eden, the classical Golden Age and the tradition of the *locus amoenus*,
or pleasant place, the whole is animated by the figure of the countess. The poem's principal conceit is that the house and grounds of
Cookham reflect her presence (or absence):

> Oh how (me thought) against you thither came
> Each part did seeme some new delight to frame! (ll. 17–18)

The scene is infused with the animism and responsive emotion that the twentieth century has labeled "pathetic fallacy," but which, in this case, is no reductive device. For one thing it has the pastoral tradition behind it, which had long permitted the landscape to be an emblem of the speaker's emotions. In the January Eclogue of Spenser's *Shepheards Calendar*, for example, the frozen landscape quite explicitly reflects Colin's lovelorn state:

> Thou barrein ground, whome winters wrath hath wasted,
> Art made a myrrhour, to behold my plight. (ll. 19–20)

Further, Lanyer is careful to make her own emotional projection clear, effecting what Peter L. Thorslev, Jr., has called, speaking of Wordsworth, "the poetry of surmise."[35] This is the language of "me thought" and "seeming," the explicit recognition that the poet is constructing (in Sir Philip Sidney's terms) an animated second nature:[36]

> The Walkes put on their summer Liveries,
> And all things else did hold like similies:
> The Trees with leaves, with fruits, with flowers clad,
> Embrac'd each other, seeming to be glad. (ll. 21–24)
>
> . . . .
>
> Oh how me thought each plant, each floure, each tree
> Set forth their beauties then to welcome thee. (ll. 33–34)
>
> . . . .
>
> How often did you visit this faire tree,
> Which seeming joyfull in receiving thee,
> Would like a Palme tree spread his leaves abroad,
> Desirous that you there should make abode. (ll. 59–62)

This language of acknowledged simile and poet's surmise supports, personalizes, and at the same time distances the poem's pathos, as when the poem turns to final valedictory and departure:

> And you sweet Cooke-ham, whom these Ladies leave,
> I now must tell the grief you did conceave
> At their departure, when they went away,
> How every thing retaind a sad dismay:
> Nay long before, when once an inkling came,
> Me thought each thing did unto sorrow frame. (ll. 127–32)

The poet projects onto the landscape of Cookham both her own and her ladies' grief at their departure, gathering the landscape into their feelings, but also objectifying those feelings by projecting them outward. The summer world of pleasant walks, song, meditation, and reading, symbolized by the full leafy shade of the favored oak, now turns first to autumn then winter as departure is first announced and then taken. The leaves change color and wither, the rains come, but these emblems of sorrow have no effect:

> This being vaine, they cast their leaves away,
> Hoping that pitie would have made you stay:
> Their frozen tops like Ages hoarie haires,
> Showes their disasters, languishing in feares: (ll. 141–44)
>
> .   .   .   .
>
> But your occasions call'd you so away,
> That nothing there had power to make you stay. (ll. 147–48)

The poem moves toward a formal leave-taking, as the countess commits the pleasures of the place "to noble Memory" (l. 155), beginning with the favored oak under which "many a learned Booke was read and skand" (l. 161) with young Anne Clifford. The countess repeats (as the poet records) those happy memories, and concludes by kissing the tree. In an extended conceit, the poet tells of kissing the tree herself, to "bereave" it of the countess's kiss,

> So I ingratefull Creature did deceive it,
> Of that which you vouchsaft in love to leave it.
> And though it oft had giv'n me much content,
> Yet this great wrong I never could repent:
> But of the happiest made it most forlorne,
> To shew that nothing's free from Fortunes scorne,
> While all the rest with this most beauteous tree,
> Made their sad consort Sorrowes harmony. (ll. 171–78)

The poem itself undercuts the apparent sentimentality of this passage, as it inscribes "noble Memory" and offers recompense for "Fortunes scorne." The role of the poet is to take this sad moment, inspired by the (indirect) kiss of the countess, and make "Sorrowes harmony." The bereft tree and all the natural world of Cookham join to provide the "sad consort," a background music to the poet's words very like the recorder consorts of father and uncles and husband and son with which Lanyer was surrounded for much of her life, or like the music and spectacle that give aural and visual resonance to the poetry of a Jonsonian masque.

The house and grounds of Cookham shrink to dead winter, as Lanyer gives absence a vivid presence at the end of the poem. The consort of sounds that moved from happy to sad harmonies now die away completely in the emptiness of departure:

> Delightfull Eccho wonted to reply
> To our last words, did now for sorrow die. (ll. 199–200)

What seems death, however, receives new life in the poem itself. Lanyer concludes the poem with explicit reference to her role as eternizer of the place, the history, and the countess, to whom the poet is linked by Platonic chains of virtuous love:

> This last farewell to *Cooke-ham* here I give,
> When I am dead thy name in this may live,
> Wherein I have perform'd her noble hest,
> Whose virtues lodge in my unworthy breast,
> And ever shall, so long as life remaines,
> Tying my heart to her by those rich chaines. (ll. 205–10)

Jonson could have found in this poem several devices compatible with his view of the role of the poet and poetry. Penshurst (still standing in Tonbridge, Kent) was and remains the ancestral estate of the Sidneys, in Jonson's time the home of Sir Robert Sidney and his family.[37] Celebrating the home was a way of celebrating the Sidneys, seen as embodying values Jonson chose to make exemplary. For all their dedication to particular noble persons and places, both "Cookham" and "Penshurst" extol general virtues: delight in an ordered nature, stewardship, learning, and piety. In both poems the poet shares those virtues, gaining strength in them from a right appreciation of the social order the place symbolizes, and performs the important social role of recording and affirming them. "Penshurst" has the same basic purpose as Lanyer's poem: to paint a verbal portrait of a place and a time. Its tone is celebratory, however, where that of "Cookham's" is valedictory. Lanyer's crown manor is an Edenic world lost through "occasions" and "Fortune," memorialized but not recoverable. Jonson's family estate is a classical model of right order, still in place and promising (through the much touted chastity of its mistress) the continuance of that order.

There are other interesting contrasts between the two poems. Time of year is one: "Cookham" moves from summer through autumn to winter, while in "Penshurst," like Spenser's Garden of Adonis (*FQ* 3.vi), it is spring and autumn. Another difference is the movement across terrain suggested by each poem. Both emphasize the estate's beautiful natural setting, but Lanyer's picture moves from low to high—walks, copses, and streams, up to hills and the particular hill where, seated under the magnificent oak,

> . . . you might plainly see,
> Hills, vales, and woods, as if on bended knee
> They had appeared, your honour to salute. (ll. 67–69)

Jonson's poem, on the other hand, moves from high to low, starting with

> Thy *Mount*, to which the *Dryands* doe resort,
> Where *Pan* and *Bacchus* their high feasts have made,
>   Beneath the broad beech, and the chest-nut shade. (ll. 10–12)

The iconography is similar, but its meaning very different. The oak praised in "Cookham" symbolizes retirement and contemplation, for example, while the special oak in "Penshurst" represents fame and worldly recognition. It was planted at the birth of the most famous Sidney of all, Sir Philip (1554–86), and used to blazon the names of beloved mistresses:

> That taller tree, which of a nut was set,
>   At his great birth, where all the *Muses* met.
> There, in the writhed barke, are cut the names
>   Of many a *Sylvane*, taken with his flames. (ll. 13–16)

While the copses and birds of "Cookham" offer shelter and accompany the idealized life of learning and song, those of "Penshurst" offer venison, pheasant, and partridge for happy feasting:

> Thy copp's too, named of *Gamage*, thou hast there,
>   That never fails to serve thee season'd deere,
> When thou would'st feast, or exercise thy friends (ll. 19–21)

. . . .

> . . . and *Sydney's* copp's,
> To crowne thy open table, doth provide
> The purpled pheasant, with the speckled side:
> The painted patrich lyes in every field,
> And, for thy messe, is willing to be kill'd. (ll. 26–30)

Lanyer's emphasis throughout the poem is on reading and retirement, while Jonson's is on food and hospitality. The social activities at "Cookham" are reading aloud and singing; at "Penshurst," hunting and eating. The poet situates himself in the poem by dining exquisitely (ll. 61–71), enjoying the same hospitality offered king and prince (ll. 76–86).

Women in Lanyer's poem exist alone, forming society, centering nature, and praising God. In Jonson's poem, fathers send harvest tribute to the Sidneys by way of

> . . . their ripe daughters, whom they would commend
> This way to husbands; and whose baskets beare
> An emblem of themselves, in plum, or peare. (ll. 54–56)

Though the lady of the house is absent when king and prince arrive, the readiness of hospitality proves

> . . . her high huswifery;
> To have her linnen, plate, and all things nigh,
> When she was farre. (ll. 85–87)

The lady of Cookham observes the laws of nature and meditates on their Creator:

> . . . you the time in meditation spent
> Of their Creators powre, which there you saw,
> In all his Creatures held a perfit Law. (ll. 76–78)

Her religion comes from walking with "Christ and his Apostles" in the "sweet woods" and is expressed by placing "holy Writ" on a tree, for meditation, and singing "holy Hymnes to Heavens Eternall King" (ll. 81–88). The lady of Penshurst observes the laws of society, protecting her family against the presumed lawlessness of most women. Religion at Penshurst is a social, not a natural expression:

> Thy lady's noble, fruitfull, chaste withall,
> His children thy great lord may call his owne:
> A fortune, in this age, but rarely knowne.
> They are, and have been taught religion. (ll. 90–93)
>
> . . . .
>
> Each morne, and even, they are taught to pray. (l. 95)

The speakers and implied audiences are equally different in the two poems. Lanyer's voice is that of the poet as preserver of a shared memory. The poem begins in a personal voice, emphasizing ties to the place and the people the speaker celebrates. Only gradually does the poet detach from personal lament and objectify the picture before her, returning at the poem's conclusion to situate herself in the action of the poem (by kissing the tree) and state explicitly her role as memorializer. Her direct address is to Cookham; the immediate implicit audience is the countess of Cumberland and her daughter. The larger implicit audience is the community of good women generally, who will see the pleasures and virtues of a female coterie in harmony with nature.

Jonson's voice, by contrast, is of the poet at the center of society, who organizes and speaks its public values. The poem begins with what purports to be objective description and only takes on a personal voice to give the authority of experience to the claim of the Sidneys' hospitality. While again the direct address is to the estate, the immediate implicit audience is Sir Robert Sidney, and the larger implicit audience is the patriarchy, including the king as its head. Lanyer's world is matrilinear, mother and daughter, natural but readily dispersed by the "occasions" of men, consoled by religion. Jonson's patriarchal world is constructed by men to secure an ordered hierarchy, reinforced by religion.

Aemilia Lanyer and Ben Jonson had much in common, including an appreciation for classical learning and music, a desire to be around and influence higher-born friends and patrons, and an aspiration to represent and memorialize the values of their worlds. She was of slightly higher social standing, a gentlewoman and wife of a gentleman captain. In her youth she enjoyed access to a reigning monarch, as Jonson was to have access to the Jacobean court. Ultimately Jonson had the advantages of gender, including a more complete education and a more visible and accepted role in the courts of both James and Anne. Yet he read and appreciated women who wrote, including the countess of Bedford and Sir Robert Sidney's daughter, Lady Mary Wroth, and may have felt no compunction about borrowing from them.[38] About Lanyer, closest to him in social class and milieu, he may have felt the least compunction of all.

5

LANYER AND ENGLISH
RELIGIOUS VERSE

Religion defined the social, political, and intellectual life of medieval and Renaissance Europe. From the imperialist folly of the Crusades to individual sacrifices, from cathedrals and epics to vestments and sonnets, religion also infused and transported the period's artistic imagination. Today many find it hard to grasp the ubiquity and power of religion in the sixteenth and seventeenth centuries. It underlay virtually every assumption about the nature, purpose, and value of life, and what appear to us as small differences within a hegemonic worldview were reasons for debate, imprisonment, and even martyrdom.

The seventeenth century is the great age of English religious verse. Stimulated in part by the Protestant focus on the Word and in part by the vivid piety of the Counter-Reformation, poets struggled to articulate their personal relationship with the divine. Religious verse was of course not new to England in this period. The greatest portion of extant medieval English verse is occasioned by religious themes, but they represent a religion so integrally a part of the rhythms of human life that the sacred and secular are often barely separable. *The Second Shepherd's Play* is a celebration of Christ's Nativity, but it is also a jolly comedic romp, and even Chaucer's *Canterbury Tales* have an overlay of pious intention. Petrarchan love lyrics seem remote from religion, until we remember the Christianized Neoplatonism that subsequent writers (such as Ficino and Spenser) derived from the last third of the *Canzoniere*.

Through the sixteenth century religious lyrics were characteristically translations and imitations of the Psalms. Considered the "compendium *par excellence* of lyric poetry" by Reformation lyricists, the Book of Psalms appeared in over three hundred English editions by 1640 and provided models for a wide range of topics and approaches to religious experience and feelings.[1] Lanyer grew up surrounded by these verses. In addition to the Sternhold-Hopkins common meter *Whole Booke of Psalmes* (1562) which had a long life as the principal hymnal of Protestant worship, she would have known Anne Vaughan Lock's sonnet sequence based on Psalm 51, and she cites the Sidney-Pembroke Psalms as an important model for her own verse.[2]

Poets such as Lanyer, Donne, and Herbert move toward a more personalized religious expression. As the energy of the Reformation drew away from issues of national to issues of individual identity, it seems to have promoted a new intensity in the religious lyrics of the late sixteenth and seventeenth centuries. The break with Rome and subsequent schisms, the access to a vernacular Bible, the emphasis on individual conscience all served to make religious interpretation more subjective and therefore more tenuous, vexed, and urgent. Even Catholic writers are forced into a more considered and dangerous piety, as Church and State were thought to be inseparable and recusancy therefore treasonous.

Lanyer writes of religion in the midst of this ferment and at the beginning of the great age of English religious poetry. Her central poem, *Salve Deus Rex Judaeorum*, summarizes and challenges key Protestant beliefs and presents a view of Christ's passion in some details not unlike Counter-Reformation piety. In this she rehearses some of the varied religious discourse of the period, at the same time challenging the authorities by which it was traditionally dispensed: men in power.

This chapter situates Lanyer as a poet among a few of her key Protestant and Catholic predecessors; her best-known contemporary among writers of religious verse, John Donne; and two of her brilliant successors, with whom she had affinities, Herbert and Milton.

Sixteenth-Century Religious Verse

Two important differences between Protestant and Catholic doctrine recur consistently in both popular and polemical literature of the sixteenth century: whether salvation is a function of faith or of works, and whether Christ exists memorially or corporeally (the doctrine of "transubstantiation") in the sacrament of bread and wine. Protestants believed that faith in Jesus Christ alone brought salvation, though good works would issue, through God's grace, from a proper faith. Catholics believed that good works were pleasing to God, and a community of good works could bolster the lagging sinner; the model and mediation of saints were therefore properly invoked as part of that community of salvific work. Protestants reduced the number of sacraments ("certain and sure witnesses, and effectual signs of grace, and God's good will towards us, by the which he doth work invisibly in us") from seven to two, baptism and communion, "the Supper of the Lord."[3] The latter, the blessing and partaking of bread and wine as the body and blood of Christ, though it comes from the tradition of the Catholic mass, was carefully distinguished from Catholic teaching: "Transubstantiation (or the change of the substance of Bread and Wine [into the physical body and blood of Christ, as the Catholics taught]) . . . is repugnant to the plain words of Scripture, overthroweth the nature of a Sacrament, and hath given occasion to many superstitions. The body of Christ is given, taken, and eaten, in the Supper, only after an heavenly and spiritual manner."[4]

For Protestants (and especially for Calvinists) human nature since the fall was utterly degenerate and therefore incapable of works that could be redemptive; faith alone, itself a gift from God, could save a sinner. According to the Calvinist catechism, "all suche workes as we doe of our selves, by our Nature are utterly corrupte: whereof it followeth necessarily, that thei can not please GOD, but rather do procure his wrath, and he condempneth them every one." When the catechizing minister asks the child how the works "whiche we doe by vertue of [God's] Spirite" may be made acceptable to God, the child properly answers, "by faithe onely."[5] For Catholics, human nature became perverted and distorted but not utterly debased. A man or woman could and should be a partner with God, sharing in the good works made possible by Christ's redeeming sacrifice. When the child in the Catholic catechism asks his master why, "if Christ have satisfied his Father for the sinnes of all men . . . we have neede to doe penance for our sinnes," he receives this response:

> Christ hath satisfied for the sins of all men: but it is necessarie to aplie this satisfaction in particular to this man and to that man, which is done by faith, by the Sacraments, by good workes, and particularlie by penance: and therefore we have neede to do penance and other good works, though Christ have suffered, and wrought for us.[6]

These doctrines had implications for how a poet might approach and represent religious matters. In general, a Protestant poet might reflect on his or her condition and seek God's grace, or celebrate and enhance a faith already in place in another. Since Christ is the source and only mediator of the divine, and since works could contribute nothing at all to attain salvation, Protestant verse tends to focus on the penitent's sense of sin, longing for grace, and relationship with Christ. Catholic verse, on the other hand, though it may be equally focused on the need for repentance, may invoke the mediation of saints and may treat the contemplation of Christ's and saints' lives as a holy work. Further, as Catholic iconography and doctrine is more corporeal, Catholic poetic language tends to emphasize the incarnational aspects of the divine, while Protestant language tends to be more analytic and intellectual.[7] Catholic language tends to be tropic, with symbols and extended metaphors, while Protestant language tends to be schematic, its artistry in analytical devices such as parallelism and contrast, and its passion in repetition.

The concluding few lines of Lock's second introductory sonnet to the Psalm 51 sequence illustrate the Protestant sense of sin, conveying emotion in the schematic play and repetition of key words and phrasings:

Yet blinde, alas, I groape about for grace.
While blinde for grace I groape about in vaine,
My fainting breath I gather up and straine,
Mercie, mercie, to crye and crye againe.[8] (ll. 11–14)

A similarly penitential lyric by the Jesuit poet Robert Southwell, "A vale of teares," uses rich and sensuous description to allegorize the suffering soul:

A vale there is enwrapt with dreadfull shades,
With thicke of mourning pines shrouds from the sunne,
Where hanging clifts yeld short and dumpish glades,
And snowie floud with broken streames doth runne, (ll. 1–4)
    .   .   .   .
Where waters wrastle with encountring stones,
That breake their streames, and turne them into foame,
The hollow clouds full frought with thundering groans,
With hideous thumps discharge their pregnant wombe.[9] (ll. 13–16)

These are only general tendencies. Most poets use metaphor, and all poets structure verse schematically. Lanyer is particularly interesting because her use of these devices blurs some of the doctrinal distinctions between Protestantism and Catholicism. There is no reason to believe her faith was anything other than the Reform Protestantism in which she was apparently raised, particularly given the centrality of Christ to all her extant poems, but her expression of that faith, though it contains typically Protestant language, includes visual and sensual elements more similar to her Catholic than to her Protestant predecessors.

Lanyer's references to Christ make ample use of the biblical and attributive epithets common to Protestant poetics. He is a "mightie monarch," "humbled king," "king of kings," "King of Heaven and Monarch of the Earth."[10] He is the "Paschall lambe," "this Lambe," "pure unspotted Lambe," "sweet lambe of God," "this siely lambe."[11] He is also the "Saviour in a Shepherds weed," "the Shepheard," "the rock," "the watchman."[12] Above all, he is "The Bridegroome" of the women for whom Lanyer writes.[13]

Yet Lanyer's imagery is more insistently physical than we might expect from a Protestant poet. If Lanyer is presenting the crucifixion as a text that a woman must learn to read, she encodes its meaning in the body and blood of Jesus. So she presents the figure of Christ to "All Vertuous Ladies" "In bloody torments" (l. 60) and to "Lucie, Countess of Bedford"

> . . . all stuck with pale deaths arrows:
> In whose most pretious wounds your soule may reade
> Salvation, while he (dying Lord) doth bleed. (ll. 12–14)

She assures "Katherine, Duchess of Suffolk" that Christ in his death is "writing the Covenant with his most pretious blood," presents him "Crowned with thornes, and bathing in his blood," and urges her to see his beauty, his "faire corps," in the "rose, vermillion" of his "precious blood" (ll. 47, 62, 80–82). Christ's blood drenches the *Salve Deus*, from the scripturally derived description of his agony in Gethsemane, where "his pretious sweat came trickling to the ground, / Like drops of blood" (ll. 406–08; Luke 22:44), to the imaginative vision of Christ on the cross, "His blessed blood watring his pierced feet" (l. 1176).[14] At the center of Lanyer's salvation story is a bloody Christ who hangs like the crucifix in a Catholic church.

There is no direct match in approach and vision among her older poetic contemporaries. Among Lanyer's most likely models are the two Protestant women poets already mentioned, Anne Lock (c. 1533– c. 1590) and Mary Sidney, the Countess of Pembroke (1561–1621). She would have known the former because of connections between the Bassano and Vaughan families, and of course she explicitly mentions the Psalms of the latter.[15] Among men whose work Lanyer certainly or possibly knew, Sir Philip Sidney (1554–86) and his friend Fulke Greville (1554–1628) wrote religious poems in the Reform Protestant tradition, while another Elizabethan courtier of Lanyer's time, Henry Constable (1562–1613), wrote religious sonnets that reflect his conversion to Catholicism.[16] The poems of the Catholic priest Robert Southwell (1561–95) were published shortly after his execution, and show some interesting resemblances to Lanyer's language in *Salve Deus*. The Protestant and Catholic approaches illustrated by these six poets show Lanyer to be Protestant in her basic theology, but unconventional in her poeticizing of religious materials.[17]

Here I focus principally on poems about salvation and penitence, since these are topics Lanyer and the other six poets clearly share. The models for these topics are largely biblical and often refer to the Psalms and the Canticles, or Song of Songs, as metaphoric resources. The Psalms provided a variety of ways in which the individual soul might approach God, while the Canticles were considered an allegory of the relationship between Christ and the Church, or Christ and the individual soul.[18] These several poets show the influences of both the Psalms and the Canticles, while Lanyer, in the *Salve Deus*, draws from these biblical resources and adds the element of narrative, based largely on Matthew's version of Christ's passion.

Lock's sonnet sequence on Psalm 51 and the countess of Pembroke's poeticizing of Psalms 44–150 (and her brother's of 1–43) illustrate two Protestant approaches to Englishing the biblical lyric, one of passionate repentance and the other of assured salvation. Lock's sequence incorporates and extends the language of the Psalm, taking it as an opportunity to reflect on the degradation of sin and the impossibility of redemption through works. The Sidney-Pembroke Psalms remain close to their originals but formulate each psalm into confident English. Lanyer's *Salve Deus* has both passion and confidence.

Lock's language, as her editor Susan Felch notes, "reflects that of a noncomformist molded by the catholic Christian tradition" and, despite the example I gave above of her direct, schematic poetics, her attention remains firmly tied to the physical world.[19] By contrast, Pembroke's handling even of the same Penitential Psalm (51) remains elegant and assured. Of the two, the countess's version is more "Protestant," in that it is more analytic and less iconic. Take, for example, her reading of 51:2, "Wash me throughly from mine iniquitie, and clense me from my sinne":[20]

o clense, o wash my fowle iniquitie:
clense still my spotts, still wash awaie my staynings,
till staines and spotts in mee leave noe remaynings.[21]

The lines gain their rhetorical force from a schematic device: "clense" and "wash" are repeated in the second line accompanied by "spotts" and "staynings," which are repeated with variation ("staines" and "spotts") in the third line. The repetition of "still" in the second line, which reinforces the cascading parallelisms, underscores "Till" in the third. The power of the passage comes from an artfully arrayed set of emphases; however passionate the expression, the speaker is in control, and the experience is of the mind, not the body.

The reverse is true in the Lock sonnet on the same biblical verse ("Wash me yet more from my wickednes, and clense me from my sinne," as it appears in the sidenote to the sonnet):

So foule is sinne and lothesome in thy sighte,
So foule with sinne I may be washed white
So foule I dare not, Lord, approche to thee.
Ofte hath thy mercie washed me before,
Thou madest me cleane, but I am foule againe.
Yet washe me Lord againe, and washe me more.
Washe me, O Lord, and do away the stain
Of uggly sinnes that in my soule appere.
Let flow thy plentuous streames of clensing grace.
Washe me againe, yea washe me every where,
Both leprous bodie and defiled face.
Yea wash me all, for I am all uncleane.
And from my sin, Lord, cleanse me ones againe.[22]

Devices of repetition abound, but with less self-conscious variation than in the Pembroke selection. The repetitions, often at the beginning of the line ("So foule," "Wash me"), serve a passionate insistence rather than an artful analysis, and lead to the climactic image that gives the sonnet its principal power: "yea wash me everywhere, / Both leprous bodie and defiled face." This language depicts a real scrubbing—a maternal God, cloth in hand, chafing off the ingrained dirt of an incorrigible child. The portrayal is both emotional and physical, suggesting the medieval heritage Felch notes in Lock's style. She may be closer in time, and therefore rhetorical tendency, to an iconic Catholic tradition, but, like Mary Sidney, her theology is firmly

Protestant, and her descriptive language leans away from the baroque lushness toward which Counter-Reformation verse was heading.

The distinction between Protestant and Catholic penitential verse is clear in a comparison between the poems of statesman and writer Fulke Greville and his sometime colleague, Catholic convert Henry Constable. Both poets had associations with the Sidneys. Greville, who went to Shrewsbury School with Sir Philip and became his biographer, considered him his closest friend and had at least some contact with the countess of Pembroke after Philip's death.[23] Constable knew Sidney and his widow, Frances, who became countess of Essex, and was a friend of Penelope Rich, reputed to be Sidney's first love (the "Stella" of *Astrophil and Stella*). Although he claimed not to know the countess of Pembroke personally, he dedicated a sonnet to her.[24] Greville and Constable also had associations with the countess of Cumberland's circle, with which Lanyer may have been associated as early as 1589 or '90. Greville appears to have been friendly with Samuel Daniel in the 1590s and is mentioned by name in Daniel's *Musophilus* (1599).[25] One of Constable's poems is dedicated to the sisters, Ann, countess of Warwick, and Margaret, countess of Cumberland.[26] Greville and Constable's religious poetry, whether or not Lanyer knew it the way she knew the work of Lock and Pembroke, sprang from the Elizabethan court with which she was familiar.

On the same general theme as the Lock and Pembroke versions of Psalm 51—God's redemptive power over the inevitable sins of mankind—Greville expresses the Calvinist understanding of "mans degeneration" as absolute, and God's mercy as an unfathomable doctrine of faith:

> Wrapt up, O Lord, in mans degeneration;
> The glories of thy truth, thy joyes eternall,
> Reflect upon my soule darke desolation,
> And ugly prospects o're the sprites infernall.
> > Lord, I have sinn'd, and mine iniquity,
> > Deserves this hell; yet Lord deliver me.
>
> Thy power and mercy never comprehended
> Rest lively imag'd in my Conscience wounded;
> Mercy to grace, and power to feare extended,
> Both infinite, and I in both confounded;
> > Lord, I have sinn'd, and mine iniquity,
> > Deserves this hell, yet Lord deliver me.

> If from this depth of sinne, this hellish grave,
> And fatall absence from my Saviours glory,
> I could implore his mercy, who can save,
> And for my sinnes, not paines of sinne, be sorry;
>   Lord, from this horror of iniquity,
>   And hellish grave, thou wouldst deliver me.[27]

Despite the claim that hellish horrors "rest lively imag'd" in his conscience, we are not presented those images. Instead, the poem sets out the Reform Protestant case that man is unable to help himself and depends entirely on God's grace for the transformation of mind and heart ("and for my sinnes, not paines of sinne, be sorry") that allows for salvation.

Constable, by contrast, presents icons of repentance and tells their stories in vivid imagery. Originally an outspoken Protestant, Constable converted to Catholicism around 1590 and spent most of the rest of his life in France. Before his conversion he had apparently been a favorite of Queen Elizabeth and a continental spy for Lord Burghley. Even afterwards he remained an English patriot to the extent his religion and residence away from England would allow, advising King James on continental issues. Constable had been a popular sonneteer in the 1580s. His religious poetry, which circulated in manuscript around the first decade of the seventeenth century, reflects his Catholic conviction and sensibility.[28]

Four sonnets "To St Mary Magdalen" exemplify Constable's penitential voice. Two will serve as examples here (and another in the next section of this chapter). The first of these appears among five other poems to several saints and concludes very differently from Greville's poem. Instead of an impassioned faith that calls for God's grace, Constable invokes penitential works, which will win heaven for the sinner:

> For fewe nyghtes solace in delitious bedd,
>   where heate of luste, dyd kyndle flames of hell:
>   thou nak'd on naked rocke in desert cell
>   lay thirty yeares, and teares of griefe dyd shedd.
> But for that tyme, thy hart there sorrowed,
>   thou now in heaven aeternally dost dwell,
>   and for ech teare, which from thyne eyes then fell,
>   a sea of pleasure now ys rendered.

> If short delyghtes, entyce my hart to straye,
>   lett me thy longe pennance learne to knowe
>   how deare I should for triflyng pleasures paye:
> And if I vertues roughe beginnyng shunne,
>   Lett thy aeternall joyes unto me showe
>   what hyghe Rewarde, by lyttle payne ys wonne.[29]

Not only does the poem's message emphasize works over faith (Magdalen earned heaven through her thirty years of penance), the poem's method is thoroughly Catholic, invoking the model of a saint's life rather than examining the unhappy conscience of the speaker.

Constable's religious poems often involve the mediation of saints and tend to be more narrative and pictorial than those of his Protestant contemporaries. His other three poems to St. Mary Magdalen form a short sequence at the end of the manuscript,[30] where they rely on the contrast between earthly and heavenly love, drawing on the language of the Canticles, to make their point. The first of these three signals a crucial difference between Lock and Greville's view of the total degeneracy of the human condition, and Constable's vision of the joy of repentance:

> Blessed Offendour: who thyselfe haist try'd,
>   how farr a synner differs from a Saynt
>   joyne thy wett eyes, with teares of my complaint,
>   while I sighe for that grave, for which thow cry'd.
> No longer lett my synfull sowle abyde
>   in feaver of thy fyrst desyres faynte:
>   but lett that love which last thy hart did taynt
>   with panges of thy repentance, pierece my syde.
> So shall my sowle, no foolish vyrgyn bee
>   with empty lampe: but lyke a Magdalen, beere
>   for oyntment boxe, a breast with oyle of grace:
> And so the zeale, which then shall burn in mee,
>   may make my hart, lyke to a lampe appere
>   and in my spouse's pallace gyve me place.

While Constable sees "how far a synner differs from a Saynt," Greville sees "the depth of mine iniquity, / That ugly center of infernall spirits," a place unredeemable except by "this *saving God* of mine" (sonnet 99, ll. 1–2, 6). The words that capture Greville's imagination are

"deformity," "degeneration," desolation," and "eternall doome"
(ll. 3, 8, 14, 20). Although the result, through faith, is still salvation,
made more wonderful by the distance traveled between man's sin
and God's forgiveness, it is difficult to think of Greville or any Protestant praising a "Blessed Offendour." Yet Constable has much for a
Protestant poet to admire, including his allusions to the biblical authority of the Canticles.

There is no reason to suspect that Lanyer had any contact with
the Jesuit priest Robert Southwell, but his capture and imprisonment
in 1592 were famous events, and his verse, first published in 1595, not
long after his execution, went through several editions of varying
authority before 1610.[31] The title poem of the earliest editions,
"St. Peter's Complaint," is a long mea culpa in the voice of Peter,
who has denied Christ three times just as his master predicted (Matt.
26:69–75). The purpose of the poem, as the speaker explains in the
introductory verse, "The Author to the Reader," is to set the model
of a penitent saint before the contemporary sinner:

> Dear eie that daynest to let fall a looke,
> On these sad memories of Peters plaintes;
> Muse not to see some mud in cleerest brooke,
> They once were brittle mould, that now are Saintes.
> Their weakness is no warrant to offend:
> Learne by their faultes, what in thine owne to mend. (ll. 1–6)

Like Lanyer (and George Herbert) after him, Southwell complains
about the attention poets give to the false beauties of love poetry
("Still finest wits are stilling Venus Rose. / . . . To Christian workes,
few have their talents lent," ll. 16, 18) and invokes "heavenly sparkes
of wit" to speak plainly of divine things: "Cloude not with mistie loves
your Orient cleere" (ll. 20, 21).

Throughout the poem proper, Southwell uses the extended metaphor of the ship in the storm, borrowing language from the traditional Petrarchan conceit of the lover in the storm-tossed sea (see,
e.g., Spenser's *Faerie Queene* 3.iv.8–10) and alluding to Peter's own
experiences as a fisherman and follower of the Christ who walked
on waves (Matt. 14):

> Launche foorth my Soul into a maine of teares,
> Full fraught with griefe the traffick of my mind:
> Torne sailes will serve. thoughtes rent with guilty feares:

Give care, the sterne: use sighes in lieu of wind:
Remorse, the Pilot: thy misdeede, the Carde:
Torment, thy Haven: Shipwracke, thy best reward. (ll. 1–6)

The poem suggests its Catholic theology by making grace the result of penance:

Divorc'd from grace thy soule to pennance wed: (l. 10)

. . . .

Thy trespasse foule: let not thy teares be few:
Baptize thy spotted soule in weeping dewe. (ll. 17–18)

Catholicism is more explicit in references to the standard Latin Vulgate Bible, attributed to St. Jerome (l. 40), and the intercessory role of the Virgin Mary:

When traitor to the sonne in mothers eies,
I shall present my humble suit for grace:
What blush can paint the shame that will arise;
Or write my inward feeling in my face?
Might she the sorrow with the sinner see:
Though I dispisde: my griefe might pittyed bee. (ll. 577–82)

Here is hope for a mediated grace by means of penitential work, just the reverse of the Protestant unmediated and unearned grace that comes from faith in Christ alone.

There are nonetheless some interesting similarities between Southwell's work and Lanyer's. His poem is in six-line stanzas (Lanyer's is in ottava rima) and reads like a narrative despite its single penitential voice; it concerns a piece of the passion story; and it accumulates vivid detail that produces something like the tone Lanyer evokes in her retelling of the passion. Like Lanyer, Southwell portrays Christ as the perfect lover, emphasizing his physical beauty as well as his redemptive power. In a nineteen-stanza rhapsody on Christ's "sacred eyes" (ll. 331–444), Southwell includes language from the Canticles ("O Pooles of *Hesebon*, the bathes of grace, / Where happy spirits dyve in sweet desires," ll. 379–80) and his rhapsodies on Christ's beauty anticipate Lanyer's portrayals of Christ. Here is Southwell on Christ's microcosmic eyes:

O little worldes, the summes of all the best,
Where glory, heaven, God, sunne: all vertues, starres:

> Where fire, a love that next to heaven doth rest,
> Ayre, light of life, that no distemper marres:
> The water, grace, whose seas, whose springs, whose showers,
> Cloth natures earth, with everlasting flowers. (ll. 409–14)

And Lanyer, emphasizing the magnitude of the passion:

> The beauty of the World, Heavens chiefest Glory;
> The mirrour of Martyrs, Crowne of holy Saints;
> Love of th'Almighty, blessed Angels story;
> Water of Life, which none that drinks it, faints;
> Guide of the Just, where all our Light we borrow;
> Mercy of Mercies; Hearer of Complaints;
> Triumpher over Death; Ransomer of Sinne;
> Falsly accused: now his paines begin. (ll. 641–48)

Despite Lanyer's references to "Martyrs" and "holy Saints," Christ remains her only mediator ("Hearer of Complaints"). Her Virgin Mary, unlike Southwell's, does not stand between her sins and her God. Lanyer does place an emphasis on Mary that is unusual in Protestant piety; she devotes sixteen stanzas to "The sorow of the virgin Marie" (ll. 1009–1136), including a version of the Magnificat, "the salutation of the virgin Marie" (ll. 1041–56). This portrait contains no hint of Mary as mediator or co-redeemer, but instead presents her as the chief examplar of all the womanly virtues Lanyer praises throughout the *Salve Deus*. She is the "Most blessed virgin" (l. 1025), the "Faire chosen vessell" (l. 1030), the "most beauteous Queene of Womankind" (1040) whom God raised from "poore degree" to "Servant, Mother, Wife, and Nurse / To Heavens bright King, that freed us from the curse" (ll. 1086–88).

In their portrayal of women generally, however, there is a strong contrast between the two poets. Despite his invocation of a mediating Virgin Mary (a much more distant figure than Lanyer's weeping mother), Southwell has nothing good to say about women. St. Peter agonizes over his own responsibility for the sin of denying Christ three times on the morning of the crucifixion, but he also manages to blame the young women who identified him as a follower of Christ: "A puffe of womans breath bred all my feare" (l. 150). The voice of Peter later complains that while "the blaze of beauties beames" were "*Davids*, *Salomons*, and *Sampsons* fals" (ll. 307, 302),

. . . gratious features dasled not mine eies,
Two homely droyles were authors of my death:
Not love, but feare, my sences did surprize:
Not feare of force, but feare of womans breath.
And those unarm'd, ill grac'd, despisde, unknowne:
So base a blast my truthe hath overthrowne. (ll. 313–18).

Southwell's Peter describes himself as worse than those biblical figures who were moved by beauty, since his downfall comes from ugly,
weak, and insignificant women. The speaker pauses to make the
point that women of every kind are the cause of evil generally:

O women, woe to men: traps for their falls,
Still actors in all tragicall mischaunces:
Earthes necessarie evils, captivating thralles,
Now murdring with your tongs, now with your glances,
Parents of life, and love: spoylers of both.
The theefes of Harts: false do you love or loth. (ll. 319–24)

This seems an excessive response to the women of the biblical
story (described simply as one and another "maide" in the Geneva
translation, "damsel" in the King James, and "maidservant" in the
Douai), who merely comment that Peter was one of Christ's follow-
ers. But it is part of a long line of gratuitous clerical castigation of
women from at least St. Jerome forward. A similar patristic misogyny
moved Chaucer's wife of Bath to throw her fourth husband's book
into the fire and, more than two hundred years later, provoked
Lanyer to her ingenious "Eves apology" (*Salve Deus*, ll. 761–832). As
Pilate's wife tries to persuade her husband not to authorize Christ's
crucifixon, she makes the point that, whatever Eve's culpability,
Adam's is at the base of it, and the men who would crucify Christ
assume an even more grim responsibility:

If any Evill did in her [Eve] remaine,
Beeing made of him [Adam], he was the ground of all;
If one of many Worlds could lay a staine
Upon our Sexe, and worke so great a fall
To wretched Man, by Satans subtill traine;
What will so fowle a fault amongst you all?
    Her weaknesse did the Serpents words obay;
    But you [men] in malice Gods deare Sonne betray. (ll. 809–16)

While Protestant misogynists can be as vigorous as Catholic ones, Southwell is the only poet within the group I am looking at here who condemns women categorically. Sidney and Greville, for example, distinguish between human and divine love and beauty, as Spenser had done (see chapter 2), but there is no universal condemnation of women in their renunciation of earthly love. Sidney longs for the light of Christian truth and seeks to cast away that which fades:

> Leave me o Love, which reachest but to dust,
> And thou my mind aspire to higher things:
> Grow rich in that which never taketh rust:
> What ever fades, but fading pleasure brings.
>
> Draw in thy beames, and humble all thy might,
> To that sweet yoke, where lasting freedomes be:
> Which breakes the clowdes and opens forth the light,
> That doth both shine and give us sight to see.
>
> O take fast hold, let that light be thy guide,
> In this small course which birth drawes out to death,
> And thinke how evill becommeth him to slide,
> Who seeketh heav'n, and comes of heav'nly breath.
>   Then farewell world, thy uttermost I see,
>   Eternall Love maintaine thy life in me.[32]

Greville similarly distinguishes between earthly fire and heavenly light. Confronted with passion, he advises endurance or renunciation:

> The Earth with thunder torne, with fire blasted,
> With waters drowned, with windie palsey shaken
> Cannot for this with heaven be distasted,
> Since thunder, raine and winds from earthe are taken:
> Man torne with Love, with inward furies blasted,
> Drown'd with despaire, with fleshly lustings shaken,
> Cannot for this with heaven be distasted,
> Love, furie, lustings out of man are taken.
> Then Man, endure thy selfe, those clouds will vanish;
> Life is a Top which whipping Sorrow driveth;
> *Wisdome must beare what our flesh cannot banish,*
> *The humble leade, the stubborne bootlesse striveth:*
>   Or Man, forsake thy selfe, to heaven turne thee,
>   Her flames enlighten Nature, never burne thee.[33]

These efforts to reject passion are compatible with Lanyer's attempt to move beyond false to true beauty:

That outward Beautie which the world commends,
Is not the subject I will write upon,
Whose date expir'd, that tyrant Time soone ends:
Those gawdie colours soone are spent and gone:
But those faire Virtues which on thee attends
Are alwaies fresh, they never are but one:
    They make thy Beautie fairer to behold,
    Than was that Queenes for whom prowd *Troy* was sold. (ll. 185–92)

Despite her appreciation for the Virgin Mary and her richly descriptive penitential language, Lanyer remains more closely identifiable in doctrine and sensibility with her Protestant predecessors than with the Catholic Southwell. The sensibility and language in Constable's religious sonnets, however, resonate in Lanyer's *Salve Deus* and may help us to see how the work of yet another Catholic (turned Protestant), John Donne, compares to Lanyer's verse.

Lanyer and Donne

The figure of Christ the bridegroom offers an interesting point of departure for considering how male and female poets, whether Catholic or Protestant, envision salvation and their personal relationship to Christ. The bridegroom in the Christian interpretation of the Canticles is always Christ, but the bride may be either the church as a whole, invariably depicted as female, or the individual soul (whether of a man or a woman), depicted in a posture of female subservience to and union with Christ. Beyond those conventions, Catholic and Protestant imaginations differed considerably in how they negotiated the allegory. In general, the Protestant exegetes used the allegory of the celestial wedding to interpret a historical and personal narrative of pilgrimage, while the Catholic tradition saw the bride as the perfected church or the soul in mystical union.[34]

The last of Constable's poems to Mary Magdalen portrays the transformed penitent as a model for the soul's ultimate fulfillment in Christ. This poem extends the image of the celestial wedding, on which so much of Lanyer's *Salve Deus* also depends, transforming

Mary Magdalen into the exemplary bride of Christ and allowing the
(male) poet to see what his own happy union will become:

> Sweete Saynt: Thow better canst declare to me,
>   what pleasure ys obtayn'd by heavenly love,
>   then they which other loves, dyd never prove:
>   or which in sexe ar differyng from thee:
> For lyke a woman spowse my sowle shalbee,
>   whom synfull passions once to lust did move,
>   and synce betrothed to goddes sonne above,
>   should be enamored with his dietye.
> My body ys the garment of my spryght
>   whyle as the day tyme of my lyfe doth last:
>   when death shall brynge the nyght of my delyght
> My sowle uncloth'd, shall rest from labors past:
>   and clasped in the armes of God, injoye
>   by sweete conjunction, everlasting joye.

The image of Christ the bridegroom mating with the reformed Christian soul takes a more violent turn in the well-known Donne sonnet, "Batter my heart, three person'd God":

> Yet dearely I love you, and would be lov'd faine,
> But am betroth'd unto your enemie,
> Divorce mee, untie, or breake that knot againe,
> Take mee to you, imprison mee, for I
> Except you enthrall mee, never shall be free,
> Nor ever chast, except you ravish mee. (ll. 9–14)[35]

These are Catholic and Protestant versions of the same desire: that
the soul of a man be like the body of a woman and achieve its union
with Christ. For Constable the wedding night is "the rest from
labors past" as well as the "uncloth'd" enjoyment of "sweet conjunction" with Christ—the reward for good works, as well as the gift of
spiritual consummation. Donne's poem is more reminiscent of Anne
Lock's in the violence of its imagery, and, although its implicit physi-
cality may be more like the Catholic tradition in which Donne was
raised, it is Protestant in its plea for a grace that will overcome the
worthless degradation of the longing soul and in its use of spousal
imagery to describe the struggle of pilgrimage rather than the ecstasy
of union.

Another of Donne's "Holy Sonnets" offers a more considered look at the relation between bridegroom and bride, Christ and the church, in the confusing world of Reformation and Counter-Reformation:[36]

> Show me deare Christ, thy Spouse, so bright and clear.
> What! is it she, which on the other shore
> Goes richly painted? or which rob'd and tore
> Laments and mournes in Germany and here?
> Sleepes she a thousand, then peepes up one yeare?
> Is she selfe true and errs? now new, now outwore?
> Doth she, and did she, and shall she evermore
> On one, on seaven, or on no hill appeare?
> Dwells she with us, or like adventuring knights
> First travaile we to seek and then make Love?
> Betray kind husband thy spouse to our sights,
> And let myne amorous soule court thy mild Dove,
> Who is most trew, and pleasing to thee, then
> When she is embrac'd and open to most men.

Like his "Satyre III," this sonnet is a plea that the pilgrim be guided toward the true church. It also offers a distinctively male twist on the Canticles imagery. The speaker identifies not with the bride (as in the Constable poem), but with the bridegroom: "let myne amorous soule court thy milde dove." The wit of the poem depends on the paradox of a bride/church who is "most trew" to Christ "When she is embrac'd and open to most men." Donne may have written his "Holy Sonnets" while he was contemplating holy orders, in which case his association with Christ in this poem may have had the particular resonance of priesthood. Conservative theologians continue to argue against women priests by claiming that the earthly gender of Jesus means that only a man can represent the full manhood of Christ's priesthood. Donne assumes a more general male privilege in this sonnet, however ("most men"). Men are like Christ, and in that sense can love (as well as be) the true church.

Lanyer, too, genders Christ by making him, in contrast to both Constable and Donne, specifically the bridegroom of women: of "all vertuous Ladies in generall" (l. 9), of Susan, dowager countess of Kent (l. 42), of Lady Anne, countess of Dorset (l. 15), and most particularly of Margaret, countess of Cumberland (*Salve Deus*, e.g., ll. 77, 1305–44). Lanyer's women are the correct gender for the traditional Christian allegorizing of the Canticles. Like a mortal bride, they are women and can love the bridegroom without the nervousness Donne's wit betrays. As the bride, they also most particularly represent the true church and can therefore figure salvation to individual souls. This is precisely how Lanyer portrays the countess of Cumberland: she is the true bride, therefore the true church, whose model is salvation for those who would follow her.

> . . . in thy modest vaile do'st sweetly cover
> The staines of other sinnes, to make themselves,
> That by this meanes thou mai'st in time recover
> Those weake lost sheepe that did so long transgresse,
> Presenting them unto thy deerest Lover;
>> That when he brings them back into his fold,
>> In their conversion then he may behold
>
> Thy beauty shining brighter than the Sunne,
> Thine honour more than ever Monarke gaind,
> Thy wealth exceeding his that Kingdomes wonne,
> Thy Love unto his Spouse, thy Faith unfaind,
> Thy Constancy in what thou hast begun,
> Till thou his heavenly Kingdom have obtaind;
>> Respecting worldly wealth to be but drosse,
>> Which, if abuz'd, doth proove the owners losse. (ll. 1394–1408)

The countess is no saint or icon, but a living example of the redeemed Protestant soul whose faith accomplishes the redemption of others. Her portrayal brushes closer to Constable's mediating Mary Magdalen, and his picture of blessed union, than to Donne's Calvinist impotency in "Batter my Heart," and his historical journey in "Show me deare Christ," yet the countess is also on a pilgrimage. Her exemplary blessedness remains part of an earthly journey, "Till thou his heavenly Kingdom have obtaind."

If a man can be the bride of Christ, a woman (Lanyer suggests) can also defy gender expectations. She can have honor and wealth greater than a king (ll. 1402–3) and can display "Love unto [Christ's] Spouse," the church as a whole. She is both the "Deere Spouse of Christ" (l. 1170), herself the figure for the whole church, and the lover of both church and Christ, presenting redeemed "weake lost sheepe" (l. 1397) to the sacred bridegroom. Lanyer has taken the opportunity offered by the Canticles to imbue the countess with rich symbolic resonance: she is both priest and bride, mediator in history and image of transcendent perfection.

In the image of Christ the bridegroom, and of the bride as both church and individual soul, Lanyer and Donne offer interesting contrasts in the gendering of religious imagery. Another poem that illustrates gender differences between these near contemporaries is one of the few works by Donne that was printed during his lifetime, *An Anatomy of the World* (the "First Anniversarie"). Like the *Salve Deus*, it was published in 1611.

While the *Anatomy* is a funeral elegy and *Salve Deus* purports to be a narrative of Christ's passion, both are long lyrics about what Arthur Marotti calls "loss and the need for recovery."[37] Both poems seek patronage by expressing sympathy for a high-born family. In the "Anatomy" Donne offers sympathy to the Drury family for the loss of their daughter, Elizabeth, who died at the age of fourteen in December 1610; in the *Salve Deus* Lanyer sympathetically laments what the countess of Cumberland has suffered, first, over her separation from her husband and then, after his death, from the loss of her daughter's expected patrimony. Both poems concern the evil and injustice of the world, yet there are interesting differences in how they portray gender and assert authority in the poetic enterprise.

Donne's portrayal of Elizabeth Drury (whom he had never met) as an Astraean perfection whose abandonment of earth signals the world's decay was controversial in its own time. William Drummond of Hawthornden reports that Ben Jonson "told Mr. Donne that if [the *Anatomy*] had been written of the Virgin Marie it had been something," an accusation that apparently prompted Donne to reply "that he described the Idea of a Woman, not as she was."[38] The relation between the poet and the woman who is the subject of his poem is never a relationship between John Donne and Elizabeth Drury, but between the artificer and an idea of perfection.

Barbara Lewalski has glossed Donne's use of "Idea" by reference to his sermons, where "the Idea of Mankind" is "the image of God," or, more particularly in the *Anatomy*, the figure of Elizabeth Drury represents "the restoration of the image of God in man through grace."[39] Donne has therefore infused enormous symbolic force into an image of virtuous womanhood, which his poem will presumably display as an occasion for admonishing the world against its decay. His presentation of that image and his authority to rail against the world's decay are intertwined, even fused, in the poem.

In a prefatory commendation,[40] Joseph Hall comments on the late Elizabeth Drury's good fortune in finding so effective and authoritative an elegist:

> And thou the subject of this wel-borne thought,
> Thrise noble maid; couldst not have found nor sought
> A fitter time to yeeld to thy sad Fate
> Then whilst this spirit lives, that can relate
> Thy worth so well. (ll. 11–15)

The young woman has managed to die at a time when she can provide the occasion for this man's pen, Hall suggests, and he goes
on to make explicit the virginal page she presents to the worthy
pencil:

> Admired match! where strives in mutual grace
> The cunning Pencill, and the comely face:
> A taske, which thy faire goodnes made too much
> For the bold pride of vulgar pens to touch. (ll. 17–20)

   Donne's power is sexual, just as Elizabeth Drury's value as an
"Idea" depends in large part on her virginity. As Donne notes in an
accompanying poem, "A Funerall Elegie," she "soone expir'd"

> Cloath'd in her Virgin white integrity
>   For mariage, though it doth not staine, doth dye.
> To scape th'infirmaties which waite upone
>   Woman, shee went away, before sh'was one. (ll. 74–78)

To be a woman is to be tainted by sexual conquest. Better to be con-
quered instead, Hall says, by the masculine authority of the poet.
   By lauding her virgin purity, Donne inevitably connects Elizabeth
Drury with the Virgin Mary; Elizabeth, too, is a "Queene" for whom
heaven is as "her standing house" (ll. 7–8). Not unlike Lanyer's figure of the countess of Cumberland, Donne's Elizabeth Drury is a type
of the co-redeemer who would erase original sin, but here it is Eve's
sin that specifically needs to be overcome and is (ironically) overcome
by her descent to earth as "the weaker Sex":

> She in whom vertue was so much refin'd,
> That for Allay unto so pure a minde
> She tooke the weaker Sex, she that could drive
> The poysonous tincture, and the stayne of *Eve*,
> Out of her thoughts, and deeds; and purifie
> All by a true religious Alchimy. (ll. 177–82)

Donne uses the image of idealized virginal purity to assert his own authority as a poet in terms that suggest important differences between what a man could claim and what a woman, such as Lanyer, might find or claim through her own idealization of another woman. Donne offers his poem on Elizabeth Drury as a tribute to her and to the virtue she represents not only to the penitent soul but to the recorder:

> . . . blessed maid,
> Of whom is meant whatever hath beene said,
> Or shall be spoken well by any tongue,
> Whose name refines course lines, and makes prose song,
> Accept this tribute. . . . (ll. 443–47)

Yet it is not the "Idea of a woman" that authorizes Donne's lines. His right to inscribe the example of perfection, warn against earthly decay, pay tribute to virtue and castigate vice, and to do it all in verse rather than sermon or history, comes from a more powerful inspirational source:

> . . . if you
> In reverance to her, doe thinke it due,
> That no one should her prayses thus reherse,
> As matter fit for Chronicle, not verse,
> Vouchsafe to call to minde, that God did make
> A last, and lastingst peece, a song. He spake
> To *Moses*, to deliver unto all
> That song: because he knew they would let fall,
> The Law, the Prophets, and the History,
> But keepe the song still in their memory. (ll. 457–66)

God, not Elizabeth Drury, authorizes the poet. Lewalski suggests that we may bridge the gap between Elizabeth Drury as the inspiration for the poem, and the divine authority Donne claims here, by reference to Donne's theory of "Idea": "for Donne the Idea of a man, or of a woman, is—quite precisely—the image of God. . . . If, then, Donne declared his intention to praise Elizabeth Drury not as she was but rather as the Idea of a Woman, we may suppose that he undertook to praise the image of God created and restored in her."[41] This would situate the power of God, Donne's ultimate authority, in his subject. But his subject is a deliberate cipher, an unknown

woman, and the poem is about decay and disappointment, not
about transformed perfection. The woman is gone and was never
a "woman" in the first place. Her virginity made her a clean page
to write upon; the image of perfection resides in her absence, not
her presence. What fills the void is the authorial voice which finds
its authority in the same voice that inspired Moses. The poet is made
bold by Moses' example, and concludes his poem by asserting the
poet's primacy over his subject matter:

> . . . such an opinion (in due measure) made
> Me this great Office boldly to invade.
> Nor could incomprehensibleness deterre
> Me, from thus trying to emprison her.
> Which when I saw that a strict grave could do,
> I saw not why verse might doe so too.
> Verse hath a middle nature: heaven keepes soules,
> The grave keepes bodies, verse the fame enroules. (ll. 467–74)

The example of Moses, God's authority, allows the poet to "invade" and "emprison" his subject in the artifact of verse. What lasts
is not the person but the song, not the object of imitation but mimesis itself, not the decaying physical presence but the mnemonic power
of the record. Verse "enroules" the fame—but whose fame? In the
Anatomy, Donne dominates his ostensible subject and becomes himself the authority for his vision of the world. He becomes God's
image, redeemed through a new creation, his own. He engenders
his subject and disengenders her as part of the process of asserting
his own poetic authority, and he aligns himself with the voice of God.

In Lanyer's work the relation between subject and authority is
different. While the godly authority that Donne ultimately claims for
himself distances him from his subject, making him a transcendent
divinity in relation to his poetic creation, Lanyer merges her authorial
voice with the subject(s) and process of her poem, making her an
eminent creative force within the territory of her creation. Just as her
gender connects her with her great patrons, mediated through "Eves
Apologie" in her poem to Queen Anne (ll. 73–78), for example, or
through a mutual effort at divine poetry in her poem to the countess
of Pembroke (ll. 201–04), so it infuses the gendered point of view she
brings to the passion story, including her portrayal of Christ.

The *Salve Deus* begins where Donne's *Anatomy* concludes: by
claiming the eternizing role of verse. After elegizing the departed

Queen Elizabeth (ll. 1–8), Lanyer turns to the living object of her praise, the countess of Cumberland:

> To thee great Countesse now I will applie
> My Pen, to write thy never dying fame;
> That when to heav'n thy blessed Soule shall flie,
> These lines on earth record thy reverend name. (ll. 9–12)

Donne's portrayal of the unknown Elizabeth Drury is hyperbolic and (Jonson at least believed) incidental, but Lanyer's attention to the countess, her virtues and her suffering, is grounded in the living reality of the countess's "sad soule, plung'd in waves of woe" (l. 34). Though the topic of her poem is Christ's passion, the poet pays considerable direct attention to the countess; roughly 500 of the poem's 1840 lines address her directly, describe her situation (e.g., "Thou from Court to the Countrie art retir'd," l. 161), or praise her virtue and faithfulness. The central passion story is framed by catalogs of women who failed to find the true good or sought it imperfectly, so the countess's own devotion to Christ may be contrasted with, yet gain force from, a historical community of suffering women.

Lanyer's central authorizing strategy is to make the situation of women—the countess of Cumberland, the women in the poem's frame, the women who accompany Christ through the story as Lanyer tells it—inseparable from the passion itself. Even Christ becomes a figure for female experience, both as object of the female gaze and, as Janel Mueller has pointed out, as a feminized character whose words and silences are misconstrued by the men in the poem:

> They tell his words, though farre from his intent,
> And what his Speeches were, not what he meant. (ll. 655–56)

A female identification with Christ, Mueller suggests, authorizes Lanyer to interpret Jesus's actions. She cites "the pattern of fundamental misprision exhibited by all of the males in the story, friends and foes alike, while the female poet unfailingly understands what and who Jesus is." Lanyer's Christ, "like the ideal woman of the Puritan manuals, is silent except when induced to speak, and modest and taciturn when he does; he is gentle, mild, peaceable, and submissive to higher male authorities."[42]

Lanyer's authority for her version of the biblical passion—for her anatomy of the world's decay and redemption—lies in her identification with, and ability to interpret, the passion of Christ. She who has the power to understand has the authority to speak, an assumption that runs throughout the *Salve Deus*. She portrays that understanding as quintessentially female, from the voice of Pilate's wife which moves imperceptibly back to that of the narrator (ll. 749–912), through the tears of the daughters of Jerusalem and the sufferings of the Virgin Mary (ll. 968–1136), to the particular insight of the countess of Cumberland (ll. 1329–68).

For both Lanyer and Donne, authority resides ultimately with God, but Donne identifies with Moses and an Old Testament divinity who imposes law from the mountaintop. Lanyer's identity is with the women of the New Testament who understand a God who enters his own creation in order to save it. If, according to Donne, Elizabeth Drury "tooke the weaker sexe" to redeem Eve's sin (*Anatomy*, l. 179), by contrast Lanyer claims that her weakness (like Paul's) is an opportunity to demonstrate the power of this humble Christ:[43]

> But yet the Weaker thou ["my deare Muse"] doest seeme to be
> In Sexe, or Sence, the more his glory shines,
> That doth infuze such powerfull Grace in thee,
> To shew thy Love in these few humble lines. (ll. 289–92)

Lanyer's fusion with her subjects proceeds only up to a point. The creator never disappears entirely into her creation, nor does the claim of weakness abrogate the force of her vocation. As visionary and interpreter of Christ's passion, the poet is the giver who offers the gift of Christ crucified to the judgment of her inspiring patron:

> Which I present (deare Lady) to your view,
> Uppon the Crosse depriv'd of life or breath,
> To judge if ever Lover were so true.
> To yeeld himselfe unto such shamefull death. (ll. 1265–68)

Even more directly, she tells "the doubtfull Reader" in her brief afterword that she was "appointed to performe this Worke." Still, Lanyer is a divinely called representative of this privileged community of female weakness, rather than an external authority etching a "middle way" between body and soul.

Lanyer sees her Creator as alive in the world, joining his creation through shared humility and suffering, and, as God's image, she joins her own creation, largely through shared gender. Donne, on the other hand, identifies specifically with a masculine authority that shares gender with God. As he would share the bride with the bridegroom in "Show me deare Christ," so he shares Christ's own incarnational function by mediating between grave and soul at the end of the *Anatomy*.

Like Lanyer, however, Donne's biblical poetics are difficult to categorize simply in Protestant or Catholic terms. He had a particular appreciation for the Virgin Mary, for example, possibly a heritage of his Catholic background. In "Goodfriday, 1613. Riding Westward," Mary is Christ's "miserable mother" (l. 30)

> Who was Gods partner here, and furnish'd thus
> Halfe of the Sacrifice, which ransom'd us. (ll. 31–32)

Although she is portrayed as co-redeemer, she still does not intercede or mediate between man's sin and God's grace. Donne's version of the passion emphasizes the distance between Christ's sacrifice and the speaker's abject sinfulness, which can be bridged only by an active grace from God:

> O think me worth thine anger, punish mee,
> Burne off my rusts, and my deformity,
> Restore thine Image, so much, by thy grace,
> That thou may'st know mee, and I'll turne my face. (ll. 39–42)

In "The Litanie," however, Mary is not only co-redeemer, she is a mediating force whose "deeds" are "our helpes" :

> For that faire blessed Mother-maid,
> Whose flesh redeem'd us; That she-Cherubin,
> Which unlock'd Paradise, and made
> One claime for innocence, and disseiz'd sinne,
> Whose wombe was a strange heav'n for there
> God cloath'd himselfe, and grew,
> Our zealous thankes wee poure. As her deeds were
> Our helpes, so are her prayers; nor can she sue
> In vaine, who hath such title unto you. (ll. 37–45)

Theologically more like Lock and Greville in the first instance, more like Southwell and Constable in the second, Donne is most like Lanyer in his willingness to take risks with both language and idea.

As risk-takers, willing to analyze biblical texts with a new eye and to challenge traditional boundaries of theology and gender, Lanyer and Donne are contemporaries in ethos as well as chronology.

Some Later Parallels:
Herbert and Milton

Lanyer may have encountered George Herbert (1593–1633) or John Milton (1608–74) in her long life, though we have no evidence that she met either poet. If she maintained contact with Anne Clifford, it is possible she crossed paths with Herbert, who was installed as rector of the parishes of Bemerton and Wilton (gifts of the Wilton-based earls of Pembroke) in April 1630, shortly after his distant cousin, Philip Herbert, succeeded his brother William as earl of Pembroke. Philip married Anne Clifford in June of that same year, and apparently the former countess of Dorset, and new countess of Pembroke, had a cordial relationship with the poet-priest.[44] By 1630 Lanyer was settled in the greater London parish of St. James, Clerkenwell, with her son, Henry, and his family, many miles from Wilton (near Salisbury, in Wiltshire). Since Milton's father was a musician and a Londoner, it is just possible that Lanyer may have met him—and possibly the younger Milton—through her husband, son, or any of her musician relatives, but there is no record of their meeting.

It seems likely that she would have been familiar with Herbert or Milton's contribution to the rich heritage of religious verse of which her own book was an early part. Herbert's *Temple* was published shortly after his death in 1633, while Milton's *Mask at Ludlow Castle* and *Lycidas* saw print in 1634 and 1637 respectively. She died less than a year before the publication of Milton's *Poems*, which appeared at the very end of 1645; she was buried on April 3.[45] Herbert or Milton may have read Lanyer's book of poems, but again we can only speculate. If Anne Clifford still had her copy, she might have shared it with Herbert. If John Milton senior were acquainted with Alfonso Lanyer, he may have seen or received a copy, since we know Alfonso presented at least one copy to a friend, Thomas Jones, Archbishop of Dublin. But Alfonso prsumably hoped for some favors from Jones, unlikely from Milton senior. The whole search for acquaintance remains highly speculative in any case.

Although there is nothing to suggest that the two great religious poets of sixteenth-century England were influenced by Lanyer's work or that they even knew of it, her poetry still provides, as it did with earlier poets, a new and useful perspective on theirs. Herbert, like Lanyer, explores images of Christ and the relation between Christ and the redeemed soul, and Milton, like Lanyer, is interested in the ideas of freedom and what constitutes virtue beyond earthly beauty. I conclude with a few comparisons between the earlier poet and the later ones.

Poets in the Catholic tradition (including Constable and South-well) could appeal to a variety of saintly models and mediators be-tween themselves and God. Mary Magdalen was popular in a peni-tential climate, the Virgin Mary remained a favorite, and other saints might be cited.[46] For a Protestant poet the only mediator was Christ. While not absent from Catholic poetry, the relationship between the soul and its redeemer in life's pilgrimage continued to be a more common concern of Protestant verse. In the early years of the cen-tury, the Scots poet Elizabeth Melvill, Lady Culros, wrote *Ane Godlie Dreame* to explore the relationship between the Christian soul and Christ in the journey of life.[47] And Greville's lyric sequence ends with an appeal to "sweet *Jesus*" to "fill up time and come, / To yeeld the sinne her everlasting doome."[48]

The connection between the speaker and his redeemer is central to Herbert's poetry, in which he recognizes and explores many ver-sions of that relationship.[49] Lanyer's various and complex portrait of Christ is a worthy backdrop for Herbert's achievement. In the *Salve Deus* her "Jesus of Nazareth" (l. 499) is, first, a betrayed man (l. 329), a "siely, weake, unarmed man" (l. 551), a humble man who embodies "virtue, patience, grace, love, piety" (l. 958). At the same time he is our "maker" (ll. 41, 420), "our heavenly King" (l. 942), and "Heavens bright king" (1088). Only the weeping daughters of Jerusalem under-stand the apparent contradictions, perceiving his divine origin, the force of his sacrifice, and his ultimate triumph: he is "their Lord, their Lover, and their King" (l. 982). The piety of women in Lanyer's poem illustrates the proper response to Christ's great sacrifice of mediat-ing love: they grieve, love, comprehend, and respond. He is both "God in glory, / And . . . man in miserable case" (ll. 1329–30), becom-ing "the Booke / Wherein thine eyes continuelly may looke" (ll. 1351–52), "the Lord of Life and Love" (l. 1362).

Herbert also explores the apparent contradictions between who Christ appears to be and who he ultimately is. "The Sacrifice" might almost be a companion to the *Salve Deus*. In Herbert's poem, Christ speaks the passion story and regards the actions of men, asking: "Was

ever grief like mine?"⁵⁰ In Lanyer's poem, when Christ goes to
Gethsemane with Peter, James, and John, he struggles to tell them
his sorrows. She interjects the apparent uselessness of the task:

> Sweet Lord, how couldst thou thus to flesh and blood
> Communicate thy griefe? Tell of thy woes? (ll. 376–77)

Herbert's Christ observes his sleeping companions:

> Yet my disciples sleep. I cannot gain
> One houre of watching; but their drowsie brain
> Comforts not me, and doth my doctrine staine:
> Was ever grief, &c. (ll. 29–32)

Through the betrayal, abandonment, trial, and crucifixion itself, men
are relentlessly cowardly or wicked, leading to ironic distinctions
between perception and reality. Herbert's Jesus is mocked by soldiers
who do not understand they are speaking the truth:

> They bow their knees to me and cry, *Hail king*:
> What ever scoffes & scornfulnesse can bring, (ll. 173–74)
>   .   .   .   .
> Yet since mans scepters are as frail as reeds,
> And thorny all their crowns, bloudie their weeds;
> I, who am Truth, turn into truth their deeds: (ll. 177–79)

There are no women in Herbert's portrayal, even with mention of
original sin. It is "the earths great curse in *Adams* fall" (l. 165):

> *O all ye who passe by, behold and see;*
> Man stole the fruit, but I must climbe the tree;
> The tree of life to all, but onely me:
> Was ever griefe, &c. (ll. 201–4)

Generic man may be to blame, but specific women are not cited for
particular scorn.

Like Lanyer, Herbert is ultimately concerned with how the redeeming sacrificial act engenders, through grace, the proper response
of love. "The Thanksgiving," which follows "The Sacrifice," begins,
"Oh King of grief!" and seeks an appropriate human reaction to so
great a sacrifice, but concludes that the distance is too great: "Then

for thy passion—I will do for that— / Alas, my God, I know not what"
(ll. 49–50). Poems that follow ask for grace and explore both the nature of Christ and the soul's relationship to its redeemer.

The Protestant triad of "Repentance," "Faith," and "Grace" assures
the connection between the soul and Christ; most of Herbert's poems
explore varieties of that connection.[51] As they are in Lanyer's poem,[52]
the soul's expectations about its relationship with this redeeming
Lord are often surprised in Herbert's lyrics. "The Collar" is a familiar example. The speaker wants freedom and abundance and thinks
it resides in disorder and resistance, only to find it in the ordered call
and submission of the final lines:

> But as I rav'd and grew more fierce and wilde
>   At every word,
> Me thoughts I heard one calling, *Child!*
>   And I reply'd, *My Lord.*[53]

Several Herbert poems consider the ironies of human expectation
and aspiration in the face of Christ's incarnation and passion. "Redemption" is an allegory of tenant and Lord, in which the speaker
knows the Lord's majesty and expects him to be in "great resorts"
but finds him among "theeves and murderers" (ll. 10, 13). More characteristic are the many poems that use mind and art to struggle toward the high complexity of the divine, only to recognize a much
simpler reality. "Easter" begins with complex stanzas tuning up to
praise the great achievement of the resurrection, and concludes with
apparently artless simplicity:

> Can there be any day but this,
> Though many sunnes to shine endeavour?
> We count three hundred, but we misse:
> There is but one, and that one ever. (ll. 27–30)

"Man" brags on the elegance of the microcosm as a "Stately habitation,"
"ev'ry thing," "all symmetrie," and asks finally that God ". . . dwell in
it, / That it may dwell with thee at last" (ll. 2, 7, 13, 50–51). The speaker
in "Jordan II" begins by "curling with metaphors a plain intention" since
"nothing could seeme too rich to clothe the sunne," only to be told
"there is in love a sweetnesse readie penn'd" (ll. 5, 11, 17). In setting personal
experience against traditional expectations, both Herbert and Lanyer
draw surprising conclusions from familiar materials.

Both poets also emphasize the personal and familiar relationship between the soul and Christ. For Lanyer it is found in the Canticles' analogy of bride and bridegroom, which she renders specific to the gender of herself and her dedicatees. Herbert's relationship with Christ is grounded in the loving friendship of a discipleship not specific to gender. "Love III" concludes Herbert's lyric sequence with an image of a (Protestant) memorial meal of love, in which "the friend" keeps overturning the speaker's expectations:

> . . . let my shame
> Go where it doth deserve.
> And know you not, sayes Love, who bore the blame?
> My deare, then I will serve.
> You must sit down, sayes Love, and taste my meat:
> So I did sit and eat. (ll. 13–18)

Of all the religious poets who wrote during Lanyer's lifetime, Herbert comes closest to a view of Christ like Lanyer's in the *Salve Deus*. Despite differences in genres, verse forms, style, and voice, they share a tone of confident exploration into the mystery of the passion and portray Christ as a real and vivid presence in their imaginations and their lives. Lanyer displaces much of the sense of Christ's companionship onto the countess of Cumberland, whereas it is the poetic "I" who does "sit and eat" in Herbert's verse, but the feeling of closeness, and of a directness and simplicity that comprehends complexity, is remarkably similar in the work of these two poets. Lanyer presents a narrative about women reading aright the central story of the human condition, and Herbert portrays a man learning to read that same story.

If women are largely absent from Herbert's verse,[54] they play a prominent role in Milton's. Lanyer's "Eves Apologie" and her portrait of women generally compare interestingly with Milton's depiction of Eve in *Paradise Lost* and of women throughout his work. Lanyer's Eve wants to give her beloved the gift of knowledge (ll. 801–2), while Milton's fallen Eve offers Adam the fruit in order to assure she does not die alone (IX.826–31). Milton's Dalila is vain and self-serving and would enjoy dominating Samson in a voluptuous bed (*Samson*, ll. 920–27). In Lanyer's poem, even temptresses such as Cleopatra and the queen of Sheba affirm great love and seek wisdom (ll. 1441, 1569–78). The shepherd-speaker in "Lycidas," if he seeks fame both earthly and divine, must reject the temptation "To sport with *Amaryllis* in the shade, / Or with the tangles of *Neaera's* hair" (ll. 68–69). By no means does he take "Knowledge . . . / From *Eves* faire hand, as from a learned Booke" (*Salve Deus*, ll. 807–8).

The debate over Milton and women has been amply considered elsewhere.[55] I want to suggest that there is more similarity between Lanyer's and Milton's approach than it might at first appear. Both retell biblical stories and take imaginative liberties with Scripture in order to comment on contemporary practices. Both intrude a personal voice that claims its authority from divine inspiration. And both challenge the traditional understanding of the fall and redemption. While Milton generally follows contemporary teaching about the sexes, including the biblical story of Eve being formed from Adam (Gen. 2:21–23), and of women's consequent secondary status ("Hee for God only, shee for God in him" [IV.299]),[56] the two poets nonetheless draw similar conclusions about female beauty as both an emblem of the divine and a serious danger.

Like Milton's Eve, Lanyer's women may be tempted by their own beauty not to look farther than surface loveliness and the satisfactions it can bring. Faire Rosamond's beauty

> . . . betraid her thoughts, aloft to clime,
> To build strong castles in uncertaine aire,
> Where th'infection of a wanton crime
> Did worke her fall. (ll. 227–30)

True beauty, represented by the devoted virtue of the countess of Cumberland, transcends Helen's, "that bred in *Troy* the ten yeares strife" (l. 209), and cowardly Cleopatra's, who "flies . . . from him [Antony] when afflictions prove" (l. 1435). Cleopatra's "Beauty wrought the hazard of her Crowne" (l. 1448). By contrast (and in the example of the countess):

> A mind enrich'd with Virtue, shines more bright,
> Addes everlasting Beauty, gives true grace,
>   Frames an immortall Goddesse on the earth. (ll. 197–99)

Milton's Eve is at first tempted by her own beauty to stay gazing reflectively. Soon after her awakening, she encounters her image in a "Smooth Lake":

                          . . . . there I had fixed
        Mine eyes till now, and pin'd with vain desire,
        Had not a voice thus warn'd me, What thou seest,
        What there thou seest fair Creature is thyself. (IV. 459, 465–68)

The voice leads her to Adam, whom she finds "less fair, / Less winning soft, less amiably mild, / Than that smooth wat'ry image"
(IV.478–80). She turns back, only to be called by Adam, through
whom she learns

        How beauty is excell'd by manly grace
        And wisdom, which alone is truly fair. (IV.490–91)

    In Milton's version, Eve's fall may hearken back to her vulnerabil-
ity to the visually appealing. The Serpent is outwardly beautiful
(IX.49–505) and his feigned affectionate indignation makes its way into
her mind, yet the beautiful fruit is the principal attraction:

        Fixt on the Fruit she gaz'd, which to behold
        Might tempt alone, and in her ears the sound
        Yet rung of his persuasive words, impregn'd
        With Reason, to her seeming, and with Truth;
        Meanwhile the hour of Noon drew on, and wak'd
        An eager appetite, rais'd by the smell
        So savory of that Fruit, which with desire,
        Inclinable now grown to touch or taste,
        Solicited her longing eye. (IX.735–43)

She is tempted by knowledge, but seduced by beauty and appetite.
    While confusing surface beauty and self-love with wisdom and
proper desire appears to be paradigmatically female in this section
of *Paradise Lost*, Adam's fall arguably stems from his own inability
to see Eve as other than a reflection of himself. The appeal of beauty
and narcissism are general, not necessarily gendered, dangers:

                          . . . . I feel
        The Link of Nature draw me: Flesh of Flesh,
        Bone of my Bone thou art, and from thy State
        Mine never shall be parted, bliss or woe. (IX.914–16)

After the fall, beauty and desire bring pain, and gender hierarchy is no longer a natural compatibility but an imposed tyranny, as Milton paraphrases God's judgment of Eve (Gen. 3:16):

> Thy sorrow I will greatly multiply
> By thy Conception; Children thou shalt bring
> In sorrow forth, and to thy husband's will
> Thine shall submit, hee over thee shall rule. (X. 193–96)

Although both poets acknowledge that Eve was tempted and deceived, they write differently the motives and consequences. Lanyer's Eve desires knowledge and has no reason to disbelieve the Serpent who offers it, while Adam, attracted by the fruit she offers him, indulges his appetite.

> If *Eve* did erre, it was for knowledge sake,
> The fruit beeing faire perswaded him to fall:
>> No subtill Serpents falshood did betray him,
>> If he would eate it, who had powre to stay him?
>
> Not *Eve,* whose fault was only too much love.
> Which made her give this present to her Deare,
> That what shee tasted, he likewise might prove,
> Whereby his knowledge might become more cleare;
> He never sought her weaknesse to reprove,
> With those sharpe words, which he of God did heare:
> Yet Men will boast of Knowledge, which he tooke
> From *Eves* faire hand, as from a learned Booke. (ll. 797–808)

In a common response to those who placed the blame for the fall entirely on Eve, Lanyer uses Eve's derivation from Adam as another reason to turn the argument around:

> If any Evill did in her remaine,
> Beeing made of him, he was the ground of all. (ll. 809–10)

Lanyer's version of the passion does not ignore the gender hierarchy, but valorizes a specifically female piety. Pilate's wife concludes her apology for Eve by implying that Christ's crucifixion will so debase men that women will be liberated from their curse of submission:

> Her weaknesse did the Serpents words obay;
> But you in malice Gods deare Sonne betray.

> Whom, if unjustly you condemne to die,
> Her sinne was small, to what you do commit;
> All mortall sinnes that doe for vengeance crie,
> Are not to be compared unto it. (ll. 815–20)

> . . . .

> Then let us have our Libertie againe,
> And challendge to your selves no Sov'raigntie;
> You came not in the world without our paine,
> Make that a barre against your crueltie;
> Your fault beeing greater, why should you disdaine
> Our beeing your equals, free from tyranny? (ll. 825–30)

The virtues Lanyer praises in her women are similar to what Adam learns to value at the end of *Paradise Lost*. The modest countess of Cumberland embodies the powerful devotion to Christ and to inward virtue that surpasses the achievements of Old Testament heroines Deborah, Judith, and Susanna (ll. 1481–1542). She is constant in "Gods true service" (l. 1516), and spends "that pretious time that God hath sent, / In all good exercises of the minde" (ll. 1566–67). The queen of Sheba, who sought wisdom from Solomon, is a "faire map of majestie and might," but only "a figure of thy deerest Love" (ll. 1609–10). The countess understands Christ's Passion and redemption:

> Pure thoughted Lady, blessed be thy choyce
> Of this Almightie, everlasting King. (ll. 1673–74)

Milton's Adam (and presumably the dreaming Eve [XII.610–13]) learn the lessons that Lanyer's countess of Cumberland already knows. "Henceforth I learn," he says, "that to obey is best, / And love with fear the only God" (XII.561–62); that God is

> Merciful over all his works, with good
> Still overcoming evil, and by small
> Accomplishing great things, by things deem'd weak
> Subverting worldly strong, and worldly wise
> By simply meek; that suffering for Truth's sake
> Is fortitude to highest victory,

And to the faithful Death the Gate of Life;
Taught this by his example whom I now
Acknowledge my Redeemer ever blest. (XII.565–573)

For both Lanyer and Milton, wisdom and virtue are true beauty, humility true strength, and "Death the Gate of Life." These cliches of Christian belief arise from different impulses and are differently presented and differently gendered. Yet both poets have a love of liberty, seen as a restored hope for the human condition after Christ's redemptive grace. For Lanyer "libertie" may seem a particularly gendered emancipation from masculine tyranny, which is how it is expressed in *Eves Apologie*, yet an idea of liberty underlies the entire poem and is implicitly connected with her advocacy of true beauty as the virtue which chooses the right lover (Christ) and the right course of action. Lanyer blesses the countess of Cumberland's "choyce" of Christ and so inscribes her freedom. Milton was of course a great advocate of freedom, "religious, domestic, and civil," and in *Areopagitica* makes a connection Lanyer might have applauded: "when God gave [Adam] reason, he gave him freedom to choose, for reason is but choosing."[57] Lanyer has Pilate's wife ask for "libertie" from the domination of men in a context that praises knowledge and suggests that men have the power to choose against the crucifixion. If they choose to crucify Christ (as historically they did and memorially they might continue to do), that frees women to choose not to submit to men. The first choice must always be, as exemplified by the figure of the countess, for Christ.

Lanyer and Milton both advocate knowledgeable choice; both put God's word and Christ's example ahead of society's rules. Milton excused the killing of a king and advocated representative government.[58] Lanyer, by contrast, merely suggested that women have the right to choose their own faith and pursue their own virtue. Milton was read, and risked imprisonment or worse at the Restoration. As far as we know, Lanyer was simply ignored.

Aemilia Lanyer is an impressive and worthy member of the group of poets who founded the great century of English religious verse. Her approach to biblical materials and doctrinal issues is original and interesting, providing perspective and commentary on the varieties of more familiar Catholic and Protestant verse. Her wit and her richly descriptive passages follow both Southwell and Greville and anticipate Crashaw as well as Milton. Her voice triangulates the complex struggle of Donne and the achieved simplicity of Herbert with a view from outside the center of worldly power, inside the center of female virtue. Lanyer was invisible when most of the current generation of professors was in college and graduate school, but it is increasingly difficult to imagine a full understanding of early seventeenth-century English poetry without her.

NOTES

Preface

1. On the vexed development of print culture and identity as an author, see Wendy Wall, *The Imprint of Gender: Authorship and Publication in the English Renaissance* (Ithaca: Cornell Univ. Press, 1993), 1–22 and passim (on Lanyer, 319–30); on the rise of professionalism, see Edwin Haviland Miller, *The Professional Writer in Elizabethan England* (Cambridge, MA: Harvard Univ. Press, 1959) and Richard Helgerson, *Self-Crowned Laureates: Spenser, Jonson, Milton and the Literary System* (Berkeley: Univ. of California Press, 1983).

Helgerson uses the term "laureate" to serve as a better term than "professional" for the development of a particular literary self-assertion that leads ultimately to a public and official laureateship (for John Dryden and later poets). He makes the point that professional is too easily contrasted with personal or private, and that "laureate" poets sought to represent a complete identity in the construction of their art and (and as) themselves (4–14). While accepting much of Helgerson's argument, I use the term "professional" both because the self-presentation through naming, important to Jonson and Milton, is less possible for a woman poet who may change her last name more than once in a lifetime, and because the distinction between public and private remained of severe importance for women in this period. Hence the *Salve Deus Rex Judaeorum* is in continuous tension between praise of particular women and of their supposed spiritual interiority.

2. On Lock, see Patrick Collinson, "The Role of Women in the English Reformation Illustrated by the Life and Friendships of Anne Locke," in his book *Godly People: Essays on English Protestantism and Puritanism* (London: 1983), 273–87; Elaine Beilin, *Redeeming Eve: Women Writers of the English Renaissance* (Princeton: Princeton Univ. Press, 1987), 61–63; Margaret P. Hannay, "'Unlock my lipps': the *Miserere mei Deus* of Anne Vaughan Lok and Mary Sidney Herbert, Countess of Pembroke," in *Privileging Gender in Early Modern England*, Sixteenth Century Essays and Studies, vol. 23, ed. Jean R. Brink, *Sixteenth Century Journal*; and Susanne Woods, "The Body Penitent: a 1560 Calvinist Sonnet Sequence," *American Notes and Queries* 5 (April–July 1992), ed. Anne Lake Prescott, 137–40. On Whitney, Dowriche, and Colville, see Beilin, 88–110; on the countess of Pembroke, see Margaret P. Hannay, *Philip"s Phoenix: Mary Sidney, Countess of Pembroke* (Oxford: Oxford Univ. Press, 1990); Beilin, 121–50; and Mary Ellen Lamb, *Gender and Authorship in the Sidney Circle* (Madison, WI: Univ. of Wisconsin Press, 1990), 115–41. On Queen Elizabeth I, see Leicester Bradner, ed., *The Poems of Queen Elizabeth* (Providence: Brown Univ. Press, 1964); Frances

Teague, "Queen of England: Elizabeth I," in *Women Writers of the Renaissance and Reformation*, ed. Katharina Wilson (Athens, GA: Univ. of Georgia Press, 1987), 522–47; on her connection with Marguerite of Navarre, see Beilin, 67–72, and Anne Lake Prescott, "The Pearl of Valois and Elizabeth I: Marguerite de Navarre's *Miroir* and Tudor England," in *Silent but for the Word: Tudor Women as Patrons, Translators, and Writers of Religious Works*, ed. Margaret P. Hannay (Kent, OH: Kent State Univ. Press, 1985), 61–76.

3. E.g., at least two noble Italian women writers were widely recognized before the middle of the sixteenth century: Vittoria Colonna (d. 1547) and Veronica Gambara (d. 1550). The poems of the talented courtesan Gaspara Stampa, arguably Italy's first major woman poet, were published shortly after her death in the 1550s. In France, Marguerite of Navarre was widely recognized as a writer as well as noble partisan of her brother, Francis I. Louise Labé (d. 1566), much-praised intellectual of Lyon, published her *Euvres* in 1555; they were prominent enough even in England for Robert Greene to publish a partial translation, *The Debate Between Folly and Love*, in 1584. See the introduction by Katharina Wilson and the essays by Frank Warnke, Joseph Gibaldi, Richard Poss, Marcel Tetel, and Jeanne Prine in Wilson, *Women Writers*; Keith Cameron, *Louise Labé: Feminist and Poet of the Renaissance* (New York: St. Martin's, 1990); Patricia H. Labalme, ed., *Beyond Their Sex: Learned Women of the European Past* (New York: New York Univ. Press, 1984); Ann Rosalind Jones, *The Currency of Eros: Women's Love Lyric in Europe 1540–1620* (Bloomington, IN: Univ. of Indiana Press, 1990).

4. Edward Arber, ed., *A Transcript of the Registers of the Company of Stationers of London, 1554–1640*, vol. 2 (London, 1875), entries for 22 Dec. 1608, 28 Jan., 22 Feb., and 25 Apr., 1609 (all dates are new style). R. B. McKerrow et al., *A Dictionary of Printers and Booksellers in England, Scotland, and Ireland, and of Foreign Printers of English Books, 1557–1640* (London: Bibliographical Society, 1910), 245–26: "From the outset of his career, [Simmes] was constantly in trouble for printing books that were obnoxious to the authorities." This includes an arrest in 1589 for his involvement with the Marprelate tracts. Between 1597 and 1604 he also printed several of Shakespeare's plays (*Richard II* and *Richard III* in 1587; *Henry IV, Part 2* and *Much Ado about Nothing* in 1600; and a second edition of *Henry IV, Part 1* in 1604). See 42–43 for the entry on Bonion.

5. For another definition of "diachronic," see Susanne Woods, "Amazonian Tyranny: Spenser's Radigund and Diachronic Mimesis," in *Playing with Gender: A Renaissance Pursuit*, ed. Jean R. Brink et al. (Urbana: Univ. of Illinois Press, 1991), 52–61.

6. On time and light cones, see Stephen Hawking, *A Brief History of Time, from the Big Bang to Black Holes* (New York: Bantam, 1988), 24–28.

7. See James Gleick, *Chaos: The Making of a New Science* (New York: Penguin, 1987) and Shelley Turkle, *Life on the Screen: Identity in the Age of the Internet* (New York: Simon & Schuster, 1995).

1. Lanyer in Her World

1. The baptismal record of "Emillia Baptist" is in the Parish Register of St. Botolph's Bishopsgate, Guildhall Library 4515/1; Baptista Bassano was bur-

ied at St. Botolph's Bishopsgate 11 April 1576, Margaret Johnson on 7 July 1587 (Guildhall Library 4515/1); Baptista Bassano's will is in the London Public Record Office (henceforward PRO), Prob. 11/58, ff. 153–54; Margaret Bassano's will is in the Guildhall Library, St. Paul's Ms. 25,626/2, f. 302; Aemilia Lanyer's burial is recorded in *A True Register of all the Chr[is]teninges, Mariages, and Burialles in the Parishe of St. James, Clarkenwell, from the yeare of our Lorde God 1551*, ed. Robert Hovenden (London, Harleian Society, 1891), 263. Mary, Queen of Scots arrived in England on 16 May 1568; references to events surrounding her early years in England and the role of Lord Hunsdon are from Wallace T. MacCaffrey, *The Shaping of the Elizabethan Regime: Elizabethan Politics, 1558–1572* (Princeton: Princeton Univ. Press, 1968), 243, 247–67, 330–53. All dates are new style.

2. International Genealogical Index, the Greater London Historical Library, published by the Church of Jesus Christ of the Latter Day Saints (hereafter referred to as "IGI, Greater London"); David Lasocki, *The Bassanos: Venetian Musicians and Instrument Makers in England, 1531–1665* (Brookfield, VT: Scolar Press, 1995), 184, 201. This treasure of information about the Bassanos includes chapters co-written with Roger Prior about Aemilia and Alfonso Lanyer.

3. Guildhall Library, St. Paul's, Ms. 25,626/2, f. 302; Lasocki, 46; George S. Fry, ed. *Abstracts of Inquisitiones Post Mortem Relating to the City of London* (London, 1896–1908), vol. 3, 145–46.

4. The record is unclear. Fry, vol. 3, 145, refers to *"Angela Holland* then the wife of *Joseph Holland,* gent., and *Emelia Bassany* daughter of the said Margaret." Margaret's own will, however, refers to Jospeh Holland as her "sonne in Law" (Guildhall Library, St. Paul's GB-lgl, Ms. 25,626/2, f. 302).

5. Except where otherwise indicated, all information on the Bassano family is derived from Lasocki, esp. xxiii–xxviii, 3–68. I have followed his conventions of naming (xxxi–xxxiv), including "Baptista" instead of "Baptist" for Aemilia's father.

6. According to his will, witnessed 3 January and proved 7 July 1576, Baptista was "a native of Venice and one of the Musitions of our Sovereigne Ladye the Quenes majestie" (PRO Prob. 11/58, f. 153).

7. *OED,* "Repute, v," 2b.

8. Lasocki, 27; Huntington Library Ms. Ellesmere 2652, f. 13.

9. Roger Prior's article, "More (Moor?) (Moro?) Light on the Dark Lady," *Financial Times* (London), Oct. 10, 1987, 17, claims this origin, and critics have been quick to accept it. See, e.g., the introduction to Lanyer in James Fitmaurice et al., eds., *Major Women Writers of Seventeenth-Century England* (Ann Arbor: Univ. of Michigan Press, 1997), which refers to Lanyer as "probably of Jewish ancestry," 23. Prior develops his case most fully in Lasocki ("The Bassanos' Jewish Identity," 92–98, and "Coat of Arms," 80–83), and I borrow his arguments for this discussion.

10. Lewalski, 137; Prior, in Lasocki, 80. For evidence of the fad, see T. Moffet, *The Silkwormes and Their Flies* (1599). I am grateful to Katherine Duncan-Jones for this reference.

11. Prior, in Lasocki, 95.

12. A. L. Rowse, *Simon Forman: Sex and Society in Shakespeare's Age* (London: Weidenfeld and Nicolson, 1974); Prior, in Lasocki, "Was Emilia the Dark Lady?" 114–39. I will have more to say about their arguments in chapter 3.

13. See, e.g., Jasper Ridley, *Henry VIII: The Politics of Tyranny* (New York: Viking, 1985), 413, and John N. King, *English Reformation Literature: The Tudor Origins of the Protestant Tradition* (Princeton: Princeton Univ. Press, 1982), 23, 76.

14. Stephen Vaughan the elder, who died in 1550, was a merchant ambassador for Henry VIII in the low countries (notably Antwerp) and an early supporter of English Protestantism. At the dissolution of the monasteries in 1538 Thomas Cromwell granted him the mansion house and considerable property around St. Mary Spital in the parish of St. Botolph's Bishopsgate. When this became his widow's principal place of residence she and the younger Stephen became neighbors of the Bassanos; the Vaughans' St. Mary Spital tenants included Sir Thomas Wyatt the younger, Kentish leader of a failed Protestant effort to challenge or overthrow Mary Tudor in 1554 (Fry, 86; Penry Williams, *The Later Tudors: England 1547–1603* [Oxford: Clarendon Press, 1995], 93–97). The Vaughan property passed to the younger Stephen at the latter's majority in 1558. Fry, vol. 1, 85–87, 178; W. C. Richardson, *Stephen Vaughan, Financial Agent of Henry VIII: A Study of Financial Relations with the Low Countries* (Baton Rouge: Louisiana State Univ., Social Science Ser., 3).

15. On Catherine (Willoughby Brandon) Bertie, dowager countess of Suffolk, and her continental exile, see Lady Cecilie Goff, *A Woman of the Tudor Age* (London: John Murray, 1930), 219–51. For further discussion of Lanyer's relation to Susan Bertie, see later in this chapter. For Simmes's career, see R. B. McKerrow et al., *A Dictionary of Printers and Booksellers in England, Scotland and Ireland, and of Foreign Printers of English Books, 1557–1640* (London: Bibliographical Society, 1910), 245–46.

16. Lasocki, 71–75.

17. Goff, 219–28, notes the story's continuing legacy in John Foxe's *Acts and Monuments*, in a popular sixteenth-century ballad, and in Thomas Deloney's *Strange Histories,* c. 1607.

18. In Patrick Collinson, "The Role of Women in the English Reformation Illustrated by the Life and Friendships of Anne Locke," *Godly People: Essays on English Protestantism and Puritanism* (London: The Hambledon Press, 1983), 280. Susan M. Felch, *The Collected Works of Anne Vaughan Lock,* (Tempe, AZ: Medieval & Renaissance Texts & Studies, vol. 185, 1999), "Introduction." See also Susanne Woods, "The Body Penitent: An Early Calvinist Sonnet Sequence," *American Notes and Queries Special Double Issue: Renaissance Studies,* 5 (Apr.–July 1992), ed. Anne Lake Prescott, 137–40.

19. Spenser refers to the countesses of Warwick and Cumberland in his review of those at court during his visit in 1589–91 (*Colin Clouts Come Home Again*, ll. 492–507), which coincides with the most likely period of Aemilia's residency as mistress of Lord Hunsdon. See later in this chapter and chapter 2.

20. King, *English Reformation Literature*, 105. These promising young scholars both died in their early teens, a tragedy for which Wilson wrote a formal consolation to the duchess (Goff, 192–94).

21. See John N. King, "Patronage and Piety: The Influence of Catherine Parr," in *Silent but for the Word: Tudor Women as Patrons, Translators, and Writers of Religious Works*, ed. Margaret P. Hannay (Kent, OH: Kent State Univ. Press, 1985), 43–60.

22. Anne Clifford's father assured his only child a rich education but pro-

hibited Latin (Lewalski, 37), whereas Cooke's daughters were famous Latinists. One of them, Lady Anne Bacon (wife of Nicholas and mother of Francis), earned a lasting role in English church history by translating its first important theological treatise from Latin to English, Bishop John Jewel's *An Apologie, or answer in defence of the Church of England* (1562).

23. Bodleian Ms. Ashmole 226, f. 110v, appears to confirm that Lanyer reported having been "brought up with the Contess of Kent." I was at first reluctant to accept this reading (Forman's hand is very difficult to decipher), but have now looked at the passage several times and had the benefit of Katherine Duncan-Jones kindly reviewing it as well. This seems the most likely reading after all.

24. It is possible that "ungovern'd" refers to Aemilia's loss of both parents, not just her father, but I think it unlikely. She refers to the countess as "you that were the Mistris of my youth" (l. 1); at eighteen Aemilia would not be considered in her "youth." Also, Susan's marriage to Sir John Wingfield in 1581 would have taken her to Lincolnshire. It is intriguing to think of Aemilia joining the dowager countess's new household at Withcoll, near her husband's aunt, the formidable Elizabeth, countess of Shrewsbury. If Aemilia was in Susan Bertie's service at that time, she very probably met "Bess of Hardwicke" and her royal granddaughter, Arbella Stuart (b. 1575), which would explain the otherwise cryptic reference in Lanyer's poem to Stuart: "Great learned Ladie, whom I long have knowne, / And yet not knowne so much as I desired" (ll. 1–2). See Leeds Barroll, in Marshall Grossman, ed., *Aemilia Lanyer* (Lexington: Univ. of Kentucky Press, 1998).

25. Roger Ascham, *The Scholemaster*, ed. John E. B. Mayor (London, 1863; rpt. New York: AMS Press, 1967), 3–4.

26. *The Poems of Aemilia Lanyer: Salve Deus Rex Judaeorum*, ed. Susanne Woods (New York: Oxford Univ. Press, 1993), 48. All references to Lanyer's works will be to this edition unless otherwise cited.

27. Thomas Wilson, *The Art of Rhetorique* (1560), in *English Literary Criticism: The Renaissance*, ed. O. B. Hardison, Jr. (Englewood Cliffs, NJ: Prentice-Hall, 1963), 41.

28. Wilson, in Hardison, 34.

29. Lewalski, 37.

30. Ascham, in Mayor, xxiii.

31. Ibid., 63.

32. The humanists considered Greek the true linguistic home of civilization (ibid., 52); "Esop," to whom Lanyer refers in "To all vertuous Ladies," l. 27, was recommended as an easy way into Greek for young children. See, e.g., Thomas Elyot's *Boke Named the Governour* (1531), in *The Renaissance in England*, ed. Hyder E. Rollins and Herschel Baker (Lexington, MA: Heath, 1954), 110b.

33. For information on the activities of the countess dowager of Kent I am grateful to Leeds Barroll.

34. Guildhall Library, St. Paul's GB-lgl, Ms. 25,626/2, f. 302.

35. PRO Prob. 11/58, f. 153.

36. Bodleian Ms. Ashmole 226, ff. 95v, 110v.

37. Bodleian Ms. Ashmole 226, ff. 95v, 110v, 201.

38. MacCaffrey (1967), 345; *Dictionary of National Biography* (*DNB*), ed. Leslie Stephen and Sidney Lee (London: Oxford Univ. Press, 1917), 3:977–79.

39. Wallace T. MacCaffrey, *Queen Elizabeth and the Making of Policy, 1572–1588* (Princeton: Princeton Univ. Press, 1981), 411, 421, 436–37; *DNB* 3:978.

40. Steven May, *The Elizabethan Courtier Poets* (Columbia, MO: Univ. of Missouri Press, 1991), 11–12. May's first chapter, "The Social Organization of the Court" (9–40), provides an excellent picture of the world Lanyer was exposed to through her association with the lord chamberlain.

41. Both portraits belong to Mr. R. J. G. Berkeley, to whom I am most grateful for allowing their reproduction, and are at Berkeley Castle. Lord Hunsdon's only surviving granddaughter, Elizabeth, married into the Berkeley family in 1596. As his only heir, she presumably received these portraits when her father died ten years later. The family does not know who the "unknown woman" is supposed to represent. It is tempting to think it might be Lanyer herself, painted shortly before she married Alfonso, but there is no external evidence to support the attribution. Katherine Duncan-Jones thinks it unlikely that a portrait of the lord chamberlain's mistress would be with the family, although one could argue that if Lord Hunsdon wanted a memento of his "long" affair with the beautiful young woman, it might well be with the family's effects, though with the memory of its sitter long since deliberately or accidentally erased. However, in a letter to me about the picture, Catharine MacLeod, Curator of the sixteenth and seventeenth century collections of the National Portrait Gallery, cautions that we cannot even be sure the sitter was a gentlewoman rather than an aristocrat, since "there were plenty of wealthy gentry and plenty of aristocrats who for one reason or another did not adopt the most extreme, lavish form of late Elizabethan costume. . . .[W]ithout documentary evidence it seems likely that the sitter will remain unidentified."

42. Bodleian Ms. Ashmole 226 f. 95v: "she hath bin un chast . . . she hath had a child in fornication"; f. 110v: "she hath a sone his name is henri."

43. Lasocki, 34, 36. Lodovico Bassano, Alvise's second son, was a resident of that parish in 1592. Among those in his own family, Baptista seems to have been closest to Alvise's sons, Augustine and Lodovico, who are mentioned (Lodovico as "Lewis") as residual heirs of the income from his property in the parish of St. Christopher le Stocks. Fry, vol. 3, 10.

44. Lasocki, 106.

45. Lasocki, 106, 34.

46. Andrew Ashbee, *Records of English Court Music (RECM)* 4 (1603–25) (Aldershot: Scolar Press, 1991), 154–55.

47. Bodleian Ms. Ashmole 226, f. 201.

48. Bodleian Ms. Ashmole 354, f. 246; Lasocki, 107–10.

49. Lasocki, 108–9; Woods, xlix.

50. Lasocki, 109.

51. Lasocki, 109–10; *RECM* 154.

52. Bodleian Ms. Ashmole 226, f. 93v: "Millia Lanier of 24 [sic] yeares in Longditch at Westmenster."

53. John Stow, *A Survey of London Conteyning the Originall, Antiquity, Increase, Moderne estate, and description of that City, written in the yeare 1598 . . . Since by that same Author increased* (London, 1603), Everyman ed. (London: J. M. Dent, 1956), 403; see the copperplate map (c. 1559), Museum of London, in Woods, map B, xliv.

54. Bodleian Ms. Ashmole 226, f. 95v.

55. Bodleian Ms. Ashmole 226, f. 110v.

56. This may refer to hope for a knighthood, the explicit issue in the next entries, but more probably means that as of 3 June Alfonso had not yet been appointed to go on the expedition put together by the earl of Essex, Robert Cecil, and Sir Walter Ralegh that would become known as the Islands Voyage. In early June 1597 Sir Walter Ralegh was received back at court after three years of disgrace and put in charge of provisioning an army of 6,000 men for this expedition, whose object was to capture Spanish treasure in Ferrol and the Azores. The success of the Cadiz expedition of the previous year sparked hope for advancement among the "gentlemen volunteers" of this new enterprise. William Stebbing, *Sir Walter Ralegh* (Oxford: Clarendon Press, 1891), 133–40.

57. Bodleian Ms. Ashmole 226, f. 122v; see n. 56. The fleet encountered storms and returned to Plymouth a few days after setting out, then sat in the harbor until setting out again on August 18. Stebbing, 134, 136.

58. Bodleian Ms. Ashmole 226, f. 201.

59. A. L. Rowse, *The Poems of Shakespeare's Dark Lady* (London: Jonathan Cape, 1978), "Introduction"; in Lasocki, Prior follows Rowse's assumptions, 114–39.

60. Bodleian Ms. Ashmole 226, f. 222v; Bodleian Ms. Ashmole 236, f. 5.

61. Bodleian Ms. Ashmole 354, f. 246.

62. Bodleian Ms. Ashmole 354, f. 246.

63. IGI, Greater London.

64. Lasocki, 107.

65. Lasocki, 107–10.

66. Lasocki, 110.

67. Lewalski, 234; Lewalski, 216 and 396, n. 21, summarizes all that we know about Margaret and Anne's occupancy of Cookham.

68. Lewalski, 136–37, 216–17.

69. Pamela Benson, in a paper delivered at the Renaissance Society of America Annual Meeting in Bloomington, Indiana, April 1996.

70. The painting, now at Appleby Castle, Cumbria, is reproduced in Lewalski, 124.

71. Lewalski, 127–33, 150–51, summarizes the courage and relentlessness of Anne Clifford's insistence on her inheritance.

72. Joan Rees, *Samuel Daniel: A Critical and Biographical Study* (Liverpool: Liverpool Univ. Press, 1964), 76, n. 19. See also G. C. Williamson, *Lady Anne Clifford* (Kendal: T. Wilson and Son, 1922), 66 and 494–95.

73. Lasocki, 104–6.

74. PRO Chancery Case, C2/ James I L11/64.

75. Woods, xxi-xxii.

76. *Grove's Dictionary of Music & Musicians: Supplementary Volume to the Fifth Edition*, ed. Eric Blom (London: Macmillan, 1961), 258a. There is some confusion over whether Henry had a son named Andrea (see also 257b), but I have found no evidence of a son with that name, unless the name "Henry" is incorrect for the son in the baptismal record.

77. IGI, Greater London; Guildhall Library 9050/6 (1633 Reg. 6, 134v; 1634 Reg. 6, 145).

78. Lasocki, 104–5.

79. *A True Register of all the Chr[is]teninges, Mariages, and Burialles in the Parishe of St. James, Clerkenwell, from the yeare of our Lord God 1551*, ed. Robert Hovenden (London: Harleian Society, 1891), 210 (Henry Lanyer) and 263 (Aemilia Lanyer).

80. Joan Rees, *Samuel Daniel: A Critical and Biographical Study* (Liverpool: Liverpool Univ. Press, 1964), 1–5.

81. Rees, 7–11; Margaret P. Hannay, *Philip's Phoenix: Mary Sidney, Countess of Pembroke* (Oxford: Oxford Univ. Press, 1990), 162–63.

82. *Colin Clouts Come Home Again*, ll. 416–27:

> And there is a new shepheard late up sprong,
> The which doth all afore him far surpasse:
> Appearing well in that well tuned song,
> Which late he sung unto a scornfull lasse.
> Yet doth his trembling *Muse* but lowly flie,
> As daring not too rashly mount on hight,
> And doth her tender plumes as yet but trie,
> In loves soft laies and looser thoughts delight.
> Then rouze thy feathers quickly *Daniell*,
> And to what course thou please thy selfe advance:
> But most me seemes, thy accent will excell,
> In Tragick plaints and passionate mischance.

Edwin Greenlaw et al. eds., *The Works of Edmund Spenser: A Variorum Edition*, vol. 7, *Minor Poems: Part One* (Baltimore: Johns Hopkins Univ. Press, 1943).

83. "Cumberland was a particularly enthusiastic participant in the court's military spectacles. . . . On Accession day in 1590 [Sir Henry] Lee resigned to Cumberland his place as the queen's tiltyard champion," May, 247; "Sir Edward Dymoke, the Queen's Champion . . . was . . . Daniel's first patron, and the association, however it began, lasted over a number of years," Rees, 5.

84. Hannay, 118–29; Rees, 50.

85. Rees, 76. George Clifford "was too occupied in making piratical voyages to the West Indies or the Mediterranean to spend much time with [Margaret], but his infidelities were notorious." Margaret had apparently developed a reputation for pious endurance well before the death of her husband in 1605, which provided for a deathbed reconciliation, though not the generous inheritance of his lands that Margaret wanted for her daughter, Anne. See Lewalski, 133–36.

86. Lasocki, 108–9.

87. Williams, 385–86, 371, 261 (on Norfolk's execution), 33 (on Surrey's execution).

88. Williams, 371, 374.

89. Alexander B. Grosart, ed., *The Complete Works in Verse and Prose of Samuel Daniel* (5 vols. (London: Hazel, Watson and Viney, 1885–96) reissued New York: Russell & Russell, 1963), vol. 1, 10. The letter also thanks Egerton for "the preferment of my brother," the musician, John Daniel, "who took the degree of Bachelor of Music at Christ Church College, Oxford, on June 14, 1604, published a collection of songs in 1606, and was a member of the royal com-

pany of the 'musicians for the lutes and voices' in December 1625" (Rees, 2). John Daniel the musician seems to have been close to his brother, who had Queen Anne sign over a patent to him in 1619 (Rees, 166). John also supervised the 1623 posthumous edition of Samuel Daniel's *Works*.

90. Rees, 150 and *passim*.

91. Linda Woodbridge, *Women and the English Renaissance: Literature and the Nature of Womankind, 1540–1620* (Urbana: Univ. of Illinois Press, 1984), 143–44 and *passim*; Jonathan Goldberg, *James I and the Politics of Literature* (Baltimore: Johns Hopkins Univ. Press), 33–54, 85–89; Lewalski, 15–43; Rees, 89–121, 147–49, 157–66. Joy over the transition from queen to king has even affected the rhetoric of some recent historians, such as J. P. Kenyon, *Stuart England* (New York: Penguin, 1978): "[James's] advent was welcome. Queen Elizabeth had long outlived men's affection, if not their fear and respect, and after fifty years of petticoat rule (since Mary I's accession in 1553), they welcomed a male ruler, and the end of female tantrums, sulks and irrationality," 48.

92. Eve Sanders, *Gender and Literacy on Stage in Early Modern England* (Cambridge: Cambridge Univ. Press, 1998), 132. See also 218, n. 58. I am grateful to Professor Sanders for pointing out the difference between these two versions, and sharing page proofs of her book with me.

93. In Grosart, vol. 1, 138.

94. Rees, 34–38.

95. First published in 1597 and reprinted with his *Works* in 1605, 1608, 1610, 1613, 1617, and 1619.

96. Facsimile of *Delia with the Complaint of Rosamond* (1592), (London: Scolar Press, 1969); all citations from *Delia* and *Rosamond* will be from this (first) edition.

97. Hannay, 116–19. Hannay admits the case is tentative, but it is as logical as anything yet put forth. See Rees, 13–21.

2. Lanyer and Spenser

1. The chamberlain was one of three chiefs of the royal household (the others were the steward, responsible for such support areas as the pantry and laundry, and the master of the horse, responsible for the royal stables). The chamberlain's areas of oversight included the chapel, with its sixty to seventy musicians, and court entertainments. Stephen May, *The Elizabethan Courtier Poets* (Columbia: Univ. of Missouri Press, 1991), 11–12.

2. Edwin Greenlaw et al., eds. *The Works of Edmund Spenser: A Variorum Edition*, vol. 7, *Minor Poems: Part One*, (Baltimore: Johns Hopkins University Press, 1943), 158. All references to Spenser's poetry are from this *Variorum Edition* (vols. 1–10, 1932–49). See Alexander C. Judson, *The Life of Edmund Spenser*, vol. 11 of Greenlaw et al., *Works of Spenser: Variorum Ed.*, 139–55, for what we know (and Judson imagines) of Spenser's visit to court.

3. Both poems were among a second group of seven, added to a first group of ten while the printing was in process (Judson, 143).

4. Described as "Faire *Marian*, the *Muses* onely darling: / Whose beautie shyneth as the morning cleare, / With silver deaw upon the roses pearling" (*CCCHA*, ll. 505–7). She is the sister of "*Theana*," who is readily identifiable as

Anne, countess of Warwick, recently widowed. Anne's late husband was Ambrose Dudley, brother of Elizabeth's favorite, Robert, earl of Leicester, and uncle of Mary Sidney, countess of Pembroke, who, as *"Urania,"* is the only lady of the court—other than the queen herself—to precede Anne and Margaret in Colin/Spenser's list of worthy ladies. See also Judson, 146–47.

5. The monument was erected in 1620 (Judson, 207; Lewalski, 139). Margaret was not at court in January 1590; she gave birth to her daughter Anne at Skipton Castle, Yorkshire, on January 30. She was probably around the court on May 1, 1589, however; Anne reports that she was conceived then in the city of Westminster (Lewalski, 126).

6. Abraham Fraunce cites from *FQ* II in *The Arcadian Rhetorike* (1588), and Marlowe borrows from Spenser in *2 Tamburlaine* (c. 1587). Some sense of Spenser's early fame can be glimpsed in the citations collected by R. M. Cummings, ed., *Spenser: The Critical Heritage* (New York: Barnes & Noble, 1971), 35–62, 277–82, and from Samuel Daniel's comments, 74–76.

7. See the references in Cummings, 49, 53, 55, 79 and *passim*. Spenser was also frequently compared with classical and continental writers, notably Petrarch; Ralegh's commendatory poem to the *Faerie Queene* contains one of the most moving tributes (Cummings, 66):

> All suddeinly I saw the Faery Queene:
> At whose approch the soul of *Petrarke* wept,
> And from thenceforth those graces were not seene.
> For they this Queene attended, in whose steed
> Oblivion laid him downe on *Lauras* herse. (ll. 6–9)

8. Spenser's female audience was important to him. Not only did his primary hope of preferment reside with his queen, but he wrote in genres—sonnets, epithalamia, romance—that were expected to appeal to women, as well as to show off his masculine force as the public poet and laureate, blazing and defining the national virtue. Spenser declares the "generall end" of *The Faerie Queene* to be "to fashion a gentleman or noble person in vertuous and gentle discipline," with "noble person" gender neutral. ("A Letter of the Authors . . . to . . . *Sir Walter Ralegh*" [usually referred to as the "Letter to Ralegh"], Greenlaw et al., *Variorum Ed.*, vol. 1, 167. Suzanne W. Hull rightly lists *The Faerie Queene* among Renaissance books intended for women readers, in *Chaste, Silent and Obedient* (San Marino, CA: Huntington Library Press, 1982).

9. *Oxford English Dictionary*. (I use the 1971 compact version of the *OED*.) References will continue to be cited parenthetically in the text.

10. E.g., W. L. Renwick, *Edmund Spenser* (London: Edwin Arnold, 1925) 125: "In *Colin Clouts Come Home Again* . . . the meeting of the poets, the Ovidian horror of the sea, the panegyric upon a monarch, the courteous commendation of friends and brother-poets, the attack on court life, the celebration of a mistress—in all these passages literary and personal motives and interests are inextricably bound up together; and we must accept them together and try to appreciate both at the same time." See also William Nelson, *The Poetry of Edmund Spenser* (New York: Columbia Univ. Press, 1963), chapter 2.

11. Judson, 155.

12. Bodleian Ms. Ashmole 226, f. 201 (2 Sept. 1597).

13. Greenlaw et al., eds., *Variorum Ed.*, vols. 1, 2.

14. See Frederick Morgan Padelford and Josephine Waters Bennett in Greenlaw et al., *Variorum Ed.*, vol. 1, 506–12, for the debate over which muse is being invoked; yet another possibility is Urania, muse of astronomy and so the "heavenly" Muse, perhaps the most closely allied to the idea of "holy" in Spenser's descriptive epithet, "holy Virgin."

15. E.g., like God, Elizabeth's dazzling "exceeding light" can only be presented veiled by allegory (2.proem.5), and she is described as "that sacred Saint my soveraigne Queene" (4.proem.4) and "Dread Soverayne Goddesse, that doest highest sit / In seate of judgement, in th'Almighties stead" (5.proem.11).

16. In May, see poems to the queen such as Essex's "To plead my faith where faith hath noe reward," 253, and Ferdinando, Lord Strange's "If ever man did live in *Fortune's* scorne," 370. See also Sir Walter Ralegh's several poems to the queen, in Agnes Latham, ed., *The Poems of Sir Walter Ralegh* (Cambridge, MA: Harvard Univ. Press, 1962): "Calling to minde mine eie long went about," "Praisd be Dianas faire and harmles light," "Like truthles dreames, so are my joyes expired," 10–12, and the Cynthia poems, 24–44.

The courtly love tradition figured the lady as a feudal lord with the lover her vassal; Elizabeth was able to use this tradition to reinforce its literal parallel in her relationships with male courtiers.

17. As in the standard doctrine of "the King's two bodies," to which Spenser often alludes in *The Faerie Queene*, e.g. in 2.proem.5:

> Ne let his fairest Cynthia refuse
> In mirrours more than one her selfe to see,
> But either Gloriana let her chuse,
> Or in Belphoebe fashioned to bee:
> 　In th'one her rule, in th'other her rare chastitie.

18. As Lewalski notes: "In the opening dedication to Queen Anne, Lanyer laments that she does not now enjoy the associations and favors of that earlier time, when 'great *Elizaes* favour blest my youth' . . . intimating that the present Queen might like to renew that happy condition" (220).

19. In the dedications, the proems, and in such passages as the Mt. Acidale of book 6.10, where the presence of the queen's glory is an explicit backdrop (6.10.28).

20. Margaret's sister Ann (not Marie) was the dowager countess of Warwick. She had been married to Ambrose Dudley (d. 1590), brother of the earl of Leicester.

21. Greenlaw et al., *Variorum Ed.*, vol. 7, 193.

22. Ibid., 657–62; Nelson, 99–100; Enid Welsford, *Fowre Hymnes, Epithalamion: A Study of Edmund Spenser's Doctrine of Love* (Oxford: Basil Blackwell, 1967), 48; Mary I. Oates, "*Fowre Hymnes*: Spenser's Retractations of Paradise," *Spenser Studies* 4 (1984), 143–69.

23. Oates, 164; William C. Johnson, "Spenser's 'Greener' *Hymnes* and *Amoretti*: 'Retractation' and 'Reform,'" *English Studies* 5 (1992), 431–43; Nelson, 102–4: "the heavenly hymns oppose Christ to Cupid and Sapience to Venus. At the same time, these oppositions declare the relationships, however distant,

between the blind generative passion of beasts and the love of Christ, between the beauty of mundane creation and the unimaginable splendor of God" (104). See also Benjamin G. Lockerd, Jr., *The Sacred Marriage: Psychic Integration in* The Faerie Queene (Lewisburg: Bucknell Univ. Press, 1987): "Spenser . . . hints to his reader [in the dedication to the countesses of Cumberland and Warwick] that his purpose in printing the two pairs of hymns side by side is to mark their similarities as well as their differences" (159).

24. Lewalski, 127. E. Legouis made the same inference in 1923: "Quant à la Comtesse de Cumberland, elle avait un haut renom de piété et de vertu. . . . Il semble naturel que cette dame malheureuse en amour et pénétrée de pieux sentiments ait exprimé devant Spenser sa crainte de l'effet que pouvaient produire sur des coeurs jeunes et tendres les hymnes à l'Amour et à la Beauté" (cited in Greenlaw et al., *Variorum Ed.*, vol. 7, 508).

25. Welsford, 18–24. Pico's ladder begins with the lover's appreciation of the physical beauty of a particular lady, moves to his mental image of her, then to a general appreciation of corporeal beauty. At the fourth step the lover withdraws to an inner contemplation of ideal intellectual beauty in the mind, then seeks to unite with the angelic mind where ideal beauty dwells, and finally, with the angelic vision, is united to God. Castiglione has Bembo describe a four-rung ladder, beginning with the lady, moving to general corporeal beauty, to intellectual beauty, and finally to contemplation of God as the source of all beauty (Baldassare Castiglione, *The Book of the Courtier*, tr. George Bull [New York: Penguin, 1976], 324–28). On Bruno's philosophy, see John Charles Nelson, *Renaissance Theory of Love: The Context of Giordano Bruno's* Eroici furori (New York: Columbia Univ. Press, 1958).

26. See, e.g., Thomas Elyot, *The Boke named the Governour* (1531), in Hyder Rollins and Herschel Baker, eds., *The Renaissance in England* (Lexington, MA: Heath, 1954): "But above all other the warks of Plato would be most studiously rad when the judgement of a man is come to perfection, and by the other studies is instructed in the fourm of speaking that philosophers used" (113b). For a review of Plato's influence, see Sears Jayne, *Plato in Renaissance England* (Dordrecht, Netherlands: Kluwer, 1995).

27. Jayne, 107–8; Margaret P. Hannay, *Philip's Phoenix: Mary Sidney, Countess of Pembroke* (New York: Oxford Univ. Press, 1990), 60–63.

28. *HHB*, ll. 120–61.

29. Welsford, 169–70.

30. Greenlaw et al., eds., *Variorum Ed.*, vol. 1, 178, 196.

31. Ibid., 496–500, 499.

32. Anne Shaver, "Una as Institutional Satire," Sixteenth-Century Studies Conference, Tempe, AZ, Oct. 1987.

33. While Lanyer could certainly read the allegory, it is Una's role as a female character in the narrative that provides the woman poet with a model for how a master empowers a sometimes marginal female presence.

34. In a blurring of women's voices typical of Lanyer, it is not clear where the voice of Pilate's wife leaves off and that of the narrator resumes. Is it at l. 840, after the wife has finally paraphrased the words in the Bible, or at l. 936, when the direct address to Pilate concludes, or somewhere in between? Lanyer

as narrator uses direct address through much of the poem, so its presence or absence is no certain measure of who is speaking.

35. Richard Helgerson, *Self-Crowned Laureates: Spenser, Jonson, Milton and the Literary System* (Berkeley: Univ. of California Press, 1983), 104–5.

3. Lanyer and Shakespeare

1. A. L. Rowse, *Shakespeare's Sonnets: The Problems Solved. A Modern Edition, with Prose Versions, Introduction and Notes*, 2nd ed. (London: Macmillan, 1973), x (henceforth Rowse, *Sonnets*); Rowse first made his announcement in "Revealed at Last, Shakespeare's Dark Lady," *Times Literary Supplement*, 29 Jan. 1973, 12.

2. S. Schoenbaum, *Shakespeare's Lives* (Oxford: Clarendon Press, 1970), 19–36. Of many useful versions of the documentary materials of Shakespeare's lives, this volume is particularly helpful in placing claims about the Shakespeare biography in an intelligent perspective, gathering as it does not only the documentary information but the legends and extreme interpretations that have dogged the tradition of bardolatry.

3. Schoenbaum, 40; Register General of St. Botolph's Aldgate 1571–93, Guildhall Library 9221; Bodleian Ms. Ashmole 226, f. 95v.

4. J. Leeds Barroll et al., *The Revels History of Drama in English, Volume III 1576–1613* (London: Methuen, 1975), 104 (henceforth Barroll, *Revels*); Schoenbaum, 37.

5. Alfred Harbage et al., *Annals of English Drama 975–1700*, 3rd ed. (London: Routledge, 1989), 56–59 (henceforth Harbage, *Annals*); Barroll, *Revels*, 60–63. The plays are: *Henry VI, Parts 1, 2, and 3, King John, The Comedy of Errors, Richard III*, and *The Taming of the Shrew*. Part of the difficulty is the sporadic records of which plays were performed at court during the 1590s. *Love's Labour's Lost* is the only Shakespeare play known to have been performed at court during Elizabeth's reign (Christmas, 1597), though others may well have been. From 1604 to 1612, however, court productions of Shakespeare are frequently recorded. Barroll, *Revels*, 80, 87–93.

6. See, e.g., for *Lucrece*, John Roe, ed., *The New Cambridge Shakespeare: The Poems* (Cambridge: Cambridge Univ. Press, 1992), "Sources," 35–41 (all quotations from poems other than the sonnets will be taken from this edition, including the dedications to Southampton) and Ian Donaldson, *The Rapes of Lucretia: A Myth and Its Transformations* (Oxford: Clarendon Press, 1982), 3–56. The countess of Pembroke published her *Antonius* in 1590, Daniel his *Cleopatra* in 1594 (it went through nine editions by 1611). The principal source for Shakespeare's play was Thomas North's popular version of Plutarch's *Life of Antony* in *The Lives of the noble Grecians and Romanes* (1579).

7. A. Wilson Verity, ed., *Thomas Heywood's Plays* (London, 1888), 328.

8. David Lasocki, *The Bassanos* (Brookfield, Vt.: Scolar Press, 1995), 108–9, quotes Bancroft's letter to Robert Cecil on behalf of Alfonso (24 August 1604) as saying "he [Alfonso] was put in the hope of your favor by the Earl of Southampton."

9. See Bodleian Ms. Ashmole 354, f. 246 (23 Sept. 1597), where Lanyer is described as "A Gentlewoman whose husband was gone to Sea with therle of Essex in hope to be knighted"; see also chapter 1; 19–20, 23.

10. Including Rowse, who tried to read the sonnets with one-to-one connections between poem and biography (*Sonnets*, "Introduction"). Some literary historians have also seen Southampton behind at least some of the sonnets, including Muriel C. Bradbrook, in *Shakespeare: The Poet in His World* (New York: Columbia, 1978) and Robert Giroux, in *The Book Known as Q: A Consideration of Shakespeare's Sonnets* (New York: Athenaeum, 1982). Many other contemporary figures have been proposed as "the young man" of the sonnets, however, most notably William Herbert, future earl of Pembroke, by, e.g. J. Dover Wilson in *An Introduction to the Sonnets of Shakespeare for the Use of Historians and Others* (New York: Cambridge Univ. Press, 1964) and J. B. Leishman in *Themes and Variations in Shakespeare's Sonnets* (London: Hutchinson, 1961), who concludes: "anything like certainty is unattainable. All that seems desirable is to try to form some impression of the *sort of man* it was to whom Shakespeare addressed these sonnets" (20). Others dismiss the identification of the friend, noting that Shakespeare was creating poems in a popular mode, not, strictly speaking, writing biography. See, e.g., Stephen Booth, *Shakespeare's Sonnets* (New Haven: Yale Univ. Press, 1977), 546–49; Kenneth Muir, *Shakespeare's Sonnets* (London: George Allen & Unwin, 1979), 152–55; and Hallett Smith, *The Tension of the Lyre: Poetry in Shakespeare's Sonnets* (San Marino, CA: Huntington Library Press, 1981), 69 and *passim*.

11. According to Rowse, however, Southampton was at Cambridge until June 1589, then in the household of Lord Burghley off and on until 1591, when he went to France to seek military glory, at age eighteen (A. L. Rowse, *Shakespeare's Southampton: Patron of Virginia* [London: Macmillan, 1965], 46–57). It seems unlikely that he spent any noticeable time at court before Lanyer found herself exiled from it in October 1592.

12. A. L. Rowse, *The Poems of Shakespeare's Dark Lady* (London: Jonathan Cape, 1978); *Sex and Society in Shakespeare's Age: Simon Forman the Astrologer* (New York: Scribner's, 1974), 99–117; Roger Prior, "Was Emilia Bassano the Dark Lady of Shakespeare's Sonnets?" in Lasocki, 114–39 (henceforth Prior, in Lasocki).

13. Rowse, *Sex and Society*, 117; *Poems of Shakespeare's Dark Lady*, "Introduction" (which repeats much of what he wrote in *Sex and Society*).

14. See chapter 1, 5–6. For examples of Rowse's rejection of criticism, see David Bevington, "Aemilia Lanyer and A. L. Rowse," in Marshall Grossman, ed., *Aemilia Lanyer: Gender, Genre, and the Canon* (Lexington: Univ. of Kentucky Press, 1998). Rowse's purported review of my edition of Lanyer's poems is another curious example of this technique; he never reviews the edition, nor even mentions my name, but simply reiterates his argument that Lanyer is the dark lady and concludes that it is too bad people still do not see the irrefutable truth of his claim. *Contemporary Review* 267 (August 1995), 110–12.

15. See chapter 2, 59, 61.

16. C. S. Lewis, *The Allegory of Love* (London: Oxford Univ. Press, 1938), 1–43, still offers the best summary of the early characteristics of the courtly love tradition. For specific examples of red and white as early as the thirteenth century, see *The Oxford Book of Italian Verse*, 2nd ed., ed. St. John Lucas and C. Dionisotti (Oxford: Clarendon Press, 1952) and *The Oxford Book of French Verse*, 2nd ed., ed. St. John Lucas and P. Mansell Jones (Oxford: Clarendon Press, 1957), e.g., (in the latter) the "Chanson" by Richart de Semilli (4, ll. 6–7):

N'est riens qui ne l'amast; cortoise est a merveille,
Plus est blanche que flor, coume rose vermeille.

For a recent study of *Venus and Adonis* in its context, see Katherine Duncan-Jones, "Much Ado with Red and White: The Earliest Readers of *Venus and Adonis*," *Review of English Studies* 44 (1993), 479–501.

17. Kenneth Muir and Patricia Thomson, eds., *Collected Poems of Sir Thomas Wyatt* (Liverpool: Liverpool Univ. Press, 1969), 5. The source is Petrarch's *Rime* 190, which begins, "Una candida cerva sopra l'erba" (reproduced in Muir and Thomson, *Collected Poems*, 266). Wyatt's poem has received considerable interest because of its probable association with Anne Boleyn, which would date it around 1527. Edwin Greenlaw et al. and Charles Grosvenor Osgood, eds., *Works of Edmund Spenser, A Variorum Edition: The Minor Poems, Part Two*, (Baltimore: Johns Hopkins Univ. Press, 1947), 223.

18. Sayre Greenfield, "Allegorical Impulses and Critical Ends: Shakespeare's and Spenser's *Venus and Adonis*," *Criticism* 36 (1994), 475–98, outlines some of the differences between the two poets' use of the story.

19. Christopher Marlowe's *Hero and Leander* (1592) is the most famous example.

20. Catherine Belsey, *Desire: Love Stories in Western Culture* (Oxford: Blackwell, 1994). She defines desire as

the location of the contradictory imperative that motivates the signifying body which is a human being in love. Desire is in excess of the organism; conversely, it is what remains unspoken in the utterance. And moreover, at the level of the unconscious its objects are no more than a succession of substitutes for an imagined originary presence, a half-remembered 'oceanic' pleasure in the lost real, a completeness which is desire's final, unattainable object (5).

Belsey identifies "absence as desire's recurring figure . . . in Renaissance lyric poetry" (15).

21. E.g., in prose, in William Painter's *The Palace of Pleasure* (1575), "The Second Novel"; Shakespeare's narrative poem (1594); and Thomas Heywood's play (1608). For a fascinating account of the story's history and its consequences for humanist values of reading and interpretation, see Stephanie Jed, *Chaste Thinking: The Rape of Lucretia and the Birth of Humanism* (Bloomington: Indiana Univ. Press, 1989), and for its history in England, see Ian Donaldson, *The Rapes of Lucretia*.

22. Painter, in Hyder E. Rollins and Herschel Baker, eds., *The Renaissance in England* (Boston: Heath, 1954), 674a.

23. Donaldson, 21–39, 103–15; Jed, *passim*, but especially chapter 2, "Lucretia's Chastity and the Alienation from Literary Material," 51–73.

24. Verity, *Thomas Heywood's Plays*, 327–427.

25. Lucrece's beauty is figured in the obligatory language of red and white, e.g., ll. 65, 71, 419–20, 477–80.

26. Nancy J. Vickers, "The Blazon of Sweet Beauty's Best: Shakespeare's *Lucrece*," in *Shakespeare and the Question of Theory*, ed. Patricia Parker and Geoffrey N. Hartman (London: Methuen, 1985): Lucrece represents "a battle

between men that is first figuratively and then literally fought on the fields of woman's 'celebrated' body" (96). But see also Philippa Berry, "Woman, Language and History in *The Rape of Lucrece*," *Shakespeare Survey* 44 (1992), 33–40: "Close analysis of her lament revals Lucrece as the deliberate rather than accidental cause of that historical change which follows her death, and which leads to the expulsion and death of the Tarquins and the establishment of the Roman republic" (35).

27. Donaldson, 28–33.

28. Booth, 549.

29. Helen Vendler, the most recent commentator at this writing, ignores everything except the language and structure of individual sonnets. *The Art of Shakespeare's Sonnets* (Cambridge, MA: Harvard Univ. Press, 1997).

30. Prior, in Lasocki, 115–16.

31. Bevington, in Grossman.

32. This sort of reading would be less objectionable if it were acknowledged as surmise, but Rowse has a habit of accruing a small amount of circumstantial possibility and then declaring an uncontrovertible truth, chastizing anyone who disagrees with him as obtuse. He cannot have it both ways: either he takes the liberty to construct a story that might fit the few facts he has, and allows others to do the same, or he must prove his case more substantially than he often does. He finds it uncontrovertible, for example, that Southampton is the young man of the sonnets, Marlowe the rival poet, and Lanyer the dark lady (introduction to the *Sonnets*, 1973), but (if one insists on trying to find a biographical figure to match the sonnet fictions) Leishman's case for William Herbert is at least as good for the young man, almost anyone could be the poet, and dark-haired ladies (even assuming Lanyer was one) were moderately unusual but not at all rare. Rowse also asserts with certainty, but often without evidence, historical occasions for Shakespeare's plays, including, for example, the countess of Southampton's wedding to Thomas Heneage as the occasion for *Midsummer Night's Dream*. (See Schoenbaum's analysis of this and other claims in *Lives*, 761–63; he notes mildly that "other historians . . . do not make positiveness an article of their creed".) A recent interesting book by David Wiles argues much more substantially for the Elizabeth Carey–Thomas Berkeley wedding of 1596 (*Shakespeare's Almanac:* A Midsummer Night's Dream, *Marriage and the Elizabethan Calendar* [London, D. S. Brewer, 1993]).

33. *Astrophil and Stella* (1991), sonnets (e.g.) 7, 20, 24, 37, 79–82, 86, in William A. Ringler, Jr., ed., *The Poems of Sir Philip Sidney* (Oxford: Clarendon Press, 1962), 165 ff.

34. Katharine M. Wilson argues for the "dark lady sonnets" as pure parody, in *Shakespeare's Sugar'd Sonnets* (New York: Barnes & Noble, 1974), 83. While other scholars of the sonnet tradition might not go quite so far, all make the point that it is misleading to try to read them out of their cultural context. See, e.g., J. W. Lever, *The Elizabethan Love Sonnet* (London: Methuen, 1956), and, most recently, Roland Greene, *Post Petrarchism: Origins and Innovations of the Western Lyric Sequence* (Princeton: Princeton Univ. Press, 1991): "The received process of the post-Petrarchan sequence makes a stable base for poets who elect to innovate against the form" (60).

35. Bevington, in Grossman, details this sequence. In Rowse's 1973 intro-

duction to *Shakespeare's Sonnets* he makes his dark lady case, featuring the visit to Forman of one "William" Lanier and an Emilia "very brown in youth"; in *Poems of Shakespeare's Dark Lady* there is no reference to the original claims. The importance of "Will" as the husband's name Rowse originally based on sonnet 135, which plays on both the proper name and bawdy references to its meaning as lustfulness and the sexual organ:

> Who ever hath her wish, thou has thy *Will*,
> And *Will* to boot, and *Will* in over-plus.

36. Rowse, *Sonnets*; even Schoenbaum and Bevington, who so patiently dismantle what Schoenbaum calls Rowse's "tissue of conjecture," do not question the assumption of Lanyer's promiscuity (Schoenbaum, *Shakespeare and Others* [Washington: Folger Books, 1985], 76, and *Lives*, 2nd ed., 556–59; Bevington, in Grossman).

37. Katherine Duncan-Jones notes the rumors that Lord Hunsdon, son of one of Anne Boleyn's sisters, was rumored to be the product of her liaison with Henry VIII (*Times Literary Supplement*, Aug. 19, 1994, 23a); Aemilia Bassano may therefore have thought herself in the sort of royal liaison described by Daniel's *Rosamond* (see chapter 1, 38–41).

38. Rowse typically misreads and then ignores his own misreadings as he silently corrects some of them in later works. In his *TLS* announcement that he had discovered the dark lady, for example, he first reported that Forman recorded that Lanyer had been "very brown in youth," but when it was pointed out that the actual word was "brave," not "brown," Rowse made the correction in his subsequent work on Lanyer but continued to assume that she was "dark." Nowhere does Forman comment on Lanyer's complexion. See Prior in Lasocki, 120.

39. Prior, in Lasocki, 119. Other quotations and arguments used by Prior are taken from Lasocki, 120–29.

40. Bevington, in Grossman, makes this point, important since Lanyer's supposed bastardy becomes a feature of Rowse's circular reading of her character from the sonnets.

41. As described by Rowse, Forman often pursued the women who came to him for help, and, by his own account, was almost as often successful in getting them to "halek" (*Sex and Society*, 51–95 and *passim*). Rowse's selections from Forman also reveal his jealousies, brutalities, and name-calling (e.g., *Sex and Society*, 86–87, 94–95, 271–72).

One of Forman's sexual relationships was with Avis Allen, about whom he apparently cared a good deal. Her death on 13 June 1597 (*Sex and Society*, 295) may help explain why in May and early June his consultations with Lanyer are matter-of-fact, but in September he tries to seduce her.

42. See, e.g., diary quotations in Rowse, *Sex and Society*, 86, 292–95. Forman's misogyny and fear of female power probably stem from his conviction that his mother "never loved him" and are clearly evident in his famous dream about Queen Elizabeth, in which he tells her that he means "'to wait *upon* you, and not under you, that I might make this belly a little bigger to carry up this smock and coats out of the dirt.' And so we talked merrily and then she began to lean upon me, when we were past the dirt and to be very familiar with me, and methought she began to love me. And when we were alone, out

of sight, methought she would have kissed me" (presented and analyzed, in its cultural context, by Louis Adrian Montrose "'Shaping Fantasies': Figurations of Gender and Power in Elizabethan Culture," in *Representing the English Renaissance*, ed. Stephen Greenblatt [Berkeley: Univ. of California Press, 1988], 31–64; the dream discussion is on 32–35).

43. This is my own modern spelling transcription of Bodleian Ms. Ashmole 354, f. 250 (see chapter 1, 26, for the original spelling). I am grateful to Katherine Duncan-Jones for correcting my original reading of "goodly bolden" to "go the bolder" and for pointing out that the second horoscope on this page, which I had strained to read as "whether to go to Lanyer's house or no" is actually "whether to purchase Langdell's house or no"—an entirely separate topic. I was happy to confirm her reading on my third review of the Forman materials.

44. The proud fair was ubiquitous in the Petrarchan tradition. A few English examples are Sir Thomas Wyatt's "How oft have I, my dere and cruell foe" (from Petrarch, *Rime* 21); Spenser's "Faire proud now tell me why should faire be proud"; and Daniel's "Faire is my Love, and cruell as she's faire."

45. Sir Walter Ralegh and Elizabeth Throckmorton suffered that fate in June 1592, and they may in fact have been already married (William Stebbing, *Sir Walter Raleigh* [Oxford: Clarendon Press, 1891], 88–89). It was a scandal neither the lord chamberlain nor Aemilia Bassano could have missed and probably contributed to her hasty marriage to Alfonso Lanyer in October of the same year.

46. Interestingly, while male opponents of Rowse's dark lady thesis, such as Schoenbaum, have tended to assume he is right about Lanyer's promiscuousness, the women who have reviewed the evidence have found nothing seriously to suggest it. See, e.g., Diane Purkiss, *Renaissance Women: The Plays of Elizabeth Cary, The Poems of Aemilia Lanyer* (London: William Pickering, 1994), xxxi–xxxii; Barbara Lewalski has also personally reviewed the diaries and agrees with my reading (personal communication; Lewalski, 213–14).

47. Lasocki, 244.

48. Another famous half-Italian young woman, Surrey's "Geraldine," has her complexion described as "bright." Frederick Morgan Padelford, ed., *The Poems of Henry Howard, Earl of Surrey* (Seattle: Univ. of Washington Press, 1928), 83 (no. 29). Padelford notes that "Geraldine" (Elizabeth Fitzgerald) was probably nine years old when Surrey wrote this little love sonnet, but that "most of his amatory verse is undertaken largely as a literary exercise, as any student of Renaissance polite verse must appreciate" (220). This playful, nonbiographical tradition in sonneteering is so well established by Shakespeare's time that I find it a wonder so many critics remain desperately interested in identifying all the real-life persons behind the characters of Shakespeare's sonnets.

A Jewish heritage for the Bassanos would reinforce the probability that they, and not just Elina di Nazzi, contributed to the dark coloring of Aemilia's cousins, and therefore possibly to her own coloring. I find the evidence for a Jewish background circumstantial but cumulatively possible (see chapter 1), but Prior's belief that the Bassanos were not only Jewish, but Sephardic, is pure speculation, and a totally untenable argument for Lanyer's coloring (Prior, in Lasocki, 97, 244).

49. Prior believes, for example, that an "Emilia" in *Othello* (Moor of *Venice*) supports the idea that Lanyer is the dark lady. One might as well say a woman

named Portia or Jessica, from *Merchant of Venice,* is the dark lady. Prior believes the presence of a (male) "Bassanio" in the latter play is also evidence
of Shakespeare's relationship with Lanyer, but while Shakespeare may or may
not have met Aemilia Bassano, he could hardly have avoided several of her
(male) Bassano musician cousins who were around court continuously through
the 1590s and beyond. Prior reaches for a unified theory of Shakespeare's works
surrounding Lanyer (in Lasocki, 131–34 and *passim,* chapter 8) which reminds
me of the many efforts to find in the plays "proof" that Shakespeare is really
someone else, or that they encode secret Masonic messages, or whatever the
pet theory is of the reader; this practice is not hermeneutics but the imposition
of a theory on the text. For responses to Rowse and the sort of approach Prior
takes, see Bevington, in Grossman; Muir, 156–58; Schoenbaum, *Shakespeare and
Others* (Washington: Folger Books, 1985), 76, and *Shakespeare's Lives: New Edition* (Oxford: Clarendon Press, 1991), 556–59. A review of *Shakespeare and Others*
in *Shakespeare Studies* 20 (1988) by Ann Jennalie Cook traces Schoenbaum's handling of Rowse's biographical methods from his first biography of Shakespeare
in 1963 to 1980, and concludes: "One can see here the shift from treating a self-
proclaimed authority on Shakespeare with an appropriate mixture of respect,
annoyance, and tact to the crushing of a gnat by a giant."

4. Lanyer and Jonson

1. For an outline of what is known of Jonson's life, see C. H. Herford and
Percy and Evelyn Simpson, eds., *Ben Jonson,* vol. 1, "The Man and His Work",
(Oxford: Clarendon Press, 1952) and George Parfitt, *Ben Jonson: Public Poet and
Private Man* (London: Dent, 1976).

2. Herford and Simpson, vol. 8, *The Poems. The Prose Works,* 82n.

3. *The New Grove Dictionary of Music and Musicians,* ed. Stanley Sadie (London: Macmillan, 1980): 2:253 ("Bassano"), 6:478 ("Ferrabosco"), 10:454 ("Lanier").
Two Laniers (probably brothers), John and Nicholas (the elder), came to the
Elizabethan court from Rouen in 1561, while the elder Alfonso Ferrabosco (originally from Bologna) came to England by way of France at about the same time,
by mid 1562. Nicholas Lanier named his first son after his brother John, and it
seems probable that his second son, Alfonso, was named after his court musician colleague, Ferrabosco. Although the elder Ferrabosco was back and forth
between the Continent and England until 1578 (when he left England for good,
leaving behind his own son, Alfonso, and at least one daughter), he was at
Whitehall in 1572, about the time Alfonso Lanier was born. The proximity of
the Laniers' and Ferrabosco's arrival in England and the closeness of the family in the second generation supports the idea of an early friendship. In the second generation, the younger Ferrabosco married Alfonso Lanier's sister, Ellen,
sometime before 1610, went into business with another Lanier brother, Innocent, in 1619, and worked with their nephew, the younger Nicholas Lanier,
composing music for court entertainments.

See also *Grove's Dictionary of Music and Musicians,* Supple. vol. to the 5th ed.,
ed. Eric Blom (London: Macmillan, 1961), 254–58, for a fuller account of the
Lanier family by Ian Spink. (Spink is somewhat confused about Alfonso Lanier,
however, attributing to him either a son or grandson named Andrea; 257b, 258a.)

4. David Lasocki, *The Bassanos* (Brookfield, Vt.: Scolar Press, 1995), xxiii; John Duffy, *The Songs and Motets of Alfonso Ferrabosco, the Younger (1575–1628)* (Ann Arbor: UMI Research Press, 1980), 17–31.

5. Herford and Simpson, vol. 8, *Epigrammes*, 130, 131, 82–83. All quotations of Jonson's poetry and prose are from this edition.

6. *Grove's Dictionary*, suppl. vol. 5th ed., 255b–257a.

7. *The New Grove Dictionary*, vol. 9, 678–79. John Johnson was appointed by Queen Elizabeth "one of the musicians for the three lutes at 20 livres a year." Payments from the queen extend to 1594, so he apparently died around 1595. *The New Grove* calls him "the earliest of the English lutenists of the 'golden age'" (679). If John Johnson was a relative of Margaret Johnson, it would help explain Margaret's protection by Elizabeth's court even after Baptista Bassano's death.

From his position in Sir George Carey's household, Robert Johnson was able to move into a position as composer with the King's Men (formerly Lord Chamberlain's Men), where he wrote songs for various Shakespeare plays, including *Cymbeline* (1609), *Winter's Tale*, and *The Tempest* (1611); he also wrote for Webster's *Duchess of Malfi* (1613).

8. They also shared a publisher around the same time. Richard Bonian brought out Jonson's *Masque of Queenes* in 1609, not long before he published Lanyer's *Salve Deus*.

9. For these and other connections among Lanyer's dedicatees, see Barbara K. Lewalski, *Writing Women in Jacobean England* (Cambridge, MA: Harvard Univ. Press, 1993), 4–8 and 213–41. For an excellent picture of the queen's role in the complex social production of the masque, see Leeds Barroll, "Theatre as Text: The Case of Queen Anna and the Jacobean Court Masque," *The Elizabethan Theatre* 14 (1996), 175–93.

10. Linda Woodbridge, *Women and the English Renaissance: Literature and the Nature of Womankind, 1540–1620* (Urbana: Univ. of Illinois Press, 1986), offers what is still the best analysis of conventions about women prevalent in the literature of the English Renaissance. See "Part I: The Formal Controversy," 13–136.

11. C. H. Herford and Percy and Evelyn Simpson, eds., *Ben Jonson* (Oxford: Clarendon Press, 1952), vol. 1, "The Man and His Work." See esp. chap. 4, "Jonson's Society, 1603–12," 48–63, in which they laud his appealing virility (52–53). Robert C. Evans makes the case for patriarchal hierarchy being inherent in the patronage system, in *Ben Jonson and the Poetics of Patronage* (Lewisburg: Bucknell Univ. Press, 1989):

> Whether placed under the care of tutors or apprenticed to 'masters'; whether educated by schoolmasters or instructed in the homes of wealthy relatives or family friends; whether educated later by different masters at the universities or Inns of Court, young men throughout the country quickly learned that the deference and service they owed their natural fathers was also expected by figures whose influence over their futures was in some ways equally strong. . . . Maturation involved initiation in countless ways into the rites and requirements of a system permeated by patronage relations. . . . His subordinate status encouraged dependency, but his need to compete could promote more self-centered, self-assertive impulses. . . . The central arena for such struggle was un-

doubtedly the court. . . . The men and women who competed there were often themselves the most powerful figures in other spheres of life or in other areas of the country, while the government bureaucracy offered numerous opportunities to those of lesser birth who were skillful, ambitious, or well-connected. Influence or a place at court automatically heightened one's psychological and pragmatic status; loss of favor there could be devastating economically and in social and self-esteem (27).

12. David Riggs, *Ben Jonson: A Life* (Cambridge, MA: Harvard Univ. Press, 1989), 3. See also his later comment: "having [in 1598] achieved a succes d'estime on the public stage, he now conceived of himself as a man of letters rather than a professional playwright. In order to realize that conception, he had to obtain the support of individual patrons, and patronage was the common denominator of all his new undertaking" (63).

13. Evans notes that "there were, in fact, two systems of literary patronage during the Renaissance: an ideal version, grounded in perfect reciprocity and noblesse oblige, that existed mostly in the minds and imaginations of the writers; and the often imperfect, inadequate, frustrating, or uncertain arrangements they encountered in everyday life" (29). Poetic strategy was of course based on the ideal. Robert Wiltenberg makes a similar point as he traces the maturation of the idea of "self-love," in *Ben Jonson and Self-Love: The Subtlest Maze of All* (Columbia: Univ. of Missouri Press, 1990).

14. Herford, Simpson, and Simpson, vol. 8, 116–20. For other examples of Jonson's play of gender in poems to women patrons see, e.g., epigram 79, "To Elizabeth, Countesse of Rutland," which praises her in praising her late father, Sir Philip Sidney, to whom destiny decreed, "No male unto him" (l. 7), 53; epigram 103, "To Lady Mary Wroth," "faire crowne of your faire sexe" (l. 1), whose most ample praise, again, comes because she is "A Sydney" (l. 10), 66–67; or epigram 104, "To Susan, Countesse of Montgomery," which turns on a comparison to the biblical Susanna, with the Countess "lent no lesse dignitie / Of birth, of match, of forme, of chastitie" (ll. 7–8), 67.

15. Herford, Simpson, and Simpson, vol. 8, 52; 242–47.

16. Herford, Simpson, and Simpson, vol. 8, 28, 40–41.

17. Riggs sees this as Jonson's solution to his central problem of self-assertion: "he was a fiercely independent individual, yet he was putting his services at the disposal of his social superiors" (64).

18. A point effectively made by Sara van den Berg, *The Action of Ben Jonson's Poetry* (Newark: Univ. of Delaware Press, 1987): "Throughout his career, Jonson dislocates and relocates authority, so that it resides not in the subject he addresses, not in the literary history he brings to bear upon an occasion, and not even in his own voice within the text, but in the relationships he inscribes among all these and with the reader. What finally matters is the authority of relationships. These ground the wit of Jonsonian art in community. . . . Wit negotiates the competing claims of occasion and history, text and tradition, poem and book, individual and community, poet and reader" (35).

19. "To the Queenes Most Excellent Majestie," l. 4.

20. Chapter 2, 43–46.

21. The liberating power of English Protestantism and some of its limits

are chronicled by several writers in Margaret P. Hannay, ed., *Silent but for the Word: Tudor Women as Patrons, Translators, and Writers of Religious Works* (Kent, OH: Kent State Univ. Press, 1985); see especially Hannay's introduction and Gary Waller's summary essay, "Struggling into Discourse: the Emergence of Renaissance Women's Writing," 238–56.

22. Cf. essays in Hannay; see also Janel Mueller, "The Feminist Poetics of Aemilia Lanyer's 'Salve Deus Rex Judaeorum,'" in *Feminist Measures: Soundings in Poetry and Theory*, ed. Lynn Keller and Cristianne Miller (Ann Arbor: Univ. of Michigan Press, 1993).

23. Richard Helgerson, *Self-Crowned Laureates: Spenser, Jonson, Milton and the Literary System* (Berkeley: Univ. of California Press, 1983), 184.

24. Ibid.

25. See Lewalski, "Exercising Power: The Countess of Bedford as Courtier, Patron, and Coterie Poet," in *Writing Women*, 95–123: "Lucy Harington Russell (1581–1627), wife of Edward, third Earl of Bedford, was the most important and most powerful patroness of the Jacobean court, except for Queen Anne herself" (95).

26. Lewalski, 99. Bedford was, for example, paired with the queen in the dance of the *Masque of Blackness* (Ben Jonson, *The Characters of Two Royall Masques*, 1608, f. B4).

27. "The lady who speaks this dramatic monologue has not been identified," according to William B. Hunter, *The Complete Poetry of Ben Jonson* (New York: Norton, 1968), 84 n. 1. Whatever the sources behind the poem, it stands as a fictional monologue for which identifying the lady would be beside the point.

28. G. R. Hibbard, "The Country House Poem of the Seventeenth Century," *Journal of the Warburg and Courtauld Institutes* 19 (1956), 159–74, outlined the tradition and made the claim for "To Penshurst." His assumptions have been largely followed by subsequent editors and critics, including Hunter, *Complete Poetry of Ben Jonson*, 75; Raymond Williams, *The Country and the City* (New York: Oxford Univ. Press, 1973), 27–34; and William A. McClung, *The Country House in English Renaissance Poetry* (Berkeley: Univ. of California Press, 1977).

29. Alastair Fowler, *Kinds of Literature: An Introduction to the Theory of Genres and Modes* (Cambridge, MA: Harvard Univ. Press, 1982), 154.

30. Although *Salve Deus* is dated 1611, it was in print by 8 Nov. 1610, the date on Alfonso's presentation copy to Thomas Jones (the Chapin Library copy), placing the composition of "Cookham" anywhere from after Anne Clifford's marriage to Dorset on 25 Feb. 1609 (Lanyer alludes to the marriage in the poem) and the book's publication. "To Penshurst" did not reach print until 1616 (as the second poem in *The Forrest* section of Jonson's *Workes*), but an allusion to James with Prince Henry strongly suggests that the poem was composed before Henry's death in November 1612. This is in any case what Jonson's editors and critics have long assumed, such as Hunter, *Complete Poetry*, 80, n. 23, and George Parfitt, ed., *Ben Jonson: The Complete Poems* (Baltimore: Penguin, 1975), 508. Parfitt, in a later essay, "Poetry by Women," in *English Poetry of the Seventeenth Century*, 2nd ed. (London: Longman, 1992), 241–43, attempts to dismiss Lanyer's poem as a country-house poem (not enough sense of a specific place, no "sociopolitical dimension"). I disagree on both counts, though I concede a

much different take on sociopolitical reality in Jonson than in Lanyer. This is doubtless an argument that will continue.

31. Barbara K. Lewalski, "The Lady of the Country-House Poem," in *The Fashioning and Functioning of the British Country House*, ed. Gervase Jackson-Stops, Gordon J. Schochet, Lena Cowen Orlin, and Elisabeth Blair MacDougall (1989), 261–75 (here she outlines the background for the genre and relates "Cookham" to poems by Lovelace and Marvell as well as Jonson), and *Writing Women*, 234–41:

> Lanyer's poem looks back to several classical and Renaissance poems which contributed to the development of the country-house genre. One is the *beatus ille* tradition praising a happy rural retirement from city business or courtly corruption, with its origins in Horace's Epode II, and Martial's Epigram III.58 on the Baian villa. In Lanyer's version the male speaker and the virtuous happy man are replaced by women. Another strand contains landscape or topographical descriptive poetry, such as Michael Drayton's *Polyolbion*, and, more generally, classical and Renaissance pastoral and Golden Age poetry. Closest of all are poems built upon the controlling topos of the valediction to a place, the best-known example of which was was Virgil's First Eclogue. Read against that model, Lanyer's poem makes the pastoral departure a matter of social and domestic rather than state politics (235).

32. T. S. Eliot, "Tradition and the Individual Talent," *Selected Essays 1917–32* (London: Faber & Faber, 1932). This 1917 essay has had enormous, though frequently unacknowledged, influence on twentieth-century English studies; Harold Bloom's influential *The Anxiety of Influence* (New York: Oxford Univ. Press, 1973) and Helgerson's *Self-Crowned Laureates* (1983) both owe something to Eliot; for a recent study in this line, see Raphael Falco, *Conceived Presences: Literary Genealogy in Renaissance England* (Amherst: Univ. of Massachusetts Press, 1994).

33. E.g., Catherine Belsey, *Critical Practice* (London: Methuen, 1980), and Stephen Greenblatt, *Shakespearean Negotiations: The Circulation of Social Energy in Renaissance England* (Berkeley: Univ. of California Press, 1988).

34. See chapter 1, 29–31.

35. For a full discussion of how such "phenomenological exercises" situate the English romantic poets, see Thorslev's *Romantic Contraries: Freedom versus Destiny* (New Haven: Yale Univ. Press, 1984), e.g., 82–83.

36. Sir Philip Sidney, *An Apology for Poetry*, ed. Geoffrey Shepherd (London: Nelson, 1965): "Only the poet, disdaining to be tied to any such subjection [to the limits of natural laws], lifted up with the vigour of his own invention, doth grow in effect into another nature, in making things either better than Nature bringeth forth, or, quite anew, forms such as never were in Nature . . . so as he goeth hand in hand with Nature, not enclosed within the narrow warrant of her gifts, but freely ranging within the zodiac of her own wit" (100).

37. Sir Robert Sidney (1563–1626), who inherited the estate from his father, Sir Henry Sidney, in 1586, married the wealthy heiress Barbara Gamage (1562–1620); they had at least nine children, of whom five lived past childhood. The eldest and most famous, Lady Mary Wroth, and her sister, Katherine, were married and living away from Penshurst by 1610, but at least three others were still at home. The portrait of Penshurst was of an exemplary patriarchal estate.

38. See, e.g., poems to Lady Mary Wroth, epigrams 103 and 105, and, especially, 28, *Under-wood*.

5. Lanyer and English Religious Verse

1. Barbara Kiefer Lewalski, *Protestant Poetics and the Seventeenth-Century Religious Lyric* (Princeton: Princeton Univ. Press, 1979), 39–53 and *passim*.

2. Anne Lock, "A Meditation of a Penitent Sinner: Written in Maner of a Paraphrase upon the 51. Psalme of David," appended to Lock's translation of Calvin's sermons *Upon the Songe that Ezechias Made after he had been Sicke* (1560, in Susan Felch, ed., *The collected Works of Anne Vaughan Lock* (Tempe, AZ: Medieval & Renaissance Texts & Studies, 1999), 62–71); Lanyer refers to the Sidney-Pembroke Psalms, which circulated in numerous manuscript copies in the first part of the seventeenth century, as "rare sweet songs" and "holy sonnets" ("The Authours Dreame," ll. 117, 121).

3. From the "Articles of Religion" ("The Thirty-nine Articles") of the Anglican Church, article 25, "Of the Sacraments." See also articles 11–14, on justification and works, e.g., from article 11, "Of the Justification of Man": "We are accounted righteous before God, only for the merit of our Lord and Saviour, Jesus Christ by Faith, and not for our own works or deservings." These articles became the official doctrine of the English church in 1571. For a summary history, see Massey Hamilton Shepherd, Jr., *The Oxford American Prayer Book Commentary* (New York: Oxford Univ. Press, 1950), 600–1.

4. Article 28, "Of the Lord's Supper."

5. *The Catechisme, or maner to teache Children the Christian Religion. Made by the excellent doctor and pastor in Christes Churche John Calvin*, (London: Jhon [*sic*] Kyngston, 1582), sigs. C2–C3.

6. *An Ample Declaration of the Christian doctrine. Composed in Italian by the renowned Cardinal: Card. Bellarmine*. Translated into English by Richard Ha[y]dock D. of Divinite (Rouen, c. 1602), sigs. C2. Sig. C2v: [It is as if Christ worked hard to] "gaine so much money, as were sufficient to pay al the debts of this citie, and should put the same in a bank, to the end it should be geven unto al such as should bring a warrant from him: this man had surely satisfied for all . . . & yet manie might remaine stil in debt, for that they would not, either for pride, or for slouth, or for some other cause, demand his warrant, and carrie it to the bank, to receive the money."

7. Diane McColley has captured this distinction neatly in juxtaposing two versions of God the Father's presence in creation by the Flemish engraver Jan Collaert after Maerten de Vos. In the first (more "Catholic" version), the background shows a robed figure lifting up his hands by a seashore, creating the heavens; in the middle perspective, another God figure sits on a rock with his hand pointed toward an array of Edenic animals: and, in the foreground, yet another, a vigorous bearded patriarch, blesses Eve as she emerges from Adam's side. In the second version, published later by a different printer, the scene is the same except that a sun-like oblong inscribed with the Hebrew name for God intertwined with the Latin "Pater" replaces the blessing patriarch, and the figures on the rock and seashore have disappeared. The Protestant version rejects an anthropomorphic God in favor of a more abstract "Word." Diane

McColley, *A Gust for Paradise: Milton's Eden and the Visual Arts* (Urbana: Univ. of Illinois Press, 1993), figs. 15 and 16 (see also 21–35).

8. Felch, 65.

9. James H. MacDonald and Nancy Pollard Brown, eds., *The Poems of Robert Southwell, S.J.*, (Oxford: Clarendon Press, 1967), 41. All citations are from this edition.

10. "Queen Anne," l. 44; "Arbella," l. 12; "Duchess of Suffolk," l. 42; *Salve Deus*, 474.

11. "Queen Anne," l. 85; "Ladie Anne," l. 117; *Salve Deus*, ll. 319, 411, 572.

12. "Authors Dreame," l. 218; *Salve Deus*, l. 560; "Ladie Anne," l. 131; *Salve Deus*, l. 467.

13. "Vertuous Ladies," l. 9; "Ladie Anne," l. 115; *Salve Deus*, ll. 77, 1018, 1305.

14. See also *Salve Deus* ll. 677, 728, 741, 750, 896, 1012, 1017, 1111, 1135, 1143, 1188, 1204, 1254, 1302.

15. See chapter 1; "The Authors Dream," ll. 117–32 and sidenote.

16. Lanyer lauds Sidney in "The Authors Dream," ll. 138–44, but places the countess of Pembroke "farre before him . . . / For virtue, wisedome, learning, dignity" (ll. 151–52). Greville's poems apparently circulated widely before being printed in his *Works*, 1633 (they are mentioned in Puttenham's *Arte of English Poesie*, 1586). See Geoffrey Bullough, ed., *Poems and Dramas of Fulke Greville, First Lord Brooke* (New York: Oxford Univ. Press, 1945), vol. 1, 33–42 (though it is not clear whether the religious verses were circulated early). Citations from Greville are from this edition. Citations from Constable are from Joan Grundy, ed., *The Poems of Henry Constable* (Liverpool: Liverpool Univ. Press, 1960). Grundy concludes that Constable was probably at court in 1588 and 1589 (26).

17. For persuasive arguments on aspects of Lanyer's unconventional view of the passion, see Janel Mueller, "The Feminist Poetics of Aemilia Lanyer's 'Salve Deus Rex Judaeorum,'" in *Feminist Measures: Sounding in Poetry and Theory*, ed. Lynn Keller and Cristianne Miller (Ann Arbor: Univ. of Michigan Press, 1994), and Catherine Keohane, "'That Blindest Weakenesse Be Not Over-bold': Aemilia Lanyer's Radical Unfolding of the Passion," *ELH* 64 (1997), 359–90.

18. John King, Barbara Lewalski, and Louis Martz have described and analyzed the richness and variety of the sixteenth and early seventeenth-century biblical poetics which fed the development of religious poetry in early modern English. See John N. King, *English Reformation Literature: The Tudor Origins of the Protestant Tradition* (Princeton: Princeton Univ. Press, 1982); Barbara K. Lewalski, *Protestant Poetics and the Seventeenth-Century Religious Lyric* (Princeton: Princeton Univ. Press, 1979); Louis L. Martz, *The Poetry of Meditation: A Study in English Religious Literature of the Seventeenth Century* (New Haven: Yale Univ. Press, 1962).

19. Felch, introduction. "Despite her unswerving commitment to reformed and anti-Papist sentiments, Lock's [dedicatory] epistle [to the Duchess of Suffolk] is not iconoclastic. In both its allegorical use of biblical materials and conservative rhetoric, it remains firmly embedded in the venerable tradition of English devotional writings." Although there remains some question about whether the sonnets are by Lock, Felch argues for her authorship, as have other recent commentators, e.g., Thomas P. Roche, *Petrarch and the English Sonnet Sequences* (New York: AMS Press, 1989), 155, and Michael Spiller, *The Development of the Sonnet: An Introduction* (New York: Routledge, 1992), 92.

20. All citations are taken from the Geneva Bible (1560) unless otherwise noted. *The Geneva Bible: A Facsimile of the 1560 edition*, intro. Lloyd E. Berry (Madison: Univ. of Wisconsin Press, 1969). For the definition of "Protestant" in the sense described, see, e.g., Lewalski, *Protestant Poetics*, 78–83.

21. All citations are from Margaret P. Hannay, Noel Kinnamon, and Michael Brennan, eds., *The Works of the Countess of Pembroke*, (Oxford: Oxford Univ. Press, 1998). Psalm 51, ll. 5–7, transcribed by Noel T. Kinnamon from the Penshurst ms.

22. Felch, 66.

23. Bullough, *Poems and Dramas*, vol. 1, 2–9.

24. Grundy, *Poems of Henry Constable*, 24, 150–51, 154–55, 157.

25. Daniel credits Greville with publicizing his early work, and possibly, as Bullough suggests (19), even introducing him to the Pembroke circle. He became tutor to the countess of Pembroke's sons in the early 1590's and, some years later, to the countess of Cumberland's daughter, Anne Clifford (see chapter 1). In *Musophilus*, Daniel addresses Greville:

Thy learned judgement which I most esteem
(Worthy Fulke Grevil) must defend this course [i.e., Daniel's discursive verse],
By whose mild grace and gentle hand at first
My infant Muse was brought in open sight
From out the darkness wherein it was nursed
And made to be partaker of the light. (ll. 743–48)

26. Bullough, *Poems and Dramas*, vol. 1, 18–19; Grundy, *Poems of Henry Constable*, 146. The sisters were apparently close, and common dedications not uncommon (see, e.g., Spenser's dedications cited in chapter 2, 55). For a summary of the relation between the two sisters, see Victoria A. Wilson, *Society Women of Shakespeare's Time* (London: The Bodley Head, 1924), 138–43.

27. Sonnet 98, "Caelica," in Bullough, *Poems and Dramas*, vol. 1, 143–44.

28. Grundy, *Poems of Henry Constable*, 53–59, 101–2.

29. Ibid., 187–88.

30. Ibid., 191–92.

31. MacDonald and Brown, *Poems of Robert Southwell*, lvi–lxxvi.

32. "Certain Sonnets" 32, Sir Philip Sidney, *Poems*, ed. William A. Ringler (Oxford: Clarendon Press, 1967), 161.

33. Sonnet 86, Bullough, *Poems and Dramas*, vol. 1, 135–36.

34. Lewalski, *Protestant Poetics*, 59–69.

35. C. A. Patrides, ed., *The Complete English Poems of John Donne* (London: Dent, Everyman's Library, 1985), 443. All citations from Donne's poems are from this edition.

36. Patrides, *Poems of John Donne*, 448.

37. Arthur F. Marotti, *John Donne: Coterie Poet* (Madison: Univ. of Wisconsin Press, 1986), 236 (describing the central theme of Donne's two "Anniversaries").

38. "Conversations with Drummond of Hawthornden," in C. H. Herford and Percy and Evelyn Simpson, eds., *Ben Jonson*, 11 vols. (Oxford: Oxford Univ. Press, 1925–52), vol. 1, 33.

39. Barbara K. Lewalski, *Donne's* Anniversaries *and the Poetry of Praise: The Creation of a Symbolic Mode* (Princeton: Princeton Univ. Press, 1973), 112–13.

40. Patrides, *Poems of John Donne*, 326.

41. Lewalski, *Donne's Anniversaries*, 113.

42. Mueller, "Feminist Poetics."

43. "And [God] said unto me, My grace is sufficient for thee: for my power is made perfite through weakenes. Verie gladly therefore wil I rejoyce rather in mine infirmities, that the power of Christ may dwell in me . . . for when I am weake, then am I strong" (2 Cor. 12:9–10).

44. F. E. Hutchinson, ed., *The Works of George Herbert* (Oxford: Clarendon Press, 1941), xxxvi; citations from Herbert's verse are from this edition.

45. The date of publication is given as "On or before 2 Jan. 1646" in *A Variorum Commentary on the Poems of John Milton*, vol. 2, "The Minor English Poems," ed. A. S. P. Woodhouse and Douglas Bush (New York: Columbia Univ. Press, 1972), pt. 1, 6.

46. See Grundy, *Poems of Henry Constable*, 185–92, which includes poems to "St. Mychaell the Archangel," "St. John the Baptist," "St. Peter and St. Paul," "St. Katharyne," and 'St. Margarett," as well as the two Marys. Southwell's poems often focus on St. Peter (a second poem called "St. Peter's Complaynte," "St. Peter's afflicted minde," "St. Peters remorse," 29–31, 33–35). See also William Alabaster (1568–1640), who has poems to Christ and the Virgin Mary, but also St. Augustine and St. John the Evangelist. G. M. Story and Helen Gardner, eds., *The Sonnets of William Alabaster* (Oxford: Oxford Univ. Press, 1959), 19, 42.

47. Elizabeth Melvill (Colville), Lady Culros, *Ane Godlie Dreame*, Edinburgh, 1606.

48. Bullough, *Poems and Dramas*, vol. 1, 153.

49. Lewalski, *Protestant Poetics*, 294–96: "The speaker is forced to give over his foolish and presumptuous (Catholic) efforts to achieve an imaginative identification with the crucified Christ and to participate in his sacrifice by imitation, turning instead to a proper Protestant concern with the meaning of Christ's sacrifice for his own redemption and his spiritual life. In this interest he explores the relationship which is the theological ground of all the others— Christ as Savior and the speaker as his redeemed. . . . The speaker is related to Christ also as servant to lord, or sometimes subject to king, and the terms of this relationship are also transmuted by love." Lewalski also notes Herbert's exploration of the Christ-speaker relationship as "father and child" (295), "but the primary relation explored through these poems is that of loving friends, not fixed in the Canticles' relation of Bride and Bridegroom but exchanging the roles of lover and beloved" (296).

50. Hutchinson, *Works*, 26–34. At two points the refrain changes to "Never was grief like mine": at the moment of God's apparent forsaking (l. 215) and at the end (l. 251).

51. Hutchinson, *Works*, 48–51, 60–61.

52. E.g., when the countess of Cumberland finds the true presence of her Lord in the humble and sick, ll. 1345–68.

53. Hutchinson, *Works*, 153–54.

54. The notable exception is his poem on "Marie Magdalene," Hutchinson, *Works*, 173.

55. See, e.g., Julia Walker, ed., *Milton and the Idea of Woman* (Champagne-Urbana: Univ. of Illinois Press, 1991); references to earlier debates run throughout its notes.

56. Merritt Y. Hughes, *John Milton: Complete Poems and Major Prose* (New York: Odyssey Press, 1957). All references to Milton are from this ed.

57. "Second Defense," in Hughes, 831a; "Areopagitica," in Hughes, 733a.

58. E.g., in "Eikonklastes" and "Ready and Easy Way," in Hughes.

INDEX